Praise for *Out in the Army*

"*Out in the Army* is the most moving book I have recently read.
James Wharton is such a direct and honest writer that he brings
you to the verge of tears not only when you expect him to but
when you don't. His love of Queen and country, his husband
and his family all come off the printed page and into your heart."
Paul Gambaccini

"*Out in the Army* is a truly unique look at a soldier's journey
from boy to man, from Wales to war. I couldn't put it down."
Antony Cotton

"A deeply moving and personal insight into life in the army. A
story of bravery, love and victory. James we salute you."
Alice Arnold

"A fascinating and charming insight into a remarkable life that
wouldn't have been possible just a few years ago."
Matthew Cain, Culture Editor, *Channel 4 News*

"This acutely observed account of rocket attacks, scorpion
bites and blistering heat – populated by mates such as Shagger,
Smudge and Scoffy – could have been written a hundred years
ago. It's the coming-out story, a gay wedding and a boyfriend
who runs off with a vegan that make it a highly readable and
distinctly twenty-first-century boy's own tale."
Ben Summerskill OBE

OUT IN THE ARMY

My Life as a Gay Soldier

JAMES WHARTON

Biteback Publishing

First published in Great Britain in 2013 by
Biteback Publishing Ltd
Westminster Tower
3 Albert Embankment
London SE1 7SP
Copyright © James Wharton 2013

Some of the names used in *Out in the Army* have been changed to protect the privacy of those involved.

ISBN 978-1-84954-540-2

10 9 8 7 6 5 4 3 2 1

A CIP catalogue record for this book is available from the British Library.

Set in Adobe Caslon Pro

Printed and bound in Great Britain by
CPI Group (UK) Ltd, Croydon CR0 4YY

MIX
Paper from responsible sources
FSC
www.fsc.org   FSC® C020471

For Thomas James McCaffrey

CONTENTS

ACKNOWLEDGEMENTS

O*ut in the Army* would never have been possible without the support, love and guidance of some very special individuals.

My publisher Iain Dale has had nothing but confidence in me and my story since I first pitched the book to him in May 2012. Since, my editor Hollie Teague has given it great effort and attention. Everyone at Biteback has looked after me extremely well throughout the process of leaving the military and completing the book, and I thank them wholeheartedly.

I'm lucky to have some inspirational friends, both inside and outside the army, and all have been incredible. Jonathan Harvey, thank you for the late-night phone calls and endless advice. You put my mind at ease and answered my many questions. Another person I'd like to thank, someone who has essentially acted as my agent over the past year, is Antony Cotton; thanks for the great parties and your friendship.

Thank you Michael Faulkner for your closeness throughout my ten years in the army; I wish you all the best as you embark on civilian life.

Three chaps who changed my life are Dean Perryman, Josh Tate and Jamie McAllen. I owe you guys so much, for being there the night I finally accepted the truth about who I was, and for being loyal ever since.

A long-lasting friend, who has been patiently waiting to read this book for some time, is Donna Carmichael, a person who has given so much of her life and energy to the Blues and Royals Squadron in London. The place would fall apart without you.

In North Wales, I'd like to mention Jason Whalley; my old English teacher from secondary school Margaret Graham; and my godmother and second mum, Linda Jukes.

I'm also particularly grateful to Ben Summerskill OBE at Stonewall and Sir Ian McKellen.

The greatest soldier I ever had the pleasure of serving with also became an incredible ally over the course of my career. Daniel Abbott, I hope the army keeps hold of you for as long as possible. Other soldiers, past and present, I'd like to acknowledge are Martin 'Scoffy' Clark, Alex Cawley, Geoff Park, Rob Chell and Warren Brown.

Finally, my family. Mum, I love you so much and draw such strength from your amazing courage. I hope you enjoy this book, but please don't get too upset about some of my earlier behaviour. Phil, thanks for being a great father figure and role model throughout my teenage years and early twenties. Dad, may your recovery from illness continue and I'm glad I know you in some way today.

My brother and sister, Paul and Liza, remain enormously close and important to me, and I love you both and your families beyond belief. And finally, Nan, I love you with all my heart and I cherish each day I spend with you.

The most important person in the world to me, the man who saved my life, is my darling husband Thomas. I love you.

I wish the men of the Household Cavalry the very best of luck for the future.

1

THE GREATEST DAY

Doncaster, the horse entrusted to carry me on this great occasion, looks up. I want to look up, too, but I know it's more than my job's worth. Everywhere around me thousands of people are waiting for a glimpse of the newlyweds – even me, the lucky boy who has the honour of taking part in their big day. This is the event of the year (of several years): the royal wedding, the wedding of a future king. Millions of people on the streets and around the world are focusing on this very moment and I can't help but fantasise that they're looking at me!

I am turned out immaculately, my boots polished to within an inch of their lives, my scarlet red plume hanging beautifully off the top of my helmet, the strands waving past my eyes in the slight breeze. Doncaster and I have been checked and re-checked throughout the morning, yet I'm still nervous. This day is the highlight of my life – a day I never thought I'd see.

I say this because it has been a long journey – a journey that could have ended several times.

Waiting for the prince and his new wife, the now Duchess of Cambridge, seems to last a lifetime. I've been sat patiently, still as possible, for almost an hour, listening to the words of the Archbishop from inside the abbey through the large speakers assembled outside for the world to listen; listening to the cheers of support from all over the capital. What did my family make of it all? What about the school kids who'd often put me down as a child? What about the teachers who had spent so much time and energy on my education? Were they watching? Had they seen what had become of that young boy from North Wales, sat in full state regalia atop a beautiful large black horse?

Another hymn begins inside the abbey – and outside too – led by the very lady I'm sat here waiting for: Her Majesty. She is my one concern, the one person I am here to look after.

My sword arm begins to ache as Doncaster entertains himself with the apparatus in his mouth, rattling and jingling. I'm desperate to look around. I wonder whether the nice American family I spoke with yesterday during rehearsals are enjoying the occasion. They'd told me how supportive they were of the two princes and how they'd last travelled to the UK to see 'the funeral in 1997'. My memory drifts back to that occasion and the sorrow that filled our household following her death. An innocent ten-year-old boy sat with his mother and older sister, witnessing the events with confusion and sadness.

In the space of fifteen years I've come from the Welsh countryside to the heart of royal pageantry in London at the wedding of one of those two young boys the world cried over. I feel my own eyes dampen slightly and quickly pull myself together: this next hour is the pinnacle of my military career and I need to fully concentrate. I need to ride with certainty and commitment; getting here wasn't easy and I know that today will be the beginning of the end of my incredible journey as a soldier in the British Army.

TO START WITH...

I was born into a large English family in 1987, in a hospital bed in North Wales – the first Welshman of the family. Both my parents were from Liverpool and had met there some years before, in the late 1970s.

Both my brother and sister, Paul and Liza, were older than me by quite a gap – my sister is ten years my senior – and they had a different father to me. I was quite the baby of the family – in many ways I still am!

Our large family, the Crumlins, was formed during the First World War when two men met before the Battle of the Somme. It was the lull before the battle and, in the face of a challenge that they knew would cost the lives of thousands, the two shared a cigarette and a conversation. After weeks and weeks of bloody fighting, by chance, the two men met again at the end of the battle and became friends, tied forever by the experience they'd both shared. The men kept in touch throughout the remaining months and years of the war, and then into peacetime. One of the men, from Belfast, brought his wife and young son with him on trips to Liverpool, where they'd stay with the other man, his wife and young daughter. The two children, Gladys and James ('Jimmy'), became my grandparents.

Jimmy, my granddad, went on to join the Royal Navy and

spent most of the Second World War as a Japanese prisoner of war after his ship, the *Repulse*, was sunk in 1941. He survived, and he and my nan had many children and eventually grandchildren.

Jimmy was a huge influence on my early life. I was always fascinated with his medals and although he rarely spoke of his days in the POW camp, the family – my nan, mostly – would pass on enough for me to understand that he had suffered for all our futures.

From what I can remember, my parents, Pauline and Ronald, lived a somewhat turbulent life in North Wales while I was growing up. Dad worked in a factory but was also a window cleaner. He'd often drink his daily earnings before getting home. Mum was a saleswoman at a kitchen and bathroom hardware shop in the local town. Mum would come home at 5.30 every night to a sometimes already drunk Dad, two teenagers and a very young and energetic me. They did well and I know they only stayed together because of how young I was, but they decided to call it a day once I'd reached my teens.

Enter Phil, my stepfather. Phil met my mother as she was leaving my dad and he really swept her off her feet. Around this time, Mum was diagnosed with multiple sclerosis (MS). Fairly stressful times for one lady, I think. What Phil provided for us all was security, care and most of all for my mum, love, something that had probably been missing from her life for some time. I honestly don't know what might have happened to Mum if Phil hadn't come along. He's a very good guy, and I'm glad he turned up when he did.

Mum and I left our house, which was a very pretty property on the side of a rural Welsh hillside. We moved into a two-bedroom council flat in an area of the village that I simply saw as rough. Things were going to be very different. I felt embarrassed that my life had taken such a sudden change. My sister had already moved out with her young family, and my brother Paul used the change in our family make-up as an excuse to start out on his own too. I was now solely alone with Mum. Phil, of course, became more involved as the months passed by, and as a result I bonded with him a lot sooner than Paul and Liza did.

After the break-up my dad took a turn for the worse. He walked out of his factory job, which meant he had to depend solely on his window-cleaning round; he started hitting the bottle more than he'd ever done before in his life. He attempted to take on our old house alone, buying Mum out, but it ended in failure and the property was eventually repossessed. This added to his many stresses, which he kept all to himself. He always had done. Soon he was living in a squat and I would visit him after school most days, often finding him drunk.

While I could, I tried to keep him on the relative straight and narrow. With the help of my school, Liza and I even got him into rehab, but after his second stint he returned to the bottle yet again. Thinking about the dad I knew when I was much younger, a very playful, decent, all-round dad, and then comparing him to what he became while I was in my teenage years fills me with sadness. You'd think it'd be enough to put me off drinking.

In early 2000, I saw a poster in school about the Army Cadet Force, which was opening a new club in the local village. Most of the boys poked fun at the idea, but it really appealed to me. With the many changes going on at home and the problems I was having with Dad, I saw the cadets as a chance of escape. I went along to the opening night with my best friend Ami and we both signed up.

During my time in the army cadets I made lots of new friends from around the region, which stretched from the Welsh border with England and Cheshire to the coastal towns of Colwyn Bay and Abergele. Our group, aged thirteen to seventeen, mixed very well and would unite most weekends throughout the spring and summer. It might be a little unfair to say, but I felt like we were a collective group of slight misfits. We weren't the cool kids you found commanding the playgrounds in school. We didn't do the whole hanging around street corners thing; instead, come the weekend, we'd get together at a campsite somewhere and really let our hair down, at the same time learning all about military discipline and structure. On reflection, I can see how much of a winning recruitment tool it was for the regular army.

The trick was to get involved with as many sports and activities as possible, thus ensuring the best chance of going away most weekends. Escape. My friends in the cadets and I took part in as much as possible. In the summer of 2002, I managed to go away an incredible twelve weekends in a row, driving my headmaster Mr Davies up the wall as I needed most Friday afternoons off school to be able to do so. I competed in athletics, becoming the junior Welsh high jump champion; I was part of the shooting team, which got me away for at least four weekends in a row; I competed in endurance, which was the most prestigious activity to be involved with, long-distance marching over hills and mountains while trying to navigate. This is what I excelled in – and it made me very popular among the other cadets.

I also played the side drum in the massed band, which got me away for the remaining weekends of the summer months. It was quite a glamorous role and I mostly played before kick-off at Wrexham FC home games. The boys from school sat in the crowd looking on with interest but would still ridicule me the following Monday for looking 'gay' in my uniform banging a drum.

I'd become quite thick-skinned against schoolyard teasing. I'd always been picked on for having a slight Liverpudlian accent. My dad wandering around the village with ladders and a bucket didn't help too much, either. It was worse when he became a drunk. I remember thinking Dad had become the village idiot, the one everyone could poke fun at – and often through me in the playground.

It was during these weekends of escape that I became friendly with a boy from the coast called Aaron, who was the same age as me. The seaside was about as glamorous as it got in North Wales when you were that age and I remember being a little jealous that he seemed to be constantly on holiday, living by the beach.

It's one of nature's greatest secrets: why do people attract? What draws them together? For Aaron and me, at the age of fourteen, we didn't know but we really liked each other. Neither of us fully understood what was going on but we'd drink Pepsi and eat crisps on a Saturday night and then dash around trying to catch and then tickle the other. We'd go swimming and end up chasing each other around the swimming pool; splashing water and trying to pull each other's shorts down. It felt completely natural to behave like this. I still had Dad and his problems on my mind, and was always ready for my mobile phone to ring to be told he was dead or something. When I was with Aaron, I could relax. When we fooled around together everything else seemed to disappear. I knew what I was experiencing with him was more than just a normal friendship between teenagers. This was unique. There was a physical attraction between us and I worried that I fancied Aaron. Fancying Aaron would make me gay. I didn't want to be gay. Being gay was unheard of in our family.

Years later, when I was twenty-one, we bumped into each other in Soho. Aaron was, like me, 'out', and living life to the fullest. I was pleased he had managed to break out of his North Wales town. We spoke for hours and he told me he'd come out not long after our summer friendship. He'd realised he was gay and had accepted it a lot sooner than me.

Before I joined the army cadets, I had very few friends. Most youngsters in my area were causing trouble and having run-ins with the local police. I didn't want to get involved with that. The army cadets came along and allowed me to mix and get out there. I honestly don't think I'll ever be able to fully repay what I feel I owe to the organisation; I'd recommend it to anybody.

Most of the boys I became friends with during this time were a little older than me and, by being the kid in the group, I learned about the world through their words and actions. They were much more developed than me and were exploring their teenage feelings. Although I didn't quite understand it then, now I know it was my sexuality that attracted me to them. As soon as they all hit sixteen, they left to join the army. It was an exciting time for them, but a bit of a sad one for me – I still had twelve to eighteen months of waiting before I could do the same. The instant I could, I walked through the door of the army careers office in Wrexham, and my course in life was set.

3

A CALL TO ARMS

I, James Ronald Wharton, swear by Almighty God that I will be faithful and bear true allegiance to Her Majesty Queen Elizabeth II, Her Heirs and Successors, and that I will, as in duty bound, honestly and faithfully defend Her Majesty, Her Heirs and Successors, in Person, Crown and Dignity against all enemies, and will observe and obey all orders of Her Majesty, Her Heirs and Successors and of the generals and officers set over me.

That was the promise I swore on an August afternoon back in 2003, standing on the step of adventure in North Wales, wondering what the next few weeks, months and years had in store for me.

Though I was probably more prepared than most, I still had no idea what I was letting myself in for. I didn't know that I was about to embark on the greatest journey of my life, a journey that would see me visit some of the darkest holes earth has hidden away from the majority of its people. I didn't know that in ten years' time I'd be the happiest I'd ever been, openly gay and married to the love of my life, living in London with the most amazing friends imaginable. I certainly didn't think that I would meet the woman I'd just sworn to protect and give my life to ... but it all came to pass.

Right then, all I knew was Wrexham, a handful of friends and a girlfriend I was with to keep face and fit in. I'd never really wanted a girlfriend nor needed one, but most of the older guys in the cadets had one and when a girl asked me out, I said yes for completely the wrong reasons.

Her name was Kate and we'd been brilliant friends in the Army Cadet Force. As the time approached for me to leave North Wales and join the men and women of the British Army, she'd declared her love for me and we just became a couple. As lovely a person as she was, I never did feel right with her, particularly when we were alone and close. It was nothing compared to the feelings I'd experienced with Aaron on our weekends together. Kate and I even had a physical relationship, but it was something I really didn't feel any good at. Sex was something I just didn't enjoy. The unhappiness that befell me during those few days was noticeable to all. I didn't like having sex with Kate and I didn't really fancy her, which struck me as odd because she was a very pretty girl. I kept thinking back to Aaron and even wondered what sex would be like with him. I finally began to recognise my sexuality. I was gay. I was gay and was about to become a soldier. I didn't think the two could go hand in hand. I had absolutely nobody to talk to. I couldn't chat with Mum. How could I possibly discuss something as personal as my sexuality with my own mother? It was a very lonely time for me but I just kept it all to myself.

The long process of joining the army had started almost twelve months before. At the very earliest opportunity, I'd received my application form and filled it in at once. At fifteen years and nine months, the final part of the form was a permission pro forma which needed to be signed by my parents. Mum was not at all sure about signing me up and told me to carefully consider what this actually meant for me. In school, my head teacher Mr Davies desperately wanted me to go to college and consider a future in teaching, but I was certain that I wanted to join the army. All my friends had done so; I felt I was missing out. I'd spent the last twelve months longing for them. They'd all joined up and become real soldiers and real men – it was my turn to do the same.

Mum spent many an hour in the army careers office talking through, again and again, exactly what it was I was being signed up to do. They reassured her that there was no way I'd be going off to fight anywhere until I was at least eighteen. Also, they pointed out, there wasn't much going on in the world and that it was unlikely there'd even be a war for me to fight by the time I was old enough anyway. There was trouble in Afghanistan, but that barely made the news by 2003.

The recruitment team finally proposed a solution that made both Mum and me happy. I was to go to the Army Foundation College in Harrogate, North Yorkshire, for twelve months on a part-sixth form, part-basic training basis. They billed it as a fancy boarding school, which it kind of was.

She signed the papers and I was given dates to attend 'recruit selection', a two-day stay at a barracks during which I'd be tested physically and mentally to see if I was a suitable candidate for the army. I had two months to prepare.

Every day I'd train, whether out running in the many parks surrounding Gwersyllt, the village in which I lived, or at the local gym which I'd voluntarily painted the previous year. My life was completely placed on hold; I had to pass these tests. My GCSE revision was cancelled as the army was prepared to take me on regardless. Nothing else mattered.

The two months flew past and soon the time came for me to

go to selection. The recruitment office gave me a travel warrant which I exchanged for train tickets to a place called Lichfield. Lichfield was near Birmingham and felt like a million miles away from the rural village of Gwersyllt. I was beyond excited getting on the train that morning in my new shirt and trousers. Phil said he didn't have a tie that matched my shirt (whatever that meant) so I had money to buy a new one on the way. Mum cried tears of hope and sadness as she waved me goodbye that morning.

The first part of the process was a complete full-body medical. I'd heard lots of stories about this from the many friends who'd been through the process before me and I was nervous about the dreaded 'cough and drop' examination. Sixteen-year-olds like to keep their private parts private.

After about an hour with one of the doctors, I progressed through to the next phase: leadership. Half of the potential recruits were already heading home after failing to satisfy the doctors. I hoped it was plain sailing for me now. I'd prepared so much.

After the leadership task, something I'd practised for in the army cadets, it was on to the more physically challenging assessments. Pull-ups, press-ups, walking with heavy weights and something called a 'body mass check'. I was still on course for success.

We had the chance to mix with recruits who were some months ahead of us at the end of day one, which was a great opportunity to ask any questions and find out more about the harshness of basic training. We had to wear numbered bibs constantly as there was always an assessor watching over us. In the evening I, of course, didn't attempt to buy a drink in the bar – underage drinking would be a certain failure. You'd be surprised how many people fail because of that mistake.

We were taken back to our accommodation at about 11 p.m.,

which was later than I'd normally be allowed to stay up on a school night. I felt incredibly grown-up all of a sudden. My school buddies would be getting up in the morning and walking to school; I was away securing a different future. If I could just pass selection and be offered a job the following morning I'd be set for life; I'd be better than those boys who'd teased me for years on the playground for going to cadets.

I remember being excited but quite scared that night. I was by far the youngest person on selection. I was surrounded by fully grown men and there I was, skinny, acne-ridden, wearing clothes my mother had bought for me. I was nervous in the showers but still felt I had to act confidently. We were being watched by assessors constantly. I hoped to God they would like me and offer me a job. I'd pinned all my hopes on it.

The big morning arrived and two barriers stood between me and a potential lifetime in the British Army: a 1.5-mile best-effort timed run and a formal interview with a recruitment officer, who at the end of the process would tell you whether or not you were going to become a soldier.

I showered and then shaved, something I didn't really need to do, and prepared myself for the most nerve-racking few hours of my life. Seventy hopefuls had started the previous morning; about thirty of us remained twenty-four hours later.

I stood at the beginning of the 1.5-mile circuit, so scared my knees were visibly shaking. 'Please God let me run quickly,' I remember thinking again and again.

The whistle blew and we were off. And at a fast pace.

The training I'd put myself through, which had been watched closely by my cadet leader, Captain Bowles, was very solitary. I found it impossible to find a training partner to run with every day; most teenagers would rather play on their PlayStation, I guess. This was the first time I'd run 1.5 miles with other people.

My pacing was completely off compared to the majority; I had to run a lot faster just to keep up with these men.

The laps went by and soon we were on the home straight. Amazingly, some people had dropped out. I couldn't believe they were so unprepared. It was an instant failure to just give up. I crossed the line in about the middle section of the group. Ten minutes flat. It was the fastest I'd ever run. Surely I'd done enough to guarantee employment.

I showered again and donned my new suit for the main interview. I was looking about as good as a sixteen-year-old kid with acne could look.

As we sat in the waiting room for hours, amusingly the staff played episodes of *Blackadder Goes Forth* for us to relax to. As funny as I find that particular comedy these days, I was completely uninterested in the distraction. I do remember thinking that the officer conducting the interview could be someone just like Stephen Fry's General Melchett. The thought worried me somewhat.

As fate would have it, I was the very last person they called in for the interview. The five or so potential recruits that were called in before me had all been told they were unsuitable and that the army wasn't for them. I was sure my fate was sealed. Terrified, I almost left before facing the truth.

The day before I went away to Lichfield, some of the boys in school had mocked the thought of me becoming a soldier. They told me the army would laugh in my face and tell me to get lost. I couldn't bear the thought of having to go back to school the following day and tell them that they were right.

I was called forward and taken up some stairs to a quiet room. Once there, a senior major stood up and shook my hand.

'Mr Wharton. How d'you think you've done?'

I thought this might be the first question. How on earth do

you answer something like that? Should I go in confidently or should I use a bit of humility? How's a sixteen-year-old supposed to know the answer?

'Honestly, I think I could have shown myself in a better light throughout the leadership tasks.' I was clutching at straws really. What I wanted to say was I thought I'd done amazing, all things considered. Thankfully, I used some judgement.

'Yes, I agree... You were a little quiet throughout that stage, but considering your age and who you were up against, we marked you very highly.' Utter relief. 'There is something we are a little concerned about, however...' My heart dropped. 'You should be strides ahead of everyone in the 1.5-mile run. You're young, slim, fit and healthy. We'd have expected sub-nine minutes!'

I couldn't believe what I was hearing. The ten minutes I'd run the distance in was by far the fastest I'd ever done it. I was so proud. To hear it was what they were least impressed by was crushing. I felt my palms go moist and my collar become tight.

After some time listening to the major lecture me on how very difficult training would be for me and ultimately how under-prepared he thought I was, he looked up and smiled.

'We think you're made of strong stuff and I'm delighted to be able to offer you a job!'

The feeling of utter pride was immeasurable. I had done it! I was to become a soldier. I thought of the idiots in school who hadn't been through what I just had. They didn't have a job lined up. They weren't on their way to becoming soldiers. The jubilation I felt shaking the hand of the man who'd just given me a career was something I'd never felt before. Skinny James Wharton from a tiny village in Wales was to become a soldier. I'd done it.

I phoned Mum from outside the office to tell her the good news. I was expecting a great cheer of joy, but now I know why she didn't cry with glee. She had just witnessed her youngest child grow up and spread his wings. I'd be leaving home soon to start my new life.

In the weeks that followed, against the will of almost everybody – including the army – I completely took my mind off my forthcoming exams. It just didn't seem to matter to me any longer. Life was going to be amazing and I was revelling in the fame of being the quiet boy in school who was going to be a real soldier.

But, unexpectedly, everything changed.

On 19 March 2003, less than a month after I'd been guaranteed a job with the army, the United Kingdom, alongside the United States, invaded Iraq and sent the nation and its military to war: a dramatic time for the country but, for my household in particular, it was an utter disaster.

Overnight, my future with the army turned from being that of excitement and adventure to that of dread and uncertainty. Mum couldn't believe it and fell ill; her MS had a nasty habit of attacking her when she was most upset and vulnerable. She was bedbound for over a week and in much pain. I felt it was all my fault. I also felt I'd made a big mistake in signing up to the army on the eve of the greatest invasion our country had undertaken since D-Day. What the hell was about to happen to me?

As if by fate, on the very day we went to war, a letter dropped through our door addressed to me from the Ministry of Defence. It was my joining orders and instructions. It also contained my army number, which I was to learn, and my terms of service. This was supposed to be a huge moment of pride, but I couldn't help but feel my life was now on a countdown, ending with me being shot in a land far, far away.

I was to turn up at the Army Foundation College in Harrogate on 7 September, a whole five months away, and I would begin by earning £250 per week. £250 per week! That was more money than I'd ever had before. Wow, it was £1,000 a month. Even

Mum thought it was too much for a sixteen-year-old. What on earth would I do with that much money? I wish £1,000 was as desirable today as it was when I was sixteen.

Before the month was out, twenty-seven British servicemen were killed, and when their coffins returned to the UK draped in union flags, the sight deeply affected me and, even more so, my mum. I remember thinking what would happen if I, too, returned in that way. Mum was devastated that evening watching the images on the news. She felt the pain of those dead soldiers' parents. She'd placed herself in their shoes.

In the weeks that followed, witnessing the national outcry over the invasion of Iraq was a surreal experience for me. In school, a number of pupils organised a protest in the playground instead of going to lessons. I attended my English lesson and the teacher asked me why I wasn't outside with the rest of the school community. The answer was simple: how could a soldier-in-waiting possibly take part in a 'stop the war' protest? I was the only child in the school who abstained from the protests, which sucked because I'd have skipped lessons for any other reason!

On 1 May, President Bush made that ridiculous speech stating that major combat operations were over and that the war was at an end. The news changed the atmosphere in Phil and Mum's house, but our jubilation would be short-lived.

I spent the summer continuing with my fitness regime before the pain would really begin in the autumn. I completed my exams and busied myself with preparation for the army. I left the army cadets, which I miss to this day. Captain Bowles threw a party for me on my last night and all the other cadets brought me leaving gifts, mostly army-related, and Mrs Bowles baked a nice cake. I left with a lot of pride and promised to repay everything I owed to the organisation one day, a promise I'm still to fulfil. It was almost time to leave my youth behind me.

On the penultimate day of my childhood, Mum and Phil also threw a party so they and their friends could say goodbye and wish me well. I knew they felt they were losing a son and I understood that. We'd all had a stressful few months witnessing the troubles in Iraq and the sight of coffins being brought off the back of planes on the evening news. There were many tears that night, but none from me. I was excited. Tomorrow I'd be meeting lots of new people and my life in the army would begin.

The following morning, waved off by the neighbours on our street who had seen me grow up over the course of the previous few months, I left Gwersyllt. It didn't seem to take very long to get to the Army Foundation College. We stopped along the way but, for the most part, hardly a word was spoken by anybody. Upon arriving at the large entrance to the college, I was taken aback by how modern a place it was. Throughout my time in cadets, the army bases we used were always close to derelict. This was completely the opposite. It was immediately clear that I'd get the chance to do a lot of exciting stuff.

The whole base was open for our parents and loved ones to walk around and explore fully. They put on lunch for everyone and the staff put my mind – and Mum's – at ease as to what I could expect to gain from my time at the college. I had a smile on my face until the moment came to say goodbye.

Mum broke down. It was a huge moment in her life. Her youngest son was not only leaving home, but joining an army. The British Army. An army at war. I was only sixteen, after all. I was leaving a lot sooner than my brother or sister did. I was still the baby – even today, I'm still my mum's baby – and she couldn't hold back her tears.

Phil was quite excited for me; I remember him saying he'd probably quite enjoy staying there himself. The only person who could make my mum feel better was him and I was glad he'd be there for her.

It was a very difficult parting. As soon as she turned and walked away, it dawned upon me that I was now completely alone. I was no longer a child: I belonged to the army. Mum didn't look back once. She was just too upset to draw the affair out. As she walked, Phil comforted her and hurried her along. They left me there, on the cusp of adventure, and took my childhood home with them. I was now on my own.

4

BASIC TRAINING

I was placed in 6 Platoon, which was located on the top floor of a six-storey building, boasting views right across Harrogate and Yorkshire. There were elevators, but they were strictly for training staff use. We had to ascend and descend by foot, often running. The base itself was situated on Penny Pot Lane, a long country road leading out of the nearby town, and was surrounded by green fields dotted with the occasional block of forestry. To the north was a large reservoir, which we would run around many times in the weeks that followed. I hated that bloody reservoir.

At 6 p.m. on that first day we were all called into the corridor of our platoon lines and placed in alphabetical order right along the thin corridor. From a boy called Abraham to a boy named Williams who stood next to me at the end, there were forty-nine of us from all over the UK.

Stood the other side of me was a lad called Stephen Warren, from Tamworth originally. The two also bracketed my bed space; Warren and Williams, what a pair. We got on ... sort of, although I caught Williams trying to steal the light bulb from my desk lamp that very first night because his didn't work. It was a bad start. I never really liked him much after that. I considered him an opportunist thief.

The loud guy who seemed to be taking charge, the platoon

sergeant, a corporal of horse from the Blues and Royals, called the nominal roll and called us all cunts over and over again. He told us for the next forty-two weeks our arses belonged to him and his word was law. I wasn't sure if I liked the guy or not. I guess we weren't supposed to like him. But he oozed authority and from now on, he was dad.

He laid down a few ground rules: be on time; have the correct equipment; don't bully anyone and don't come out if you're a fag... 'I can't stand faggots,' he said. That last rule startled me. Was the army that openly homophobic? Maybe being gay just wasn't allowed. His statement rendered me totally confused and I could feel my heart shudder.

First out of the mouth of the platoon sergeant, those words seemed to be the party line in 2003: the army doesn't like faggots. I was terrified. It wasn't that long since I'd cried myself to sleep after realising that I was gay. After hearing those words, however, immediately I considered the possibility that I'd just had a phase. I was in the man's army now. Didn't every teenager experience confusion over their sexuality at some point? I forced it to the back of my mind. It was a teenage stage and now I was exchanging my youth for a life in the military. 'Faggots' didn't belong in the British Army. This was a fresh start.

In command of 6 Platoon was an officer called Captain Kilpatrick, who was an Irishman serving in the Scottish regiment of the Argyll and Sutherland Highlanders. My earliest impression of him was one of ultimate authority. He didn't come out of his office to greet us on the first day and when he did eventually emerge three or four days into our training, he simply gave us all a bollocking for looking untidy, demanding the platoon sergeant take us outside and teach us a lesson we'd 'never forget'. The platoon sergeant flew out of his office and thrashed us for an hour up and down the stairs of the barrack block. Of course, everything was all planned to break us down. I know now that the platoon staff would plan weekly on how we were to be treated, often turning the heat up and sometimes giving us a little slack. Thing was, we'd make plenty of mistakes over the course of the year and find ourselves in the bad books often enough, without the need for them to make things any more difficult.

A day of new beginnings, 7 September 2003 will stick in my mind forever. I'd been thrown into the middle of forty-eight other sixteen-year-olds. Thrilling but awfully awkward. The Scottish lads really intimidated me, mostly because they spoke with such aggression and swore in between every second word. It was scary stuff.

My earliest ally was a lad called Rich. He was from Sunderland and wanted to join the Army Air Corps. He is one of the few people in 6 Platoon that stuck true to his choice over the course of the year; most changed their minds, often to stay with a friend, or perhaps to be based somewhere specific. I did myself. I chose to follow the last person in the world you'd expect me to, our apparently homophobic platoon sergeant. His wall displays of the Household Cavalry were so colourful, littered with amazing pictures of the men of the regiment accompanying the Queen on state occasions and of the same men in small tanks, advancing on enemy positions either in the Falklands or during the very recent invasion of Iraq. He'd share stories of awesome derring-do on exercise in the middle of the night or during his lectures, which included a number of sexual health lessons. In fact, he'd always stall whatever he was teaching us to tell a tale from Bosnia or Northern Ireland. Although we'd started on a bad foot, and his anti-gay words should have turned me off him forever, as the weeks and months passed the platoon sergeant turned into a bit of a hero.

Rich was following a long line of men from his family

into the military and was about the most normal guy in 4 Section, the team of twelve men within 6 Platoon I found myself in. We became close over the opening few weeks.

4 Section was full of interesting characters. Skivington, a lad from Wigan, was absolutely obsessed with his penis and would think nothing of pulling down his pants to show it off. It was huge and I think he'd only discovered the fact upon joining the army and having to shower with other guys. It certainly caused amazement among the lads. Heterosexual teenage boys are very odd. Skiv left the army about three months later, reaching the conclusion that it just wasn't for him. I've never seen him since, which is a shame because I really liked him. I don't even remember his first name but Jesus, do I remember his antics.

A Leeds lad called Turner was an absolute comedy genius. He told brilliant stories and had fabulous jokes. Sadly, Turner also didn't stick it out and left just before Christmas. I've never seen him since, either.

In the corner of the room was a boy called Taylor from Warrington, who looked older than the rest of us, was bigger than the rest of us and spoke with a much deeper voice. He talked down to us and quickly became unpopular. He picked on the smallest guy, a lad called Vella, who was a bit of a geek. In true *Lord of the Flies* style, the eleven of us turned on him and he eventually handed in his 'Discharge as of Right'. I'm still ashamed that we didn't confront Taylor in some other way; instead we gave him a taste of his own medicine and he opted to end his career in the British Army before it had properly begun.

And then there was Junior Soldier Warren, my good friend Stephen, who, like me, was taken in by our platoon sergeant's tales of regimental life and opted to join the Blues and Royals. Stephen had the thickest Black Country accent I'd ever heard in my life. He extended every word he said by about four syllables, which was something he'd be ridiculed about through-out our friendship. During the months of basic training, Stephen and I became close, as I had with Rich and, soon, a boy called Rutter, who was moved into our room because he'd been bullying someone in another room. Strangely, we quite liked him. He was a dude.

Once I'd made my friends in 4 Section, I started to join up with lads from the other three sections that made up 6 Platoon. In 1 Section I became pally with Mike, a Liverpudlian who wanted to join the Royal Electrical Mechanical Engineers (REME). He was a nice guy and I'm sure we would have become best mates had we not been in different sections.

In 2 Section there was a boy called Jonesy who didn't stay in the army past Christmas. I was sure he was gay. We found ourselves staring at each other while changing one morning and both made our excuses once we started to get aroused. It was another fleeting experience with my concealed sexuality, though this time within the walls of the British Army. With Jonesy, I was reminded of the way I'd felt about Aaron – and I certainly didn't feel the same way about anyone else in 6 Platoon. If he'd remained in the army, I might have gathered the courage to talk about my sexuality for the first time, but when he quit training I lost my only potential ally.

Also in 2 Section was a guy called Dean Perryman, who became one of my closest friends throughout my decade-long stay in the army. Dean followed me into the Blues and Royals and we would share many adventures together.

It became apparent early on that Dean was a bit of a fighter. Often he'd fall out with one of the other lads and just simply go in tough and start a fight. One night later on in the year, Dean and Williams, the boy who tried to steal my bulb, had a fallout and decided to settle the score by meeting in the shower room late in the evening and fighting it out. As young men do, everyone went to watch the fight, which began right on cue at 9 p.m. As the two were fighting, somebody turned on the showers and they both slipped and slid in the water as they battered each other over and over. The fight ended when Dean punched Williams in the back of the head, forcing his face to smash against the tiles of the shower room floor, covering the place with blood. Finally, it was over. I'd never witnessed violence like it, but in the army aggression and combat came hand in hand, and such events soon had little effect on me.

In 3 Section, a great footballer called Robertshaw was a mate during the year though he became a little distant towards the end. I heard a few years later that Robertshaw didn't remain in the military for very long after Harrogate. Ollie Reucker was another chap in 3 Section I quite liked, an American who was later awarded the Military Cross for his heroic actions in Afghanistan. I think Ollie returned to America and is now serving in the US Army. I was casually reading a newspaper some years later when I saw a full-page picture of him. His story wowed me. He turned into quite the action man.

It's fair to say that we were quite a mix. Some of us shared common ground – most were from broken families, for a start. There was the odd character who had had a very privileged upbringing and some who had barely made it through childhood, moving from one youth hostel to another. We can't always get on with everyone but, for my twelve months at the college, I couldn't imagine experiencing the changes we each went through with a different bunch of lads.

Someone very cleverly took a photograph of us all on the first day and showed it to us at the very end. The change was unbelievable. I took many pictures over the course of the year, which I look at sometimes and consider where the boys are now, and one of the clearest messages from those pictures is that we all, every one of us, started to look more and more like soldiers as the year progressed.

In my head, we're all still sixteen.

As we were all still very young, the army invested a lot of money in our training, giving us a lot more than older recruits who were joining the army in 2003. Every recruit had to choose two activities to take part in weekly, which it was hoped we'd master and possibly even take on to higher levels. I chose skiing initially, which I would do on a Tuesday night in Sunderland, and go-kart racing, which I'd find myself doing for three hours on a Thursday. These activities were great fun and, more than anything, a chance to put the stresses of basic training out of mind for a few hours every week. The skiing activity culminated in a week-long jolly to southern France in the February, which turned out to be a great week away getting drunk, underage, in the Alps.

Mid-term we had the opportunity to swap our activities if we wished; I opted to drop go-karting and took up squash, with Perryman. The change brought Dean and me closer as friends, which was ideal as we'd both be joining the same regiment in the near future. We thrashed each other in the squash courts for six months. I considered myself a much better player but I know he'd disagree.

A highlight of our time in Harrogate was the three-day trip to Normandy visiting D-Day battle sites along the coast of northern France. The battlefield tour was billed as educational, but it was also a clever chance to get out of Harrogate and spend some time abroad. Alcohol was involved, although not officially, and we got into a lot of trouble, which we paid for once back in Yorkshire and on the moors.

I was awestruck by the enormity of the task the Allied

soldiers had faced on that June morning in 1944. Standing in the machine-gun nests that the Nazis had used to gun down thousands of invading soldiers over the beaches of Normandy was chilling. I kept thinking how it would have felt running off a boat and into such ferocity. Would I ever do similar? The stories we heard and the sights we witnessed were designed to inspire us as young soldiers. It certainly did that. I picked up a pebble from Sword beach and still have it today. I took it to Basra with me in 2007 and placed it next to my living space. It reminds me what a group of motivated young people can do and how the world was changed for ever by their heroic actions.

As my army training progressed, I remember feeling extremely close to the other boys by the time we'd reached halfway. The harshness of the experience had bonded us together and I naturally forgot and lost touch with most of the people I'd known prior to joining the army. I spoke often with the platoon sergeant as he became more forthcoming, especially to those of us who were joining his regiment, and he offered me some very frank but very honest advice as the months ticked by: 'Don't get too close to the boys, Wharton. You'll never see or hear of them again once this is all over.'

I didn't really believe him. I thought that the bond most of us had was pretty solid. We'd grown protective of each other and knew each other's weaknesses; but his words resounded and I kept them in mind as our training period drew to a close.

One night at the college sticks out in my mind. We were doing our mandatory two hours of military studies when all of a sudden a loud repetitive scream was heard coming from down the corridor. Everyone filed out into the hallway and moved through the double doors towards 3 Section's room, where the commotion seemed to be coming from.

Inside one of the boys, it appeared, had had a full breakdown and was crying and shouting uncontrollably. He was beyond the point of calming and I shouted at some of the other boys to get help.

Written on the wall behind the boy in thick black ink were the words 'RYAN IS A FAG!' and it was obvious to us all that the graffiti was the cause of his current state.

Soon enough, the training staff arrived and told us all to return to our bed spaces. We weren't told politely either. I will always remember the enraged look on Corporal Campbell's face, the corporal in charge of 3 Section, as he looked down at Ryan and back at us all.

Within thirty minutes, the remainder of the platoon staff had been called back in and were having, from what we could hear, a one-way conversation with the platoon commander, Captain Kilpatrick.

We heard the office door fling open and one of the corporals screamed, 'Corridor!' The entire platoon quickly scrambled out of various bed spaces and mustered in the long hallway ready for news.

Captain Kilpatrick exited the office and stood before us.

'You pin your ears back, fuckers, and you pin them back good!' His voice reverberated through the corridor.

'In 6 Platoon, I do not stand for bullying. In the army, we DO NOT stand for bullying. You little fuckers think you're going to pass out and become soldiers, well, I'm telling you now: YOU ARE FUCKING NOT!'

It was really bad; the worst to date. We'd been bawled at plenty over the course of the year, but this was different. This was the platoon commander being called in to deal with something late at night, hours after he'd finished for the day. He wanted blood and he promised those who were responsible that they would pay for it massively.

We were ordered back to our rooms and told to sit in silence until instructed otherwise. I returned to my room, where the boys began whispering rumours about what was going on.

'WHARTON!' The platoon sergeant's voice screamed from the office.

What the fuck? What on earth did they want to speak to me about? I had absolutely nothing to do with whatever 3 Section had been getting up to in that room of theirs.

All the boys in my room looked at me. It was written all over their faces; they thought I'd written that horrible sentence on Ryan's wall. Furthermore, I knew everyone else in the platoon would all be thinking exactly the same thing. I hurried myself to the office door and stood there like a rabbit in the headlights.

'Get in here, Wharton. And close the door!'

I was alone in the office with the platoon sergeant. The other platoon staff were elsewhere, probably making sure Ryan wasn't doing anything silly. I was invited to pull up a chair, something that had never happened before to anyone. Platoon offices were no place for recruits. I eyed up the personal effects and pictures the sergeant had on his desk: pictures of a wife, two young children. It was the first time I'd considered this man, who we each feared and admired in equal breath, as someone other than the army action man he'd portrayed himself to be.

'What's going on with Junior Soldier Ryan?'

'I don't know, Corporal O'Horse. It wasn't me!' I was terrified I was about to be booted out of the army for bullying somebody I'd rarely spoken with.

'I know it wasn't you, you idiot. Ryan says you're his only friend. He says you're the only person who doesn't bully him.'

I couldn't believe what I was hearing. Ryan had told the platoon staff that everyone hated him and that I was his only friend. Ryan had made me out to be a godsend that stuck up for him daily and took an active interest in his welfare. The truth was, however, I'd barely spoken with him; I didn't particularly like him very much and I certainly didn't consider him a friend. Why would he say those things to the platoon sergeant?

'Is he gay?' the sergeant asked. The memory of his first address to us all flashed across my mind. He'd made it very clear that he didn't like gay people. But how on earth would I know the answer to his question?

'I have no idea, Corporal O'Horse. He's never spoken about anything like that to me.'

As self-centred as it now sounds, I realised at that very moment that for the previous ten or so months none of us had held a grown-up conversation with the man I was in the middle of talking with. I felt good that I'd managed to break down some institutional barrier that prevented platoon sergeants and recruits from having grown-up discussions. I was helping with the enquiry as to what had occurred earlier in the evening. For a few minutes, I was a little more important than I'd possibly ever been.

He asked me again if I wanted to tell him who'd been bullying Ryan, but away from saying that pretty much everyone picked on him for one reason or another, I told him I wasn't of any further use to him.

Junior Soldier Ryan was officially the smallest, weakest and youngest-looking recruit in the whole platoon. He would always finish last. If anybody was late in the morning it was likely to be him and if something went wrong, which it often did, he'd resort to crying straight away. Knowing what I know now, I'd say the army wasn't suitable for him, but back then I guess I just thought he was a bit of a wuss, constantly letting the side down and causing us trouble.

The army, rightly or wrongly, puts its recruits in situations where 'it pays to be a winner'. The number of times I've heard that line shouted at soldiers over the past ten years is unreal. If somebody in a team, in this example 6 Platoon, is failing or letting the side down, the entire team is punished in the hope that it will make the individual responsible realise his actions have affected everybody. This usually makes that individual unpopular and often results in some other consequence later on, a beating or some other form of bullying from the boys in his section.

After I was unable to provide the platoon sergeant with answers, he decided that we would all be punished until someone owned up to writing on Ryan's wall. What followed was hours of misery, beginning with a run down the six flights of stairs and outside into the rain. Once there, and the sergeant could see us out of his office window, we were made to run back up the stairs and stand to attention in the corridor. This was repeated for some time. He then kept us stood in the corridor in silence, soaked and out of breath, for what seemed like hours. Eventually he sent us back to our rooms to arrange our lockers, which held all the equipment we used and which had to be kept to an immaculate standard. He inspected us an hour later, by which time it was gone 1 a.m. We had to be up at six!

After the locker inspection, and just as I was sure it couldn't get any worse, he made us all change into different orders of dress, thus destroying the locker lay-outs we'd just spent an hour arranging. We were experiencing what is affectionately known in the army as a beasting.

The clock ticked past 2 a.m. and while everyone was changing into chemical warfare outfits with respirators affixed for the second time, Ryan went to the platoon office and asked to speak with the sergeant privately. Five minutes later, it was all over. We were pulled into the corridor and told it was finished, the truth had emerged.

Robertshaw from 3 Section told me in the shower afterwards

that Ryan had admitted to writing on his wall himself. It was him all along. Crying out for attention, I suppose. The news filled everyone with anger, but everyone knew that, ultimately, we'd collectively pushed him to it. The following morning Ryan left the army and was never seen again.

I'd love to tell you that I pondered over the events of that night for days and weeks after, but, to be honest, twenty-four hours later we'd all moved on. Basic training was just so time-consuming. A long time after, I recalled the events over some beers while away on a course with other soldiers and it occurred to me that maybe Ryan was gay after all. He'd written those words on his own wall and blamed the rest of the platoon for his actions. He'd pretty much blamed everyone but me. He'd singled me out as his only ally. Why did he do that? Perhaps Ryan suspected I was gay. I wished he'd approached me directly and told me of his problems. I honestly had no idea at the time and, if he had come and spoken with me, perhaps we could have discussed our sexuality. It might have helped me to consider who I was and understand the feelings I was trying so hard to repress. I had no choice but to continue to keep my secret to myself.

Towards the end of our time in Harrogate a few of us discovered a staircase behind a boiler-room door leading up to the lofts. Once there, we had a huge space completely hidden away from the other 2,000 people in the college and, more importantly, from the staff who policed us with iron fists. Amusingly, we used to call the loft space 'Heaven', which is aptly the name of a night-club I'd discover in the future. I wished we'd found it sooner, but for the last six weeks it was the place to be once 'lights out' was called at 10 p.m. every night – very annoying if you wanted to watch *Shameless* (which everybody did), with offenders punished severely for breaking the lights-out rule.

Up until joining the army, I'd lived quite a sheltered life. Mum and Phil had tried their best to give me a proper upbringing. During my time at the college I was exposed to just about every taboo there was. Smoking. Everybody smoked. I didn't. Porn. Everybody had a DVD they guarded with their lives. Porn would be traded in the evenings and the boys would share reviews the next morning over breakfast. I became superficially involved in this black market, although I had no interest in the content of each film. I let peer pressure get the better of me where this was concerned. If the platoon staff discovered these DVDs they'd confiscate them – probably to their own rooms. I have to say, my sheltered upbringing was soon behind me and heavy drinking became the norm. After spending six weeks confined to camp, most of us were trusted to go out into the world on a Saturday afternoon. This, of course, led to the inevitable.

I joined a couple of the lads on an excursion to York one Saturday afternoon which turned into an extremely messy day out and ended with us all in a world of trouble.

We found a pub, one that was willing to serve us without ID, and settled there. Curfew was at 11 p.m. on a Saturday and that day we missed it.

The trouble we faced upon returning to the college was insane. We knew we'd messed up. It was so serious the four of us had to go and see the senior officer commanding Waterloo Company, which 6 Platoon was part of, on the Monday morning.

The platoon sergeant called us into the office. 'So, you are my four bad lads.' This was something I wasn't used to being called. I was a good lad. 'Thing is, gents,' he continued, 'the trick is not getting caught!' He recounted another tale of behaving very badly while serving in Bosnia ten years earlier and, naturally, getting away with it. A lesson was learned very quickly that morning. We got slapped wrists and were put on three-month warnings. We had to behave – or at least not get caught.

Before we knew it we were counting down to the last few weeks and days until graduation and leave. We'd soon be joining our respective regiments around the world.

Having chosen the Household Cavalry, Warren, Dean and I were to report to London after leave to begin ceremonial training and riding school. The excitement was really starting to build up. I'd never been to London and had always considered it a place where dreams came true. I'd seen the city in movies and on TV and hoped to live there one day; that day was now fast approaching.

The final challenge of basic training was 'Final Ex', a five-night exercise in the Northumbria hills testing all the skills we'd learned throughout the year. This was supposed to be the peak of testing environments, but in due course we'd all be going on much harder exercises for much longer and much further away than Northumberland.

They tested us well, attacking us throughout the night and making us travel long distances in the day. Of course the weather was awful, which I'm sure the platoon sergeant had arranged especially. He'd scream his favourite slogan at us whenever it was wet: 'If it ain't raining, it ain't training!' It was a challenging time and, as the end of our test week as soldiers arrived, it dawned on me that I was going to make it. I was going to pass out, a trained professional soldier, in front of my family.

Out of the forty-nine that began our army adventures on 7 September, thirty-nine had reached the end. Over the course of the year we lost ten guys, for various reasons but mostly because they found the army just wasn't for them. As testing a period as the whole thing was, there wasn't a single moment when I considered packing it all in and quitting. I'd made my mind up almost four years earlier that a life in the military was what I really needed, and achieving that meant basic training. Basic training was now over.

The whole family came to see me graduate a year after they'd left me at the college and, at that point, it was the proudest moment of my life. I'd gone through the army's basic training and reached the other side a tough young professional soldier. My school days felt so long ago. What were my schoolmates all doing now?

Two thousand soldiers passed out of training that day, some of whom would be fighting in Afghanistan or Iraq within six months. I didn't have that worry on the horizon for some time, as I, along with Dean and Warren, was off to the safety of London to ride with the Queen for a couple of years. The thirty-nine members of 6 Platoon marched off the square proudly that afternoon, the future quite unknown to us. We had a massive party at a venue in the middle of Harrogate, which ended with us all getting very drunk. We said our goodbyes to each other and that was that.

A year of being together every day, joking, fighting, drinking, all as one close happy family, was over. We've not been in the same room since nor are we likely to be again. It's not often in life one can say one has had a life-changing experience. I'm lucky enough to be able to say I've had a few. My first life-changing experience was over.

A few of us 4 Section boys, Rich, Warren, Rutter and me, travelled to Majorca on holiday the following week. It was a typical lads' holiday in the Med. Very messy, very late nights, lots and lots of drinking, but also our farewell to each other. A swansong, if you like.

The day we landed back at Manchester airport, the four of us knew, deep down, that we were heading to very different places and that, ultimately, it was the end. We said our goodbyes, lied to each other about meeting up at Christmas and went our separate ways. I was gutted and I think the others were too. I would miss

Rich and Rutter a lot but at least I had Warren, who was on his way to London, like me.

Unknown to me, it would be London that would offer me the chance to finally accept the truth about who I was. I'd soon find the courage to tell the world I was gay.

5

POMP AND CIRCUMSTANCE

It was September 2004. After a month of leave in the Welsh countryside, I was to report for duty with the Household Cavalry Mounted Regiment at Hyde Park barracks, London. The barracks, rebuilt in the 1960s, separated Hyde Park from Knightsbridge and was just about the craziest place to have an army base. Our next-door neighbour was the Mandarin Oriental hotel, with Harvey Nicks across the street and Harrods a few dozen yards away.

The night before, Dean, who was also reporting for duty the following day, stayed with me at my Aunt Audrey's house in East Grinstead. Their house was an hour from London by train and my Uncle Ray accompanied us the following morning as we made our way to SW7. He threw us in a cab at Victoria, which was the largest station I'd ever seen, and gave the driver £20, which I now know is about £12 too much for the relatively short drive through Belgravia into Knightsbridge.

We stepped out of the cab in the new suits we'd bought especially for that very moment and stared up at the large institution we found before us. You'll know, if you've ever walked past the barracks in Knightsbridge, that the smell of horse droppings and stable dust, which at various times of the day changes in its potency, almost knocks you off your feet. I wasn't overly impressed at this first notable point.

Sensing we were fresh meat, the cab driver ushered us over to the entrance gate, which you'd miss unless you were looking carefully, and gave us a nod of reassurance, as if he were our proud father bidding us farewell. We pushed the gate and were met by a large figure, who we assumed was angry and inconvenienced by our arrival.

'What are your names, boys?' he said with a Welsh accent.

'Wharton and Perryman,' Dean returned sharply, looking at me for encouragement.

He ticked his list and told us to drop our bags off on the sixth floor and report back to him straight away.

'Your names will be on a door!' he shouted at us as the lift door slammed shut.

Both my name and Dean's were on the same door, as was our Harrogate friend Warren's, though he was nowhere to be seen. We dumped our bags on our chosen beds and rushed back to the ground floor, which for some reason was actually the second floor in the lift; the place felt like a maze. This confusion, added to the striking smell of horses and stable life, was quite disorientating.

I remember thinking that we'd probably be told to get some uniform on to carry out some task, but on return to the guard room, the large corporal of horse who had greeted us just ten minutes earlier simply informed us to report back for duty at 9 a.m. the following morning – an incredible twenty-three hours away.

'What do we do in the meantime?' I squealed.

'What?' he asked, looking completely baffled by the question.

'Are we to stay in our rooms?' I wouldn't have minded if his reply was positive; the view from our sixth-floor window was amazing, with a clear sight of Battersea Power Station. Even the incoming Heathrow passenger jets flying overhead were exciting stuff for me.

'Guys ... it's Sunday fucking morning! Go out, have a look around. Find some girls... Go and get fucking wasted! Just make sure you're on time tomorrow morning!' And with that he slammed the guard room door shut in our faces and left us to it. It was hugely different from Harrogate, where everything we did was controlled and overlooked by a member of the training team.

With our shiny suits still on, we headed out into London. To where exactly? We didn't know.

Eventually we found ourselves in Leicester Square, which was amazing! Cinemas, theatres, bars, hundreds of people. It was a thrilling experience. To be standing in the places I'd heard of all my life was incredible. Oddly, I wanted Mum to be there. I wanted to share this adventure with my family.

We continued through some dirty-looking streets and found ourselves on Dean Street, which Dean thought was a perfect photo opportunity. I look back at the picture to this day with a little smug grin, knowing now that we'd stumbled upon the heart of gay land in the capital. Dean wouldn't have been so chuffed if he'd have known that back then. I wondered how the other boys from Harrogate were getting on. What were their first days like? Where was Warren? Had he arrived at the barracks yet?

An hour later we wandered up the Mall, which prompted me to call Mum and tell her with glee that I was about to see Buckingham Palace for the first time.

'Oh, you'll see Batman there then!' Had she actually gone mad? I thought. When we reached the Victoria Memorial opposite the palace, which I'd soon be referring to as the birthday cake, the strange comment Mum had made on the phone became clear.

On 12 September 2004, two members of the fairly extreme 'Fathers 4 Justice' climbed over the perimeter wall surrounding

Buckingham Palace, dressed as Batman and Robin, to stage a demonstration on the balcony overlooking the Mall.

Luckily for them, Her Majesty was 'out of the office', as she is most Sundays, and, therefore, they were still alive. I'm sure if it had been a Monday and the Queen was in residence they'd have been shot almost immediately by a very eager Irish Guard or police marksman. As it was, she wasn't, and Batman, now without his trusty caped crusading partner, was sat quite happily with the world's media and thousands of people looking on, include Dean and me.

It was a surreal introduction to Buckingham Palace and indeed London. We stayed in position for about an hour, cheering when a police officer on a large crane (they wouldn't climb out on to the balcony to arrest him, as that would mean transporting him through the palace to a waiting police car – no demonstrator, however noble his cause, was having a behind-the-scenes look at life in the world's most traditional institution) arrested him and removed him from the front of the palace.

After wandering around Westminster for hours, we hopped on a tube (again very exciting) and got off in Hammersmith. Our method for selecting areas of interest was simple: if it was a name we recognised and it sounded exciting, we were interested.

Though we were both still seventeen, Dean, who is younger than me by about ten months, bought me my first pint as a grown-up soldier, in a Wetherspoon's near the tube station. I felt like a real adult wearing my suit, which my mum had chosen for me, sipping on a pint of lager in Britain's capital city. It was completely surreal compared to what I'd been used to at Harrogate.

We returned to the barracks at about 6 p.m., completely forgetting that other soldiers, most of whom we'd never met before, would be on the sixth floor settling in, as Dean and I should have been all afternoon.

The corridor was a flurry of activity and someone, as is always the case in the army, had found it necessary to play extremely loud and inappropriate music. Like us, most had chosen to wear what was visibly a new suit but, alarmingly, a few had turned up to their new job in jeans and polo shirts. One or two, very worryingly, had tracksuit bottoms on. I hadn't worn tracksuit bottoms since I was thirteen. Warren had turned up by the time we returned and was unpacking his belongings in the room Dean and I had thrown our bags down in hours before. It was nice to see him after our three weeks apart.

That evening I met lots of new people. Most had little impact on me but a few of the new guys became amazing friends to me, and one or two of them over the course of the following months would change my life.

Shane Ibbetson, one of the boys in a tracksuit, was from Leeds and had apparently turned up to Hyde Park barracks earlier in the day in a police car, having got completely lost in London and needing help. I could tell immediately he was quite a character.

Another new face was Jamie McAllen. Jamie, from Romford originally, became one of my closest friends in the four or so years I knew him. We're still in touch but he called it a day on return from Afghanistan in 2008. The army lost one of its most mature soldiers when Jamie left. He was some years older than the rest of us and it felt unusual to be equal to somebody who was eight years my senior, having only served with recruits my own age in Harrogate.

Also settling into Hyde Park barracks that Sunday evening was a Mancunian called Josh Tate. Josh was only a few days older than me and we hit it off straight away.

The final notable additions to our initial meetings that night in 2004 were a couple of Fijians who had travelled across the planet to join the British Army. Trooper Babakobau, who held some authority in his native village, and his close friend Trooper Torou were incredible giants of men. Both had found themselves in the Household Cavalry and were looking forward to learning to ride. I remember them saying that they'd never touched a horse in their lives. Amusingly, neither had I!

When I think back to that autumn night all those years ago, I remember fondly how it felt meeting the guys I'd inevitably be spending my career with. I realise now that we were blinded. I thought we'd all stay together and ride horses, possibly going to somewhere like Iraq in the many years that would follow. What came to pass was something quite different. Some of us would certainly see war; some of us wouldn't. Some would find the army not for them and, very sadly, one of us would be killed in action. If someone had told me that on that Sunday evening, an evening of new introductions, I'd have probably reconsidered my future on the spot.

The course was due to last about seven months, finishing the following spring. By then we'd be capable Horse Guards, riding to a high standard on state occasions for Her Majesty and immaculately turned out for visiting heads of state and dignitaries.

It all sounded wonderful, but I had no idea what exactly lay ahead of me throughout those cold and dark winter months. It would prove to be the most testing stage of my young life.

The first part of our training was based in Knightsbridge and was all about wearing state uniform correctly and learning how to clean it for parades. It was all quite straightforward stuff, but I was amazed by just how much of the uniform there actually was. Everything needed cleaning and shining, even bits that couldn't be seen. There was utter confusion on all our faces when the corporal told us that the inside of the state helmet needed to be just as shiny as the outside. Why on earth? The point became known to us as the 'backs of brasses', and would basically earn you brownie points on inspections if you'd bothered yourself to make the hidden brass as shiny as the visible brass.

By the end of the initial four weeks, known as 'drill ride', we had to present ourselves in state kit, march around the square in front of the colonel and show that we knew how to carry our swords correctly. I took pretty much everything on board quite quickly, but already there were weak links in our team, causing us all extra work which, as in Harrogate, affected everyone and made those individuals quite unpopular.

There were a lot of opportunities to get out and explore more of London as the four weeks of drill ride progressed. It was very usual to head out of an evening or on a Sunday, when we'd generally have downtime. If I caught sight of two men walking hand in hand or two lovers embracing, long-suppressed feelings would re-emerge and I'd struggle not to stare at whoever the two people were. I still wasn't ready to accept my sexuality, let alone talk to anyone in the army about it.

Soon it was time to move to the Household Cavalry training wing in Windsor, home of the famous riding school. It was another very pretty place I'd never seen before, but somewhere I'd be seeing an awful lot more of in the future. This was home for the next five months, taking us through Christmas, my eighteenth birthday and into the spring months.

The first horse I ever sat on was called Sebastian, who was huge at seventeen hands, big, black and beautiful. I was one of the lucky boys who had a friendly horse; some weren't so fortunate and were introduced to all things equine by an unfriendly beast who kicked and bit. The experience was scary enough as it was; a horse that was vile and nasty made the entire situation a million times worse.

On the first day we sat on our mounts in the riding school and Tim, our riding instructor (who would become a very close friend later), told us that if we just 'squeezed' our legs, our horses would walk forward. And they did. Within three days, Tim had us trotting, turning left and right as well as backwards, and even taught us how to stop. By the end of week one, I was one of the few clever guys who hadn't fallen off.

A few weeks later, by which time we were cantering around the indoor school at a lightning pace, I still hadn't 'come off'. I was the only soldier in the entire ride who hadn't bitten the dirt by crashing to the ground. Tim would soon change that.

It turned out the boys had had quite enough of me gloating about my bottom seemingly being glued to the saddle so, en masse, they approached Tim to see if he could change things. Of course, he easily could.

The following day Tim had us doing individual riding exercises which were designed to make us all competent riders on our own. My turn came and I began to kick on into a nice trot. At the corner, I slipped into canter and began to circle, picking up pace doing so. Abruptly, Tim, with a grin half-fixed on his face, threw his schooling whip at Sebastian and me, causing the horse to bolt upright on his hind legs and obviously causing me, at that very junior level, to crash to the ground with an almighty thud.

The wind was taken out of me and I ached all over. Sebastian was having a fit at the other end of the school while the boys were all laughing and cheering with joy at my downfall. Tim casually walked over to me in his sharp riding staff blue attire, picked me up and asked if I was OK. I gave him a nod and smiled.

'Told you I'd get the fucker,' he said to the rest of the class, to which they applauded excitedly. I made my walk of shame to Sebastian and jumped back on.

Riding school was full of amusing events like that. As awful as it sounds, there was something very funny about seeing one of your mates being thrown out of the saddle and crashing to the ground or into the wall with a loud thud. I saw one soldier break his leg on one such fall and even with the horrific screams of pain coming from the man's mouth, some of the boys still atop giggled in the commotion. I put it down to a nervous thing. We were all quite close to injury and some suffered incredibly; the only thing to do was laugh. If you didn't laugh, you'd cry with fear.

Drinking was becoming the norm for most of us in the evenings. We'd finish in the stables at about 4 p.m., clean whatever kit was needed for the following morning and then head out to the nearby town centre of Windsor for food and drinks at about 7 p.m. Most of us were still underage, but our eighteenth birthdays were each drawing closer. The exception to this was Jamie, of course. I felt a bit sorry for him, being twenty-five and only having a bunch of seventeen-year-olds to hang around with. He was the same age as most of the corporals set above us. He was even older than Tim, who, quite against the rules, would join us for drinks most evenings. How we used to stay out to the early hours and then get up to ride horses with very little sleep is beyond me.

In November, the training wing was tasked to provide a dismounted guard at Windsor Castle for the state banquet celebrating the Entente Cordiale, marking a hundred years of Anglo-French relations. We rehearsed long for this exciting role and spent many hours making our boots shiny.

The event would happen on the same day as the State Opening of Parliament at which we were also tasked to provide a 'staircase party', lining the stairs at the Sovereign's Entrance for the Queen and Duke of Edinburgh to walk up before Her Majesty donned the Imperial State Crown and robes. Again, there were many rehearsals involved for the role, and many an afternoon was spent at the Palace of Westminster in the days leading up to the Queen's Speech. Soon, the busy period was forgotten about completely as an immense feeling of anticipation shot around us all. This was our first attempt at being professional Household Cavalrymen.

The day before, we carried out a full rehearsal of both the State Opening of Parliament and the Entente Cordiale celebration. It went perfectly and the excitement was barely containable among us boys. After the practice, we were treated to a behind-the-scenes tour of both the Houses of Commons and Lords. It was a real treat and I sat in the Prime Minister's seat while our host wasn't looking, which Dean found rather amusing.

We had to get from the Sovereign's staircase at Westminster to the entrance of Windsor Castle within a short space of time, something that would prove difficult in the West End and along the M4 at rush hour on a Thursday afternoon. The solution was simple: we would be provided with a police escort and rushed through the busy streets and along the motorway back to Windsor. Things were just getting better and better.

I rang home and told Mum of my position on the stairs so she could spot me on the telly easily. The whole family was watching and recording the moment to keep forever.

The day finally arrived. I figured that if the events of the day didn't go well, or if for any reason I didn't enjoy what was being asked of me, I might as well resign and think of something else to do. The pressure that went with being inspected to such a high standard, before being placed in front of the Queen's eyes, was really concerning. Nobody wanted to fall at this first post. Turn-out and smartness was supposed to be my bread and butter as a cavalryman. The Queen was going to pass by me and look me square in the eye. I needed to keep cool and calm. Failure was not an option.

We dressed ourselves in the uniform we'd spent the previous weeks preparing. An officer I'd never seen before inspected every inch of us. The majority of us passed with flying colours; some of us, as was often the case, failed at the early hurdles and found themselves in trouble. Some didn't have their boots shiny enough; others had forgotten to shine a piece of hidden brass. Everything was expected to be immaculate.

The rest of the regiment was being inspected on the main square while we made our way over to the waiting coach that would take us to Westminster. The regiment would leave after us and make its way to Buckingham Palace to collect Her Majesty. Then they'd escort her to the Sovereign's Entrance where she would disembark her state coach and walk up the steps to the robing room, passing me on the way. The BBC were capturing every moment of the occasion and any mistakes would be highlighted by the commentators amassed in a TV studio somewhere.

I was in position thirty minutes before the Queen was due to arrive. All I had to do was stand perfectly still on my step, looking ahead at the Life Guard, in his sharp red tunic, standing opposite me across the staircase. The Life Guards were one half of the Household Cavalry and were formed a year before us in 1660. Because of that fact, they were the senior regiment of the British Army. The clock ticked away as my thoughts drifted to what was about to happen. What would the Queen look like this close? What would she smell like? Would she stop and talk to me?

A fanfare of trumpets burst into life and a hundred horses could be heard trotting along the concrete outside. In an instant the trumpets and horses were silenced. I couldn't help but picture what was going on just outside: the sound of a carriage door closing; the mutterings of an elderly duke to his dear wife; the sound of the carriage now leaving the entrance to this incredible edifice. The Queen was about to enter the building. I imagined the royal standard flying above Westminster Palace, customary to the arrival of the monarch.

'Household Cavalry... Royal salute. Carry swords!' This was the order we'd all been waiting for. My arm shifted instinctively and my sword bolted upright. From the corner of my eye I began to make out the small figure of Her Majesty ascending the staircase, the Duke of Edinburgh in his formal naval uniform holding on to her arm as she walked. Every single one of us grew an extra six inches taller with the company we now found ourselves in. My heartbeat accelerated and I felt the hairs on the back of my neck stand on end.

The Queen looked amazing. More amazing than I'd ever seen her on TV. She moved herself elegantly and with purpose, taking in all that was going on around her. I felt her eyes drift over me and my uniform. I couldn't help but watch her as she went, enjoying every millisecond of my time with her. These were my few precious moments with the Queen. I was proud to my inner being and I wanted the experience to last forever. Then she passed by and made her way into the robing rooms to don the state robes and take the crown on her head.

Within forty minutes, the Queen had addressed her Parliament and was ready to head back to Buckingham Palace. The boys outside would deal with that. Before that, however, I had the privilege of standing bold while Her Majesty walked down the stairs and out to her waiting carriage once again.

On the return trip down the stairs, the Queen passed by more quickly. I suppose it was 'job done' and she was now looking forward to lunch back at the palace. I enjoyed the few seconds when she passed me by and I wondered when I'd next be so close. Would it be later on that day at the French celebration at Windsor Castle?

Within minutes the Queen had gone, followed soon after by the crown jewels, which would make their way back to the Tower of London under close guard. We were marched off the staircase and out to our waiting coach. It was full speed ahead to Windsor Castle with blues and twos.

I've lived in west London for some years now, but never have I been able to get to the M4 without stopping at a traffic light or some arrogant taxi driver pulling out in front of me. That afternoon, with our flashing blue-light escort made up of two cars and what seemed like endless motorbikes, we set off from Parliament Square and didn't come to a halt at all for the thirty or so miles to Windsor Castle. It was crazy. I most enjoyed looking at the baffled faces of onlookers as they saw us go. Who was in that coach?

When we arrived at the castle I was surprised to see a medium-sized anti-French protest going on outside the gates. What were they protesting about? We took up our positions in earnest as somebody came around and touched up our brasses. I stood at the top of the steps next to the main entrance to the area of the castle where the state dinner was being hosted by the Queen. I noticed early on that there were film crews capturing the event from within the castle walls. I overheard one of the cameramen say it was for a BBC project. Thoughts of TV stardom entered my tired head. I'd been wearing full state kit for some hours and my body ached.

It was dark with rain falling heavily as guests began to arrive. Many cars pulled up opposite to where I was positioned and important people disembarked, most of whom I didn't recognise. Suddenly, another blacked-out saloon pulled up and out of it came Arsène Wenger. Stood there in the pouring rain this celebrity sighting raised my spirits again.

More cars arrived and people made their way into the castle from the pouring rain. Then I noticed flashing blue lights on the front of a car as it entered the centre quadrangle of the castle grounds. When it pulled up opposite me, a very smart Tony Blair stepped out of the vehicle. He dashed up the steps and stood next to me, trying to shelter from the downpour while he waited for his wife Cherie, who I could see was putting a final touch of lipstick on in the back of the car.

'Good evening,' he said to me. 'Terrible weather!'

It wasn't just a slight shower, the rain was throwing it down, and I'm sure the Prime Minister felt very sorry for me standing there soaked to my skin.

'Good evening, Prime Minister' were the only words that came into my head and with them the pair walked past me and into the castle. Unbelievable. I had held a conversation, albeit a brief one, with the Prime Minister. I couldn't believe it. I couldn't wait to tell Mum on the phone.

The guests were to enjoy a full royal banquet in the presence of the Queen and both Prime Minister Blair and President Chirac. We, meanwhile, simply got back onto our coach and returned to the barracks, which was only five minutes away, without any supper waiting for us.

In bed that night I considered just how incredible the day had been. From putting on the kit for our first official occasion to standing on the staircase and catching that amazing first glimpse of our Queen. The excitement of the police escort to Windsor and the surprise of having the briefest of conversations with the Prime Minister. These kinds of things didn't happen to people like me. I wanted to tell the world and relish the feeling of euphoria for as long as possible, but there wasn't time. The next morning we were back at the riding school, though there would be plenty more opportunities to mingle with the royals in future. One thing was very clear though: I had loved every minute. I was certain I'd made the right choice. The Household Cavalry was definitely for me.

†

The nights we spent in Windsor over the winter months were some of the greatest of my life. The entire ride would go out on a Friday to the hotel opposite Windsor Castle, which held weekly karaoke nights. Jamie, Josh and I would sing week in, week out, culminating the evening with a rendition of 'California Dreamin''. Josh always took the lead.

Christmas was on us soon enough and with it my eighteenth birthday on New Year's Day. My three friends took me out and we drank the night away in some dodgy bar in Slough. What an eighteenth! The four of us had certainly become close over the winter months, Dean, Josh, Jamie and me. The variety of experiences we faced together drew us closer, and this time I allowed myself to get attached because we'd be together in the regiment for the long term. Warren had drifted away from Dean and me slightly, for no other reason than he'd become friendlier with a few of the other guys. The thing about constantly meeting new people, moving around the country with the army and making new friends, is that mates sometimes drift apart. I was starting to become used to it.

The end of riding school was fast approaching and Tim turned up the heat for the final few weeks to ensure we were all at the required standard before handing us back to the regiment in Knightsbridge for ceremonial duties. We'd nearly made it.

Riding school is followed by a final four weeks of training back at Knightsbridge, known as the dreaded 'kit ride', which teaches the soldier how to ride a horse in full state uniform, as opposed to the traditional riding style learned at Windsor. It's a horrible experience. The four-week package is considered one of the most gruelling phases of a soldier's career, with daily inspections ensuring turn-out is to the required standard for state occasions.

In the weeks that passed in the run-up to kit ride, I'd become quite down about things. It wasn't the job, not at all. I really enjoyed riding and being part of a great organisation. But something was amiss. Over the winter months I'd joined in with the fun of being one of the lads, but had been uninterested in some of the activities Jamie, Josh and Dean were getting up to while out on the town, mostly involving girls. I'd started to think quite a bit about one of the guys, after hearing a rumour about him apparently involving some gay men's magazines that were spotted in his room. Once I'd heard the rumour, I realised that my interest in him was more than just the usual curiosity. Those feelings I'd hoped were just part of a teenage stage hadn't actually gone anywhere. Of course they hadn't. I was fed up of pretending not to feel a certain way. I didn't know what to do, who to turn to or where to look for help. But with so much work to do preparing to finish riding school, I just couldn't deal with it all. I continued on and attempted to pick myself up. But it wouldn't be long before everything came to a head.

I rarely slept for the entire month of kit ride. I was just too busy ensuring my kit was immaculate enough. My jackboots, breastplate, state helmet and my white leather buckskins had to gleam for the morning inspections. I also had my own horse, Agincourt, to care for and keep in pristine condition.

Soldiers had been broken during kit ride and we'd all been told the horror stories from the past. The equipment we were using was so expensive everybody was told to take out private insurance, just in case a sword was stolen or lost.

One of the early stories passed onto us in the bar at Knightsbridge was about a young lad who, a year before, somehow lost his state helmet, sword and scabbard and even his red plume while trying to get ready for the following morning's inspection. He didn't raise the alarm and report the loss; without insurance he knew he'd be met with a bill which would run into the thousands. Instead, he decided to throw himself out of the seventh-floor window in an effort to make all his problems go away. How could things possibly get that bad? How could things be *allowed* to get that bad?

We heard lots of awful stories like that. I often wondered whether they were just tall tales from the older boys, trying to scare us kids. These days I laugh at some of them although I can vouch for a lot of them, too. I've told stories myself to the younger lads who are new to the game which I'm sure are probably just as intimidating.

At the end of each week of the kit ride, a large formal inspection took place on the regimental square, each more important than the last. The first of these hurdles was an inspection by the kit ride officer, a junior officer in the regiment who was administratively in charge of us while in kit ride. We sailed through his inspection and he gave us the nod to progress through to the second week, at the end of which would be our first major challenge: the riding master's inspection.

The riding master was the most feared man on camp. He was ultimately in charge of all things equine, which in the Household Cavalry Mounted Regiment was everything. His name was Captain 'Dickie' Waygood and he went on to train the British Olympic equine team for the 2012 games after leaving the army.

Up until that point I'd been doing rather well and had been appointed the coveted position of 'Leading File', meaning I rode at the front of the ride with everyone else following on behind. I was so chuffed and Mum used the news as ammo back home in Wales.

During the week leading up to the RM's inspection, things started to get very difficult when one or two of us stopped achieving the standards expected and the riding staff cranked the heat up on us. People started to break. When the RM's inspection dawned, we were all hanging on to what little morale we had left.

Without morale we were dead in the water. No sleep, not much food, certainly no free time to relax. Morale was the only thing keeping us going. Well, that and Pro Plus. On that morning, my morale finally went.

After twelve long hours of cleaning my jackboots (and paying £100 to one of the older lads to finish them off for me) I walked into the square for inspection, holding Agincourt's reins as I went. Without warning, someone dropped something making an enormous noise, spooking my beautifully groomed horse. In an instant I found myself crawling on my hands and knees in a puddle of dirty rainwater and horse crap. I was gutted.

Once back on my feet, I stormed out of the main gate and into Hyde Park. The guards on the gate watched in utter surprise at the sight of a young soldier marching off into the busy London park in full state uniform. I had completely blown my top. All my hours of sleepless kit cleaning had been trashed. I thought my career in the Household Cavalry was over before it had even begun and it wasn't even my fault.

I sat myself down on a park bench next to an old man and his dog. He looked me up and down. I had tears rolling down my face, a sword in one hand and my now water-stained state helmet in the other. 'Don't let the bastards get you down, son,' he said.

I'm not at all spiritual but right then it felt like I was talking to my granddad, Jimmy. It was as if that old man on the park bench was always meant to be sat there waiting for me that Friday morning.

I pulled myself together and walked off back towards camp, from which a member of the guard was now running. When he reached me he checked I was OK and I was taken to the doctor. Although I felt like I'd calmed down, I was still visibly shaking. I had no control over my emotions. The doc told me to relax over the weekend and think of other things apart from horses and jackboots, which he then extended to everyone in the ride. As glad as I was about being granted some downtime to recuperate from the heavy pressure of kit ride, I was sure I'd blown my chances of passing out and joining the men of the regiment. If anything, I'd proved that I couldn't handle the pressure. I'd failed at keeping a calm head on my shoulders and taking everything in my stride, two hugely important traits for a soldier. Fortunately, Tim assured the riding master that I would have passed the inspection had it not been for the horse being spooked by the loud noise and the rain water. He believed him and allowed me to progress through.

That weekend, all the loose ends of my life came together.

Dean, Jamie, Josh and I headed out to forget about the stresses of kit ride on the Saturday afternoon, finally settling in Fulham where we watched the opening match of the 2005 Six Nations rugby tournament with Wales taking on England. Wales beat England before going on to win the grand slam the following month. I got drunk celebrating with my three English friends after the victory. Later, and after many beers, we got into a discussion about the events leading up to that evening, in particular the riding master's inspection the previous day.

They asked me if anything was wrong and why exactly I had snapped before the inspection. I told them that it was just the stresses of kit ride and not to worry about it, but they had an agenda. I knew this conversation had been coming my way for weeks. Some time before, Jamie had passed an innocent comment to me about my lack of interest in women. He didn't linger on the thought at the time, but I now realised that he wasn't just making an off-the-cuff remark. He was trying to let me know that he understood I was different.

Dean, who knew me so well, pointed out that my actions the previous day were completely out of character and Josh spoke about how very different he thought I'd been acting in general. They kept asking me if I wanted to get anything off my chest, at which point Dean just announced he thought I was gay and that I was struggling to come to terms with the fact.

I couldn't believe someone was actually saying those words to me. Nobody had ever mentioned such a thing. A bit of me wanted to take offence but the other side of me felt something quite different. Something I hadn't really felt before. Liberation.

The three sat there in silence, staring at me. I couldn't find the words I thought I should respond with; instead, I found the words I'd longed to say for years. 'Yes. I'm gay.'

I wish I could express what it felt to finally say those words. I'd said something that I'd never said before, although I'd known for some time. The biggest problem in my life was accepting the fact that I was gay. Since the age of sixteen I'd known for sure, but had convinced myself upon joining the army that it was a phase that might pass as I became a soldier. Every time my repressed sexuality came to the surface, I'd swallow it down and keep it locked up. At last I'd opened the door – and I was out!

Jamie still to this day insists he'd known for months about my hidden sexuality. I'd often play it down but it was obvious: Jamie had known all along. The truth was out. What next? Was I about to be beaten up? Was I about to find myself alone in west London, deserted? In the ten or so seconds of silence that we all found ourselves in, each trying to capture our thoughts, hundreds of possible outcomes flashed through my mind. Loneliness. Bullying. Rejection. Loathing. Repulsion. What was going to happen now?

Dean stood up and opened his arms to hug me. To me, he was the greatest person in the world at that moment. I was glad to have someone like him. He and the others promised to stand by my side. They reaffirmed their friendship with me and congratulated me again and again for coming out.

The night continued and we all agreed to hit the following week and the dreaded inspection on the Friday head-on. We were going to finish this course together and become fully trained Household Cavalrymen.

Right then, I felt empowered by my announcement and the support my close mates had displayed to me. Thoughts of the remaining weeks of kit ride disappeared off my radar. I felt on top of the world. My recent anxiety was inextricably linked to my unhappiness in myself. I had been unhappy since my early teens, ever since I'd hidden my real self. I was finally ready to embrace who I was. I wanted to be gay.

The third week started with a bump on that very early Monday morning. The riding staff had decided that, after our weekend off, they were really going to put us through some pain, riding in the indoor school in full state kit at 8 a.m. By the time I'd sweated it out in the saddle for a few hours and returned to the stables, the gossip from the weekend had started to circulate. Initially I was a little upset that my closest three friends had somehow let slip the news but I knew them well and I was sure they wouldn't have done it maliciously. In the end, they were probably doing me a favour.

While I was taking Agincourt's kit off and feeding him his breakfast, some of the older lads in 2 Troop – to which I belonged – asked me if it was true what they'd heard. I wasn't sure how to handle this sort of question and I'm grateful to the troop corporal who overhead and told the boys to leave me alone and continue on with their work. But that corporal wasn't there all day and, though I hadn't been beaten up yet, which a little bit of me expected on that Monday morning, I was anxious about any further reaction. Was this how it would be forever, now? Would my sexuality be the only thing people would think about when they heard my name? I really worried that my entry to the regiment would be completely marred by this recent run of events.

As I was walking along the square to the lift, somebody I didn't know opened his window from many floors above and shouted, 'Hey! Are you the gay guy?'

The whole of the barracks, and probably half of west London, heard his shout. I felt crushed by the audacity of his question. The lad in question, known as Pikey, had been at Knightsbridge for some time and was someone I knew harboured a lot of influence among the lads. If he was picking on me, everybody would pick on me. By the time I'd got out of the elevator and into my room, I'd been asked five times if the rumours were true. I collapsed on my bed trying to make sense of it all. How should I respond?

And then there came a knock at my door.

On opening, I found one of the older lads from my troop stood holding two cups of coffee.

'Alright? Can I come in?' He didn't wait for an answer. 'I'm Faulkner. I'm in your troop!' Faulkner handed me a coffee as he sat and made himself comfortable.

Faulkner, whose first name was Michael and who was originally from Wimbledon, had a year's experience on me, having left Harrogate just before I'd arrived. He'd settled well into the regiment and was a soldier with a reputation for high standards. I'd already eyed him up as a bit of a role model within the Blues and Royals, and now here he was sat in my room.

He'd heard the rumours like everyone else and had taken it upon himself to come and talk to me. I was touched by his early concern. He asked me if it was true what he was hearing in the stables. Once I'd confirmed it, he told me to admit it to the lads who were asking.

'They're only asking because they're interested. It's probably new to a lot of them. No one will pick on you if you just tell them the truth.'

I told him how the events of the morning had played out, and even about Pikey shouting down to the square from the highs of the barrack building, but he squashed all my concerns and gave me a pat on the back. His words struck a resounding chord and I decided to follow his advice.

I hadn't really made any new friends since getting back to Knightsbridge. Like everywhere, it took time to become integrated. Dean had been set to work in 1 Troop and Josh was sent to 3 Troop. Jamie and I had been kept together, which was something I was delighted about. He had a lot of life experience and a very natural ability to turn any potentially difficult situation on its head. While the regiment was going about its business we still had to finish our kit ride training; we just didn't have the time to mix with our new colleagues. When Faulkner brought himself into my life and my problems that Monday morning, checking I was OK and offering support, I was genuinely grateful. I really liked him and I'll never forget his early thoughtfulness.

I returned to work and started telling the many curious soldiers that yes, I was the gay guy, to which most replied 'Cool!' with surprised expressions plastered on their faces.

Week three passed by and, with the added endless questions from the lads – 'When did you find out you were gay?' 'Have you ever slept with a woman?' – as well as the dreaded adjutant's inspection on the Friday morning, it was an incredibly stressful time. Even so, for the first time in months, even with everything going on, I felt amazing. The lads, Jamie in particular, made a point of telling me how much I'd cheered up. Clearly coming out was very healthy to my well-being. I felt like a new person, with a new lease to go on and do whatever I wanted. I felt free from a lifetime of lies.

The final week of kit ride was a little different for us. Due to the low number of soldiers in the regiment at the time, us new boys were required to up our game somewhat and fill the empty spaces in a state escort for the Italian Prime Minister's visit on the Tuesday.

Our 'passing-out parade' wasn't due until the Thursday and, again, many members of my family were making the trip from Wales to see such an occasion. The deal from the riding staff was that if we turned out to the standard required for the escort on the Tuesday, we would all certainly pass out on the Thursday, in front of our families. However, if any of us were not at a suitable standard to escort the Queen and the Italian Prime Minister, we would fail the course and have to do the whole thing all over again. That would have been a catastrophe.

Our first insight into the many hours and days of preparations London's soldiers put in to making a royal escort as amazing as they are known to be was a huge eye-opener, waking us up to the realities of the job we were about to be proficient in.

On the Monday morning, the entire regiment was to rehearse the parade in full at 4.30 a.m., meaning we had to be at the stables at 1.30 a.m. to wake the horses, feed and groom them, and then carefully fit their saddles and furniture, before running upstairs to our changing rooms and placing all our clean kit on. Following all of this, we would collect our mounts and make our way on to the square to await the colonel's personal inspection. The whole process took hours.

Faulkner, who'd taken it upon himself to look after me a bit, taught me the previous day that because it was still going to be pitch-black at that time of the morning, I didn't really need to clean my kit properly. I wondered about this advice for some time and decided to follow it, quite unsure if it was true or not. To be fair, the advice went in the face of all we'd learned throughout the winter months of our training.

At 3 a.m., when I pitched up with my horse on that dark Knightsbridge parade square, I found that his advice was fully correct. We all, the horses included, looked dazzling. The artificial light that was beaming on us from the front and back made us look brilliant. Even the dullest of shines on a jack boot was magnified by the floodlighting.

The colonel started his inspection, during which he would speak to every man on the parade while checking the cleanliness of his horse and kit. This would take about fifty minutes, something we were all fully aware of as it had been published on orders the previous evening. The older lads, I found, would take this figure as sometimes an hour, sometimes an hour and a half, and divide it by the number of men on parade. For example, Faulkner would say that there were fifty minutes to inspect 220 men so that was just over twenty-two seconds to inspect each man. The lads would, as would I, soon come to depend on this formula to determine how much effort needed to be put into the kit cleaning prior to going on parade.

The colonel stood in front of me as I was introduced by the orderly corporal.

'Trooper Wharton, colonel. He's still in kit ride.'

The colonel's eyes lit up and he threw a jolly greeting at me.

'Trooper Wharton, welcome to the regiment!' He was extremely cheerful for 3.30 in the morning. He patted my horse and continued on to the next guy.

About thirty minutes later, the regimental corporal major (or RCM) shouted to us all to wake up and prepare to move off. After a little more ceremony we headed out of the ceremonial gate, right onto South Carriage Drive and eventually onwards to Buckingham Palace and down the Mall. At the bottom of the Mall, which was lined with Irish Guards and other service personnel, we formed up on Horse Guards Parade, facing a stage that was not quite yet completed. The Italian-themed decor was still being assembled. At about 4.30 a.m., the sun slowly started to appear from beyond the many buildings that made up the Whitehall skyline.

Many men, all fairly overweight, wandered around the assembled troops, pointing their sticks and telling people off for not standing still enough or for nodding off while sat on their horses. Without warning, the massed band fired up and started playing the national anthem. We all carried our swords while the officers performed a royal salute. A beautiful black Bentley pulled up right next to the steps of the half-constructed stage and a few royal imposters got out. The band finished and we all returned our swords to the slope, the blade just resting on the front of my shoulder. Soon another saloon, followed by a number of brand-new silver Mercedes minibus vans, entered Horse Guards from behind us and made their way to the stage. Once opposite the stage and the pretend Queen, a group of men exited the car and slowly climbed the few steps onto the platform. Only when they were all on the stage and stood next to the 'Queen' did the band play the Italian national anthem.

All the vehicles had disappeared and soon they were replaced by a few, very regal, carriages of state that would take the royal party and our Italian guests up the Mall and into the palace, with us providing a full military escort as they went.

Before I knew it, I was forcing myself into my saddle, trying desperately not to fall off with the pace we were travelling at as we accompanied the carriages along the Mall. It was here I, and every mounted soldier, learned to sit deep and consider the long-lasting effects of being 'binned' on the Mall. The empty saddles club was one organisation I didn't want to be a part of.

We made it to Buckingham Palace and formed up quickly, carrying our swords as the carriages drove into the centre section of the great building, which is hidden from view. There wasn't much left to do now, but the garrison sergeant major (or GSM), a huge Welshman called Billy Mott, was unhappy with how we'd formed up and accused us of looking sloppy. He demanded we go around the birthday cake, named so because of its grand appearance and resemblance to a giant cake, and try again.

Before long we were heading up Constitution Hill and making our way slowly back to Hyde Park barracks. It was now about 5.30 a.m. and the boys were already talking about knocking off and re-cleaning all their kit, which wouldn't be the case for me. Me and the other kit ride boys were to be back on top of our horses at 10.30 to rehearse our passing-out parade for the Thursday morning.

By the time I was back on top, I could barely keep my eyes open and had to resort to eating packets of Pro Plus, topping up their effect with cup after cup of espresso from the on-camp shop. The riding staff, renowned for being extremely unreasonable, screamed at us for hours for not getting things right. Of course we were making mistakes; we'd had next to no sleep for the best part of a month. Eventually, at lunch time, they released us to go away and prepare for the following morning's inspection.

By the time I was sat on my horse for the Italian state visit the following morning, I'd been awake for a ridiculous thirty-five hours. Because Agincourt was such a sweaty horse I had spent hours cleaning his reins and saddle, washing his coat, combing his mane, sponging his face and shampooing his white sock. Endless hours. Then I had to clean my personal kit. And at the same time, I had to stop to answer everybody's questions about my sexuality and put up with the banter that was now accompanying those questions. Sleep just didn't come into it but we all carried on regardless.

At 11 a.m. we sat and watched the Italian Prime Minister, Mr Berlusconi, arrive at the now perfectly assembled stage on which the Queen and the Duke of Edinburgh were stood. They exchanged a few initial pleasantries and were soon whisked away along the Mall, as we'd rehearsed the previous morning. The whole thing passed by excellently. They always did. Even though I felt paralysed by fatigue on that first occasion, I'd go on to ride in many escorts in the future, and each time I did, they would become easier and easier. But on that first occasion, boy, did I worry about the job I'd decided to commit myself to.

As promised, all of us went on to pass out in front of our families on the Thursday morning. It was a wondrous occasion, one that my nan travelled from Liverpool to witness first-hand. Personally, I don't remember much about the day, I was far too close to the edge of exhaustion to take anything in, but the pictures looked great.

After passing out, we were given seventy-two hours off. Time off in Knightsbridge is never given in days. There is just too little of it. I returned to North Wales with my folks and did nothing but sleep throughout the entire period. My body was exhausted.

During the three days back home I considered telling my mum about my recent announcement in London, but every time I built up the courage to tell her I'd lose my bottle and think better of it. By the end of the weekend I'd concluded that she just didn't need to know yet. So I left it.

Becoming a member of the Household Cavalry had taken seven months of constant attention since starting out at drill ride in September. It's incredible how much we'd all grown in that time, even Jamie, who was already in his mid-twenties. The training had taken us all from fresh-faced, newly trained soldiers to gentlemen of the Household Cavalry, ready to take on the ancient role of escorting the Sovereign, carrying ourselves smartly and with meaning. I can't think of a finer finishing school to my youth, nor a better group of people to endure the hardship with.

6

I'M OUT!

After passing out of kit ride in the April, I began to settle into my job as a mounted dutyman to Her Majesty the Queen, and soon became quite good at it, too. Once I'd figured out how to balance my work and social life, I found Knightsbridge a rather exciting place to be.

Every morning, and without fail, I'd be in work for 6 a.m. I'd be riding through the streets of Chelsea or Paddington by seven and back in for breakfast by 8.30. Once all this was done and if I wasn't on guard, I simply had to help out in the stable yard until noon, at which point we'd break down to skeleton crew and finish for the day. The crews that worked the afternoons would always be two lads that were in trouble for some reason or another, usually for being late in the mornings. If you were just five minutes late, you'd immediately lose your afternoon off. There were always people late and they were usually the same faces. Being a punctual guy, most afternoons I'd spend an hour cleaning kit, just so I'd always be ready or near enough ready if a fast ball came, which they often did; then I'd spend the afternoon out of base.

Since coming out, I had a great urge to explore the new-found freedom I'd afforded myself. I spoke at length with Jamie, seeking his invaluable advice, and he encouraged me to head out and attempt to make some friends. A Londoner himself, he told me where to find gay bars and gay guys in and around the capital. I plucked up some courage and went out into the unknown.

Venturing just a few stops on the tube and a short walk away, I spent a very nervous afternoon popping in and out of the shops and bars of Soho. I must have looked very wide-eyed to passers-by as I uncertainly walked through the door of my first ever gay bar, a weathered-looking pub called the Duke of Wellington. It was about 2.30 in the afternoon and about ten to fifteen men sat on the tables and benches. I quietly ordered a pint of lager and sat myself in the corner glancing through a scene magazine while I felt the glares of the men look over me. It's a sight I've now seen many times: a young, fresh-faced man, pretending to look occupied with a magazine or, nowadays, his mobile phone, trying to ignore the men that are eyeing him up. I was terrified to make eye contact with anybody but, despite my anxiety, I still felt exhilaration. For the first time ever I was spending time focusing on nothing but my sexuality. I loved it.

I finished my first drink fairly quickly and as I waited at the bar for the barman to pour me another, a young mixed-race lad started a conversation with me. Although fairly useless at general chit-chat — I had no experience, after all — I somehow held his interest long enough for him to want to pay for my drink. He followed me to my table and we carried on chatting at length; he asked me questions and I answered them. I liked the guy and was happy to have him keep me company. An hour or so later, he signalled his intention to return home and asked if I wanted to join him. I desperately wanted to go with him, but I was just too scared to do so. My heart battled with my brain and I considered just how long I'd waited for an opportunity to present itself like this. I considered how blatant the guy was being: without explicitly spelling it out, it was clear what he had in mind. I decided to decline his offer. I knew I was more than ready to do it but I was just too scared about wandering off somewhere with a complete stranger. Looking deflated, he scribbled his number on the corner of a page in the magazine that was sat before us and asked me to give him a call sometime. With that, he leaned over and kissed me. My first ever kiss with another man. My heart felt like it was about to beat out of my chest. The kiss seemed to last for minutes, although in reality it was actually over quite quickly. As soon as he walked away and out of my life, I regretted not taking the chance and accompanying him.

I returned to Soho again and again on my afternoons off from work and soon made a few friends. Sometimes, in the early evening, I'd return to the barracks and see if anybody wanted to go out later in the night. Towards the end of riding school and following my coming out, I'd become close to the soldier who had had rumours spread about him. Though I wondered whether the rumours were true, I didn't cross the line and just ask him whether or not he was gay. Then, one night, we both found ourselves out with a large group of soldiers in the West End. After many drinks I approached the situation and asked him, face to face, if he was gay or not. He looked at me for some seconds before making a response and in those moments I considered I had the whole thing wrong. But he confirmed it. He told me he was gay and he begged me not to say anything. The two of us ditched the rest of the guys and I took him to a gay bar nearby, one that I'd frequented quite often in the previous weeks. That night, we danced away together and had more fun than either of us had ever had before. One thing led to another and in the early hours of the Sunday morning the two of us kissed. It felt amazing, so much more amazing than the kiss with the guy in the pub two weeks earlier. We left the club and caught a cab back to the barracks. With the door locked and wedged shut just in case anybody walked in while we were together, he spent the night in my room. I'd never had a physical experience with anyone other than Kate – and I had been a young teenager, too. Though nothing to do with her, I had hated every minute of the things we did together, all because I wasn't heterosexual. With my closeted soldier friend that night, the things we did felt completely natural. I'd waited for years to experience something like this. I thought of chasing Aaron around at fourteen and being attracted to Jonesy during basic training. At eighteen years of age, I'd finally experienced a sexual encounter that mattered to me.

With my new-found confidence I just wanted to keep on having fun. There was always someone who would want to go out. My circle of friends from the regiment, which was by now growing in numbers, would generally insist on starting off at a straight venue, usually in Leicester Square, before demanding I take them to a gay bar conveniently nearby. Faulkner, in particular, found something of an 'untapped source' of single women in gay bars, usually out with a gay friend who I'd then find myself talking to, just so he could initiate conversation with the girl. We'd repeat this action night after night, and soon it just became the norm for us to go to a gay bar together, acting as each other's wingman.

As young, wide-eyed eighteen-year-olds go, I soon found that I was very popular with gay men on the scene. I was on the receiving end of drink offers and chat-ups almost constantly. Soon, and once I'd got a little more worldly wise, it was me chatting up the guys, the guys I wanted to chat up, and offering to buy drinks. In the initial weeks and months after I'd come out, I lost a lot of innocence as I quickly got swept up in scene life.

My soldier friend had moved back into the closet somewhat and I was faced with a situation where I could carry on a secret relationship with him, constantly having to double-check the door was locked to preserve his anonymity, or support him purely as a mate and keep our past experiences secret. I wanted to spend more time on the scene and meet other guys. The difference between us both was that I wanted to spread my wings, but he still hadn't found the courage to accept who he was. We stopped sleeping together and I looked elsewhere. The reservations I held on that first day in Soho were gone. I went out looking for guys.

Six months later, ashamedly, I was on the scene every night, going home with somebody different each time. I'd go to whatever part of town my sex mate lived, spend no more than an hour there and then jump into a cab, returning to Knightsbridge just in time for work. After a quick shower and shave, I'd be mucking out my horse and getting ready for either morning exercise or Queen's Life Guard.

Queen's Life Guard is the one role that the regiment has to provide on a daily basis in the capital. It's the daily guard that leaves Hyde Park barracks at 10.30 each morning and returns twenty-four hours later having conducted a duty for the Queen at Horse Guards Parade.

A typical day for a soldier going on 'Queen's' would be quite a long one: stables at 6 a.m. as normal but then immediately on top for a warm-up exercise for the horses – and for the men. This exercise, in the indoor riding school, was taken by the corporal of horse who was taking the guard on duty later that morning, and was an opportunity for him to account for all his men.

When the Queen is away, the guard is made up of ten troopers, one corporal and one corporal of horse, who assumes command. On weekdays, when the Queen is mostly in residence at Buckingham Palace, the guard is beefed up with a trumpeter, a warrant officer and a commissioned officer. On these occasions the commissioned officer is naturally in command. The guard will also carry a standard on guard with them, a large flag with the regiment's battle honours listed on it. The Queen presents a new standard every ten years. Iraq and Afghanistan are both on the new one.

After the exercise, and assuming all is correct, the guard then goes for breakfast before slowly fitting all of the immaculate kit, cleaned the previous afternoon, onto the horse. At 9.30, the ongoing guard begins to muster on the square and at 10 a.m. the orderly officer begins his inspection.

These inspections were what made or failed people in Knightsbridge. Every guard would be inspected fully and the findings recorded. If a soldier was found to be in bad order, he would be punished, normally by having to complete another inspection later that night while at Horse Guards. If a soldier was found to be in such a bad state that the orderly officer didn't feel he could go on public display, he was replaced by the waiting man, who stood in full kit behind the guard – a substitute, if you like.

If a soldier was 'ripped off', a phrase used to describe a soldier being removed from the guard for being in bad order, he was usually jailed on the spot for a few hours, before facing his squadron corporal major (or SCM). The SCM would hand him a bollocking, the sort that you wouldn't forget, and decide what further action to take. This happened to me once, during my first few guards after kit ride, and the SCM (who I won't name) screamed at me and punched me in the stomach. I'd received what the other lads called a 'sucking chest wound' – and boy, did it hurt. After my 'chat' in the office, I was driven to Queen's Life Guard where I was to re-clean my kit fully and present it for re-inspection at ten o'clock that night.

I made sure it never happened again but on this occasion the problem had become complex. I'd been cleaning my kit for the guard as normal, but there was still a lot of reaction going on with regard to my coming out. I couldn't stand still for five minutes without someone coming up to me and asking a load of questions about my sexuality. I didn't mind at first, but soon rumours were circulating about me and the closeted soldier I'd been involved with, after he'd stupidly told one of the boys while drunk one night in a pub. Gossip was something I found particularly stressful, and the whole thing just made me want to stop cleaning my kit and lock myself away in my room. The rumours and constant questions were preventing me from doing my job properly, and failing the guard inspection was an unfortunate consequence of the situation. Soon enough, though, everything died down.

After the inspection, the guard would leave Hyde Park barracks at exactly 10.30, with the trumpeter sounding as it did (assuming the Queen was in London) and the whole regiment would stand to attention while the guard exited through the ceremonial gates.

At a slow pace, the guard would make its way along South Carriage Drive, saluting the memorial for the 1982 Hyde Park bombing as it went. Soon, it would pass through Wellington Arch at Hyde Park Corner and move onwards towards the palace and the Mall. The trumpeter would sound the royal salute as it passed, notifying the Queen that her guard was on its way and about to be changed. We'd reach the bottom of the Mall and slowly walk onto the gravel at Horse Guards, just as the chimes of Big Ben were sounding 11 a.m. This was what was expected of us, to be just getting in place opposite the off-coming guard as the bell sounded. Sometimes we'd pull it off; often we'd be early or, worse, late. Unluckily for the guard, the general who commands all things ceremonial in London lives in the office that overlooks Horse Guards Parade, above the centre arch. There was never any way of bluffing being late for guard change. The thousands of tourists awaiting the arrival of the oncoming guard were very unforgiving if it was later than 11 a.m.

Then followed half an hour of not a lot. While the corporal of horse was having the guard handed to him behind the scenes in the building of Horse Guards, the remainder of us would stand outside while the tourists took photographs of us atop our beautiful horses. The corporal of horse would get a security brief and be told of the Queen's movements. I used to find it incredible that a very blatant folder entitled 'The Queen's Movements' was just left around for any of us to read. I used to enjoy a little nosy into what she was up to and where she was off to.

At 11.30 the guard change would be completed, with the off-going guard, members of the Life Guards (known by us as the 'Tins'), leaving Whitehall and making their way back to Hyde Park barracks along the route we'd just followed. Horse Guards was then home for the next twenty-four hours, until we were replaced by the Tins the following morning. This has gone on for centuries and will probably continue forever, or at least until this country no longer has a royal family.

Interestingly, the guys didn't overly mind going on Queen's. It was also very useful if you had no money, as your meals were provided free of charge while in Whitehall. Those that did mind would often pay other soldiers to do their guards. In 2005, the going rate for a weekday guard was about £50. At a weekend, that went up to about £80. If it was a payday guard, soldiers would pay anything up to £150 to someone for covering their duty. Prices for Christmas Day and New Year's Eve guards went off the scale. It was very simple to orchestrate, too. If, say, I needed to get off my guard due to me needing to be somewhere, like on a date for instance, I'd ask the boys in the troop if anybody was free and willing to cover the duty for me. The offering soldier would name his price and the money would be handed over. To finish the deal, you'd just notify the corporal of horse, who would cover your back if the other lad didn't turn up.

Knightsbridge was full of little scandals like this. Soldiers paying soldiers to cover duties was nothing compared to some of the incredible deals that went on. On one occasion, someone lost their state helmet, which would have cost about £2,000 to sign for on loss. One of the other lads had found it, although we all knew he'd actually stolen it in the first place, and was forcing the poor guy to buy it back off him at a reduced rate of £300. This was quite common.

There were also corporals telling younger soldiers that their boots weren't shiny enough and that they would be in a lot of trouble if they were to go on parade with them, but then offer to fix the problem for £100. Often the younger soldiers would listen to these corporals and pay up. The worrying thing is that the hierarchy in 2005 certainly knew about it. All that mattered to them was making sure the guard left the barracks every morning at 10.30 in good order. They didn't care how the boys got there. Imagine if the Queen looked out of her window and didn't see her guard passing by on time. The fallout would be awful. The colonel didn't need phone calls from the palace like that.

In 2005, the Household Cavalry Mounted Regiment was in the newspapers all the time for something or other. I remember settling into the regiment early on and reading about some of the older boys in my troop on the front page of a very popular national newspaper. It worried Mum more than it did me, and I'd have her on the phone often, double-checking that I hadn't been involved with the drugs and the sex orgies that were being reported in the media. Of course I hadn't, but I certainly saw first-hand the crazy things she was reading.

The biggest story of all was the group of Life Guards who were pictured on the front page of the same newspaper for having an orgy in the barracks with a hooker who had filmed the whole thing on her phone. The paper had somehow come by this footage and had filled their pages with its images. Some of the lads were quite young but others were much older and perhaps should have known better. One was even a married senior corporal of horse. The colonel blew his top big time over what he was reading and gave us all a huge telling-off on the main square, but it didn't stop the behaviour.

A week later there was another front-pager, this time about some of us Blues and Royals buying cocaine off an undercover reporter one night in a nearby bar, then going on parade with the Queen the following morning. Again, the colonel, probably under a lot of pressure from his superiors, gave us a huge telling-off. The offending soldiers were dealt with severely and discharged from the army after a spell in military prison. The headline was replaced the following day with another, about a horse in the Life Guards being forced to drink alcohol by some of the soldiers. Enough was enough. There followed a period of tough treatment by the chain of command within the regiment. We found ourselves working late, starting early, and on top of our horses in full kit more often. Unsurprisingly, around this time our commanding officer changed, and things eventually died down as many new soldiers filtered through and into the troops. It certainly was a tough time to start out as a new guy.

Soldiers going on parade hungover, or even still drunk, was a normal occurrence back in 2005. I was often sobering up while bouncing around in my saddle, sometimes not too far away from the Queen, but we always managed to hold a high level of professionalism. Back then, and even today, most of the mistakes on a parade rehearsal, or even an actual parade, were made by the junior officers who led us.

The officers at Hyde Park barracks lived the life of Riley. They didn't have to do anywhere near as much work as the soldiers under their command. Firstly, every officer would have his own trooper as an orderly. It would be this young trooper's responsibility to make sure every single piece of equipment his officer needed in his daily business was ready. He would also be responsible for getting the officer dressed, because an officer wasn't expected to dress himself. All of these orderlies were then collectively responsible for ensuring that all the officers were wined and dined to a high standard in the officers' mess. Some troopers would also take care of the officers' horses, ensuring they were fully groomed and tacked up so the officers could just climb on and ride away. The amount of running around the young soldiers would be made to do just so their officers were looked after accordingly was quite disgusting. There were two very different classes of people operating in that officers' mess; it was very much a modern *Downton Abbey*.

My late nights continued and I soon had my first credit card, which was solely used in places like G-A-Y. Soon after, I took out a loan to help me fund my adventures. I held no other hobby or interest apart from hitting the gay scene and sleeping with as many men as possible. Of course, now I know that I was suffering from addiction and that my life depended on my endless drinking and nights of sex; still, the regiment had its soldier and, whatever state I was in, I was always on time. Hidden behind all that uniform and tradition, as long as I could reasonably point my horse in the right direction and carry my sword correctly, everything was fine. Nobody ever gave me any hassle for being hungover in work.

As time went by I started to become aware that a few soldiers were taking an interest in me for other reasons. On the first such occasion, a Life Guard who was the same age as me started smiling at me and winking suggestively while in the on-camp bar. After a few beers I spoke with him and he told me quickly that he wanted me to invite him back to my room. He wanted to explore his sexuality and I guess I was his chosen playmate. I decided not to go into Soho that night and instead stayed put with my new friend. I took the guy back to my room and allowed him to satisfy fully his curiosity. I did this on and off with him for about twelve months; afterwards he would always insist he was straight. Until the next time, of course.

These little episodes with 'straight' soldiers didn't always go smoothly. One night, while enjoying a sports night in the bar, I was again 'hit on' by a soldier, who, by the end of the night, was begging me to join him back in his room. I was a little reluctant, because I'd never really liked the lad. He was a little older and a bit of a troublemaker, but under the influence I accepted his offer and joined him.

Once back in his room, a few floors above my own, things started to progress. His room was quite standard for a soldier in Knightsbridge: Abi Titmuss posters, his favourite football team standing behind their silverware. The room smelt every bit like a young man's space, which, I noticed, he didn't share with anybody else. I could tell he was nervous, but so was I every time this happened with a so-called straight soldier. He took his top off and started to undress me. In an instant, he had a change of heart and, instead of pulling my boxer shorts down as I had expected him to, he reached for an iron pole and whacked me across the back. I fell to the floor and he started kicking me, mostly in the face. In the few moments I lay huddled on the floor, trying to protect my face, the thought of how this scene would look in a movie played out in my mind. There was absolutely nothing I could do to stop his relentless attack on me and I think I just gave up all hope of trying to find the strength to fight back. Somehow I managed to crawl to the door and out into the corridor, but his kicking and beating with the bar continued. I thought someone would hear the commotion and come rushing to my aid as soon as I got myself into the corridor. The lad was screaming words like 'queer' at me but nobody seemed to hear or, if they did, they decided to leave me to it. By the time somebody finally came to help, the fight, even though it was never in me from the start, had completely left me, as had all energy to stop the ordeal. I think if he'd have continued on for just a few minutes more, he'd have faced a murder charge. I looked horrific. The blood was oozing out of me. The guard room was called and the guy was detained on the spot; meanwhile an ambulance was called for me. I have no memory between being rescued and waking up in Chelsea and Westminster hospital. I was in a very bad way.

Nurses treated the cuts and bruises while doctors examined me and sent me for many scans. Faulkner and another guy, Seamus, had heard the news and rushed to see me at the hospital. I was really embarrassed to see them both, but they were worried about me and wanted to know everything that had happened. They told me that the lad had been arrested.

I was released from hospital a day later, quite black and blue from the episode, and was taken into the regimental corporal major's office. Incredibly, he wanted to double-check I definitely wanted to take the incident further. I couldn't help feeling at that moment that the chain of command wanted the whole thing swept under the carpet. I stood my ground and told him I wanted to make a full complaint. There was absolutely no compassion in his voice and he felt thoroughly inconvenienced by the whole event.

The thing that hurt me most was knowing that, yet again, the whole regiment was talking about me. Although I was the victim in the incident, I felt as though I'd brought it upon myself by agreeing to go along with his advances and by joining him in his room. I had to recollect the entire story again and again for people in the regiment: the colonel, the squadron leader, the

SCM, the RCM, my troop leader. Each would want to know the full circumstances leading up to the event. When the military police turned up, again I found myself answering some very personal questions. This was very new ground for them, and I felt almost as guilty as my attacker was. Incredibly, if this had happened six years prior, it would have been me facing discharge from the army, regardless of the situation. It was clear the police were dealing with an incident that they had had little to no experience in tackling. These were, after all, the same officers who had arrested suspected gay soldiers in the past.

I was given a week off to rest and decided to stay with my auntie and uncle in East Grinstead, who looked after me excellently. I was very lucky to have close family nearby.

The soldier, who admitted everything, was later court-martialled and fined £1,200 for his actions that night. He remained in the army and I had to put up with him walking around the barracks for the rest of my time there. I was a little more cautious about who I went home with from the bar from then on. Three months after the event, while out clubbing in a gay venue in central London, I saw the guy who'd attacked me kissing another man in the corner of a dance floor. I realised just how messed up some people were over their sexuality. I just hope the poor guy didn't meet the same fate at the end of the night that had befallen me.

†

The summer of 2005 in London started off as a hot one and I spent many an afternoon relaxing in Hyde Park enjoying the rays and the many sights that came with the hot weather, mostly topless men. The summer was shaping up to be quite fantastic when, all of a sudden, things in the capital took a sudden turn for the worse.

On 6 July, many other soldiers of the Household Cavalry Mounted Regiment and I crammed into the bar over lunch to watch the live announcement of the 2012 Olympic Games host city. Our main contender was Paris and we were laughing and enjoying many a classic historic put-down of France – our regiment having played a pivotal role in the Battle of Waterloo. Suddenly the Sky News cameras panned live to the key moment.

When the envelope was opened and the word 'London' was exclaimed, a great cheer roared throughout the bar, and indeed across the entire city. We'd given the French one final stuffing and snatched the Olympics from Paris's grasp in the dying seconds. We were all delighted. I remember wondering where I'd be in 2012. It seemed like years and years away at the time.

Londoners raised a glass in celebration that night, and we all took it as a hell of an excuse to head out and have a few glasses, too.

Back at the barracks we were in the middle of a busy period, known fondly in the regiment as 'silly season', and, in particular, we were preparing for the forthcoming sixtieth anniversary of VE and VJ Day, which was fast approaching on the Sunday.

The day after the Olympic announcement, on the Thursday, I was in work bright and early, as always. After riding, I was directed by one of the troop corporals to start washing off all the horses with the other lads. We usually washed them off on the rear balcony overlooking the busy streets of Knightsbridge if the weather allowed us to and that morning, Thursday 7 July, was a very bright and sunny morning.

At 8.50 a.m., three bombs were detonated on London Underground trains in quick succession. The first at King's Cross, the second at Edgware Road and the third at Russell Square. At about that time I hadn't long finished breakfast and, blissfully unaware of the events unfolding, was just starting my first horse, a grey called Vixen.

Almost an hour later a fourth bomb exploded on a London bus at Tavistock Square. By that time, word was slowly surfacing about an event taking place involving large casualties. No one had mentioned the 'b' word yet. The media was mostly reporting that there had been a power surge, as a result of which trains had derailed. When the Tavistock Square bomb went off, everybody knew that London was under attack.

Immediately we were put on the highest alert. Everyone was ordered to their rooms to collect their fighting equipment. Webbing (which holds a soldier's essential kit, such as ammo, water and rations), combat helmets and even camouflage paint were all collected and taken down to the assembly point on the main square. The commanding officer and his few senior officers were now using the bar and Sky News as their single source for intelligence. Nobody really had a clue what was going on. The images on TV showed hundreds of injured people emerging from a number of tube stations around the capital, causing much confusion and giving the impression that more bombs had gone off than actually had. As the colonel was drawing up his battle plans in the bar in front of the TV, I was sat in my full combats on top of my green rucksack, complete with sleeping bag and emergency rations, waiting to collect my identity tags and sign a quick will.

A large stockpile of morphine injections was brought to the square, ready to be handed out to each man. I even had my gas mask attached to my person, just in case. The final addition was my rifle, which had lain in the armoury quite unused for some time. For a few very scary hours it felt like I was actually going to war on the streets of my own capital city, in England, of all places.

While I was sat on the square thinking about the awful things that were going on just down the road from us, my mobile phone rang. Mum had heard the news, like everyone else in the country, and was calling, very much in a panic, to check I was safe. I told her I was, but couldn't guarantee for how long. I'd been put in the 'fifteen-minute notice to move' section, which meant we'd be the first out of the gate when the call came. This bit of information didn't do Mum's nerves any good at all.

When we were called on the square and given a best picture of what had happened earlier in the morning, the colonel had told us to prepare for the worst and that British soldiers would be patrolling the streets of London before the day was out. We, and I certainly, felt that we were going to have to take over from the police and stop these attackers with brute force. It was still very unclear if the bombings had stopped.

As it turned out, the fourth explosion was the last of them. We all sat on the square with our kit for the call that never came. I think it would have been a very bold step for Tony Blair to have deployed soldiers carrying rifles onto London streets that morning, but we honestly expected him to do so. At about 4 p.m. we got the call to stand down. I was more than ready to take my kit off and relax but, unfortunately, the regiment had an escort to prepare for and that meant finishing off the washing of all the horses. It was incredible to return to our normal duties considering the day we'd all had signing wills and drawing out our rifles, but life had to continue.

In the days that followed, we prepared for the VE Day celebrations with no changes to plan. Early on, it was thought that the procession would be cancelled. To have the Queen in an open-top carriage only days after her city had been blasted was an obvious risk, but the Queen was not for altering her plans and, in a great show of defiance, we escorted her from the palace to the celebrations on Horse Guards as if the week had been no different from any other. Escorting the Queen that Sunday afternoon was one of the proudest and most important jobs I ever carried out within the ceremonial regiment. There was a real worry and a relevant threat of harm to the royal party, and this resounded as we left the barracks and rode along to the palace. We didn't really know what we were riding into, but it didn't matter. We proudly carried Her Majesty that day, showing the world that life went on in London. The actions of a few would not deter us from our important traditions.

London life continued, as did the guards and the state escorts for Her Majesty. My nights out also continued, once I'd brushed myself down after the gay bashing. I'd mostly go out with my new friend Ange, who worked with the vet looking after the horses in camp. In a complete surprise, out of absolutely nowhere, Tim, my old riding instructor, pulled me aside to tell me that he'd been hiding a big secret for some time. The moment he started telling me his news, I knew what was coming. Tim was gay and finally ready to tell people about it. Suddenly I had a good friend who was not only with me in the regiment but gay and very happy for the world to know. Tim, Ange and I became great buddies and would often frequent the clubs and bars of Soho.

There had been something missing in my life to that point, something that I hadn't even considered. I'd never had a boyfriend. While out one night with Ange and Tim, I met a guy who I quite liked. The feeling seemed to be mutual but instead of him wanting to come back to the barracks with me, or vice versa, he simply insisted on us meeting again in the days that followed.

It was the first time I'd ever been turned down and also the first time I was heading home to bed without a new friend. It really struck a chord.

His name was Steven, and to this day I refer to him as the one that got away. Steven liked me and wanted to spend time with me, but he certainly wasn't about to jump into bed with

me. He used to say he knew nothing about me so why would
he want to just fuck me? He rang me the day after I met him
and asked when I was next free. We made our arrangements to
meet the following evening in Leicester Square. I was going on
my first ever date and, boy, was I excited. I realised I wanted a
boyfriend. I wanted the attention and the love that came with
having a relationship.

When we met the following evening, Steven asked me if I
liked ABBA, to which I instinctively nodded; in response he
pulled out two tickets to *Mamma Mia!*

'We don't have to go if you don't want to.'

Of course I wanted to go. I'd spent over a year in London and
not seen a single show. I was beyond thrilled.

Steven, who was about three years older than me and a para-
medic, was the complete gentleman. No man had ever spent real
money on me. Nobody had ever bought me anything other than
a vodka and coke, and here he was splashing the cash. After the
show we grabbed some food and ended the night with a few
beers. It was the first time I'd been out and not been interested in
anybody but the person I was standing with. It was a perfect date,
well, when you're eighteen years old anyway. There were far worse
places we could have gone to and it ranks right up there as one of
the best dates I've ever been on.

Steven was very interested in my job and I think at first he
wasn't fully sure I was telling the truth. Eventually he believed
me and I offered to show him behind the scenes at Whitehall
when I was next on guard. I also offered him a look at life in the
barracks later that night but, as before, he outright refused to
return to camp with me for sex. Though I really admired him for
his decision I just wanted to rip his clothes off.

We carried on meeting for drinks for a few weeks after, but
still we stayed out of the bedroom. Soon he stopped replying to

my texts and stopped answering the phone. Clearly Steven had
had other thoughts and didn't want or need an eighteen-year-old
soldier. This was my first ever taste of rejection and I didn't like it.
I really fancied him, but he just didn't fancy me. Perhaps it was a
lesson I needed to learn. My ego had become rather inflated and
I almost thought I could have anybody I wanted; no guy had ever
turned me down before Steven. I realised that I was human after
all. I cheered myself up by hitting the scene with Tim and Ange,
finishing the night in somebody's flat in some unexpected part of
the city. Life went on.

Enjoying the scene as I did, I'd made many friends, including
people I hadn't slept with – or wanted to, for that matter. It was
quite nice walking into a venue and catching up with someone
who hadn't seen my embarrassing Chinese tattoo, added to the
top of my left leg at the age of fifteen, who didn't know what I
looked like with my clothes off. One such friend was a policeman
called Stuart. He was an early friend and is still someone I see
often today. I loved going out with my soldier buddies but sometimes it was quite nice to go out with 'normal' people, too. Stuart
was single and about twelve years my senior and we shared many
nights out together. Stuart was also responsible for introducing
me to a lot of other gay people and to the many other gay venues
London had to offer. One such place was in Vauxhall where I
was introduced to an entirely new crowd of people. I had nothing
against the pop scene in the West End, but it was getting a little
awkward bumping into guys I'd spent the night with and not
contacted afterwards. In Vauxhall, I could start all over again.

7

PLAYING WITH FIRE

Christmas 2005 was soon upon us. Christmases in the army are magical; whether serving abroad or, like me, in the capital, everyone comes together and celebrates the end of a long and demanding year.

The ethos of community and camaraderie is heightened as the season's festivities get into full swing. The regimental carol service usually signifies the start of this period and the troopers' Christmas lunch follows, the only occasion in the calendar when troopers are waited on by the senior ranks, before the customary food fight between us and the Tins. The seniors are usually forced to abandon the service to avoid being hit in the head with a roast potato. Then it's time for Christmas leave, with half of the regiment heading home and the other half covering duties – the palace still needs guarding over the Christmas holidays. Before New Year's Eve, those who spend Christmas on leave come back to allow the others to head home for the rest of the festive season. The system works well. I used to opt for Christmas off, celebrating in Wales with my family, and then return to London to work over the New Year period, which always placed me in the capital for my birthday on New Year's Day.

That year I spent New Year's Eve in Trafalgar Square with my gay friends, having spent the previous two weeks on leave at home with my folks. I loved catching up with them all, but it was a million miles away from my life in the city and they still didn't know about my sexuality. I couldn't wait to get back to London on 27 December. How long would I keep this secret from them?

As soon as New Year was over and 2006 was underway, work returned to normal, as did my regular nights out. Life was exactly the same as it had been for the previous year, and it was starting to take its toll on me.

One night out, I remember talking to Stuart about the experience I'd had with Steven the previous year. I told him how excited I was to have an actual love interest and, as short a relationship as it was, I had felt better in those three weeks than I had ever done before. Stuart, who adored the gay scene and had quite a bit of experience, explained to me that going out and getting drunk and then 'getting fucked' wasn't the be-all and end-all. As good as it was, there was more to life than just being a 'slag'. He introduced me to an online dating site called Gaydar, where you could search online for the gay man of your choice, arrange a date and then take it from there. However, the truth was that most men on there were actually just looking for sex from the comfort of their living room instead of in a bar in Vauxhall. Still, I agreed to get on there and give it a go.

I didn't own a computer back then, so Stu let me use his at his flat in London Bridge. I made a profile and uploaded some pictures to help persuade potential onlookers. Astonishingly, people sent me messages almost instantly. I was asked things like 'Are you a top?' or 'Are you into BDSM?' and once just the simple word 'Piss?'

I had no idea what any of this meant and I'm very grateful to my pal Stuart for taking half an hour to explain fully what all these weird and wonderful expressions meant. There was suddenly a whole new world out there – and quite a scary one at that. In 2006, there was still a little bit of taboo surrounding online dating and meeting strangers off the web but as my life was risqué enough already, I didn't really get too shocked by the things I became exposed to in this strange new technical world of hooking up with other men.

I used the internet terminal in the bar back at camp to keep up with my messages on Gaydar but two weeks into the experience, I hadn't been asked out on a proper date once. This was most frustrating. After a quick initial exchange on the site, however, I had met the same guy three times in Finsbury Park for casual sex. I was joining in with the very thing I wasn't looking for. I began to find it all a little too much.

One morning I woke early as always and a little hungover. As I scraped the slight stubble off my face with a razor, I noticed a strange sensation down below. Giving myself a quick scratch, I didn't ponder over it; I was in a rush to get sorted for work. I jumped in the shower and, as usual, began to pee. Instantly I felt the same sensation, only this time it was a hundred times worse. I'd never experienced a pain like it in all my life. It was unbearable. There was something very wrong.

I dried myself, avoiding my groin as much as possible, got dressed and headed down to the stables. I couldn't begin to imagine what was wrong with me. I'd never had any pain like that down there before in my life. What the hell was it?

Once at the stables I told my corporal of horse that I needed to see the doctor. He rang ahead to the medical centre and told them I'd be across shortly. Sitting in the waiting room, a number of fellow sick soldiers sat beside me, I glanced over the many leaflets that littered the tables and walls. My eyes kept automatically looking towards the harrowing pictures of 'STIs' and 'sexual health', and I began to wonder if my sudden pain during peeing was down to my sex life. Panicking, I thought of a million reasons why it couldn't possibly be something like that but I was fooling myself. There was one clear reason why it could have been: I'd been so foolish in recent weeks. I'd been casually meeting more guys than ever and not paying any attention to my own well-being. My stupid behaviour had caught up with me.

It turned out that I was quite ill indeed. I had to go to a special hospital in Hammersmith and get treatment, along with a number of other tests, and was taken immediately by a driver from the barracks. Travelling to hospital, I wanted to call Mum and tell her that I wasn't very well. Whenever I'd been ill in the past, Mum would look after me until I was better. But I knew I couldn't call her. I knew that she'd ask too many questions. I hated myself for the situation I was in. I hated that I wasn't able to pick up the phone and have an honest conversation with the one person in the world I should have been able to.

The doctor put me through a lot of very unpleasant tests to find out exactly what was wrong with me. It was an experience I didn't want to go through again. My penis was in so much pain already, the things he stuck into me made the whole thing unimaginable.

'Have you taken an HIV test recently?' Recently? I'd never taken one in my entire life!

'How many sexual partners have you had in the past six months?' Dozens of different faces dashed through my mind. I lied and told him that there'd been only three.

'Three in six months is an awful lot. You have to be more careful. You should have been tested.'

The doctor was doing a very good job of making me feel extremely bad about myself. Today, I'm thankful he did. I needed to be told. Something like this had needed to happen to make me understand what I was doing to myself.

I waited for the result of my HIV check fully hating myself

and the lifestyle I had chosen to lead. I remember thinking that nobody had forced me into making the choices I had done. Nobody was encouraging me to hit the bottle as much as I did, then lose control and head home with strangers. Somewhere, I'd missed the stop sign. Waiting to find out if I was HIV-positive was the lowest point of my entire life. Nineteen years old. Was I about to find out I was dying?

The doctor opened a door and called me in. I braced myself. Inside his room a lady sat waiting on a chair. She shook my hand and introduced herself as a sexual health counsellor. I was sure I was about to receive some devastating news. My heart sank and I began to shake. Everyone was so serious.

'Mr Wharton, you aren't very well. You have gonorrhoea.'

Gonorrhoea? I had gonorrhoea! I couldn't believe what I was hearing. I knew exactly what it was from the platoon sergeant's sexual health lessons back in Harrogate. How could I be so careless?

'We can treat you today. We can sort that out here, so don't panic.' I realised that he was building himself up to the main event. The HIV result. The woman kept looking at me and giving me sympathetic nods of reassurance. I considered walking out right then. I wasn't sure I was brave enough to hear the news I was about to get.

'We've tested your blood and the result has come back negative.' For some strange reason, I took negative as something bad, as something negative in itself and gave a loud gasp. For a second I thought the doctor was telling me I was HIV-positive.

'You're extremely lucky. You have to be more careful. This lady is going to spend some time with you discussing your sexual behaviour.'

The doctor gave me an injection for my little problem and I spent the next hour with the sexual health counsellor discussing the stupid things I was doing and the risks I was putting myself in.

I left the hospital in a complete mess. I called the only person in the world I could be honest and talk the whole thing through with: Faulkner. Faulkner, like the counsellor, did an equally good job of underlining how idiotic I'd been. He told me that I had to protect myself and take care. He told me off like a father would. He's always been effective at grounding people.

Following the health scare, I took a few weeks off my night-time antics. I concentrated on work more and simply returned to my room and watched movies in my spare time. The doctor had made it very clear that I wasn't to have sex with anyone for a couple of weeks, which suited me as I was in no mood to jump straight back into bed with my old habits. I needed to process where I was in life. I was still a very unworldly nineteen-year-old, but I was sensible enough to know that I wouldn't make it to twenty-one if I didn't get my act together. It was an incredible contrast knowing that in one sense I was a complete failure in terms of my own personal development, but in another, in my professional manner, I was an extremely decent royal guard. Behind the breastplate and under the helmet I wore on a daily basis in the public eye, I was actually a complete disaster.

Addiction has an incredible hold on its sufferers. I thought I'd simply erase all the bad parts of my life and return to the old James, the James that didn't need to head out on a nightly basis and drink himself into such a state he could barely string a sentence together. I found myself isolated: I had nobody to support me throughout this crucial stage. My friends, however brilliant, couldn't sort my problems out for me. Neither Faulkner nor Stuart had the answers to my issues. Soon the inevitable occurred: I ventured back onto the scene and it welcomed me back with open arms.

†

Spring dawned and with it the start of the 'silly season' at the mounted regiment. As silly seasons go, 2006 was a pretty run-of-the-mill year in terms of how busy we were putting on escorts. I looked forward to the days getting longer. Heading to the stables at six o'clock every morning was depressing enough and the darkness made it a thousand times worse.

Everyone in the army has to use all of their annual leave by the end of every March or risk losing the days they haven't spent. In Knightsbridge, the regiment simply had too many duties and responsibilities to keep, and not enough manpower to allow every man his full entitlement of annual leave. In 2006 we were very lucky to have at the top of our command a corporal major who had the balls to tell the regiment to get lost. All his men were getting their annual leave.

I went to work one Thursday morning (with a terrible hangover) and was informed straight away that I'd be going home on leave later that day, and not returning until my annual leave days were all spent. I had seven days remaining. This never happened. Men in Knightsbridge just weren't handed seven days' leave out of the blue. I cashed in one of my three free-rail warrants and rang ahead to Wrexham, exclaiming I'd be home by the end of the day.

Mid-morning, I popped into the bar and logged onto Gaydar. I had a mission. I wanted to see how many profiles there were registered in Wrexham. I had an idea there'd be about three. I didn't know anyone from my hometown who was gay; nevertheless, I searched in the hope that I'd find someone who'd like to meet up and perhaps be up for a bit of a laugh while I was home in the local area.

The search returned an incredible eighty profiles. I couldn't believe it. There were at least eighty gay men in Wrexham! I began to trawl through the profiles, spending a couple of judgemental seconds on each picture before clicking to the next. Amazingly, there was a lad on there who was in my year at school. I had no idea he was gay. I didn't fancy him at all, but couldn't help but send him a quick hello. He must have been very surprised to see a message from me.

Continuing the hunt, I eventually stumbled across a profile that immediately caught my attention: Thom from Wrexham, an eighteen-year-old hairdresser.

Considering the other profiles you'd find on Gaydar, this was like finding a diamond in a mountain of stone. He was so youthful and fresh looking, and looked like he was up for a drink and a dance, like I always was. It was nice to see a profile that had actually been put together with some thought. It wasn't anything like mine; he'd actually taken the time to put some personal information down. He stated that he loved Kylie, had a passion for fashion and designer labels, and he loved his job as a trainee hairdresser in a salon in the town centre.

After drooling over his photos and fantasising about possibly meeting up with him, I sent him a message.

'Hey, I'm a nineteen-year-old soldier heading to Wrexham for a week or so on leave. Do you fancy grabbing a drink or something?'

Admittedly, it was quite short and sweet, and I didn't think for one moment that he'd even bother to respond, but I felt excited by the possibility. I logged off, returned to work for a final few hours, packed my bags and headed to Euston to catch my train home to North Wales. As the train pulled out of the noisy station, I couldn't help but feel the grip of city life loosen from around my neck. I was heading home.

The place I'd longed to escape as a child now offered a degree of solace. London, which had promised so much freedom and joy, had in fact delivered nothing but addiction, pain and depression. The thin thread holding my head above water was getting very close to breaking point.

8

SAVED

It was getting dark as I arrived in Wrexham. As Phil drove me home from the station, I enjoyed looking at the many houses in the village that I'd grown up in before joining the army. We drove past the village pub, the Wheatsheaf, in which I'd spent many an afternoon with Dad. I quickly thought about the Tuesday I'd skipped school and sat with him while he was having his daily drink. It was 11 September, the day the world changed. Everyone remembers where they were that terrible day. I was fourteen years old and sat in a pub keeping my drunk dad company.

I glanced through the windows to see if he was in there drinking at that very moment. I couldn't see him and felt relieved but, as we drove away, I noticed his bucket from his window-cleaning round positioned just inside the entrance. He was in there after all. Some things just didn't change.

Arriving home, Mum came out of the front door followed by the family dog, Monty, to greet me. She squeezed me tightly and then looked me up and down. This was a regular occurrence with Mum. She needed to give a visual inspection and then follow it up with something like 'Oh, you've lost weight, James! Are you eating properly?'

I settled my things into my old bedroom, still pretty much untouched since I'd left three years earlier. My cabinet was crowded with the lead soldiers Dad had collected for me in years gone by. On the shelf above them lay many presentations from my days in the Army Cadet Force which were the pride of my early teenage years. Life had certainly changed since those days. It was sweet that my folks hadn't redecorated my room and changed everything around, but I kind of wished they had. I wasn't the young innocent boy who had left three years ago. I was leading a secret life in the capital, of which Mum and Phil had no idea; nobody north of London did. I wondered whether I'd find the courage to tell them while I was visiting this time. I dismissed the idea almost immediately.

After dinner that night, I asked Phil if he'd mind me using his laptop to check some emails. He set his computer up for me and left me to it. I only had one thing on my mind. I wanted to know if that gorgeous guy called Thom, who spelled his name differently, had read my message and responded. I almost didn't want to check just in case he'd read the message and not bothered sending one back. With hope I logged on.

'Hey James, I'd love to meet you for a drink. Are you doing anything on Saturday?'

I was overjoyed that he'd replied. I imagined his voice as I read his words. He'd obviously looked through my profile and liked what he'd seen. I studied his pictures again and again. He was beautiful. As crushes go, I was smitten.

I considered how our date would play out: we'd meet up, have a few drinks, I'd pay, of course, and then we'd go somewhere, maybe to his flat or something. Did he have his own place? Did he have flatmates? Maybe he owned a car and we'd go somewhere in that. I had so many questions, but I simply replied that I'd be very up for meeting him on the Saturday and asked if he had a particular place in mind. I was already conscious not to scare him off. I really wanted to meet him and for him to like me.

I considered all the possible reasons why Steven had lost interest in me the previous year. I was desperate not to let the same thing happen again.

I spent Friday preparing for our date. I went out and bought myself some new clothes and spent the remaining time wishing away the hours. The whole thing felt different from normal. Well, for a start, we'd planned to meet for an actual date as opposed to the usual 'pop around to my place for a shag' scenario. There was a chance that we both might want to see each other again.

Mum and Phil had noticed my new outfit and excited behaviour that day and asked if I was meeting someone.

I didn't lie and say I wasn't, but I was very sparse with the details and ended up telling Mum to mind her own business. She left me to it.

Saturday dawned. It was a beautifully bright morning without a trace of cloud or rain; you could tell already that the forthcoming summer was going to be great. I grabbed some breakfast and slowly got myself ready.

I wondered what Thom was doing in preparation. I bet he was probably just chilling out in his flat somewhere, watching some TV. I wondered if he'd be early, or late for that matter. I felt my experience in meeting men, although quite vast, was lacking in the actual art of conversation and holding interest. In the past, whenever I fancied somebody, I'd buy them a drink, tell them I was a soldier and, if I felt slightly mischievous, I'd even lie and say I was a virgin. That was it. Chat, taxi, bed. Today was going to be different. We were meeting at 1 p.m., at a busy wine bar chosen by him in the town centre. I assumed we'd eat and therefore spend at least an hour in conversation. Could I hold a conversation for an entire hour, trying to eat elegantly at the same time?

In the army, soldiers eat extremely quickly. Manners are left at the door. What other habits had the army taught me that made me a nightmare to date? I couldn't cook. I didn't need to. I was fairly good at tidying up, but only if my room was being inspected. Without that order, I lived in a bit of a mess. Fashion? All my ideas of fashion were taken from what all the other boys in the army wore: jeans, polo shirts, white trainers. Swearing. I realised that in most of my sentences was a swear word. Judging from his pictures and the information on his Gaydar profile, he didn't know anything about the military, and he probably assumed I was ripped with an impeccable six-pack or something. I'd been amazed how often people back in London assumed I'd be ripped like a weightlifter when I took my clothes off; there was always disappointment.

Mum offered to drop me off in town, but I thought it too much of a risk. What if Thom was waiting outside? She'd see I was meeting a boy. What if she followed me and saw I was having lunch with him? I decided to take the bus.

The bus route drove me right through the village, passing the lane that led to my old school and past the fish-and-chip shop I used to work at. As it headed out of the village towards the town, it drove past the block of flats where my father lived. It was Saturday lunchtime. He'd be out cleaning windows on such a fine day. As I went by I looked up to his living room window and saw that the light was on. That was very odd. It was a bright day, the curtains were wide open, there was no reason whatsoever why that light would be on. Perhaps Dad hadn't been home since the previous evening. I worried that he might be dead just inside that very building. Why didn't I just call on him and see if he was OK?

The town centre was about three miles away from the little village of Gwersyllt. The road passed through dozens of green fields as it meandered its way to Wrexham town centre. As the bus came to a halt opposite the bar, I regretted not getting off a stop earlier and walking the final few hundred metres. I felt like I needed to have a final few minutes to myself before heading straight in. As it was, I was now getting off a bus and walking into a busy environment for a gay date. Two young men sat gazing at each other, hopefully flirting and maybe the odd affectionate touch of the hands or feet. I was about to do this in Wrexham. Wrexham! The place I'd grown up in and never even heard of a gay couple, let alone seen one. But it was too late for that concern now.

Thom had told me the night before that if the weather was good, he'd be sat on the roof terrace. I was a little early so headed up to grab a table, able to get a good look as he walked over from the doorway.

The outside terrace was fairly quiet for a Saturday lunch time. There were a couple of girls sat next to the wall which slightly overlooked the road below, they looked like they might be out on a long drinking session; there was an elderly couple sat near me at the doorway, probably on their weekly trip out to the centre of town; and in front of me, in the middle of the terrace, was a young guy sat on his own. Fuck! It was Thom. He'd arrived early too.

He smiled at me and I walked over; as I did, I thought to myself how fit he looked. In the past, a few people I'd met online, admittedly for casual sex, looked very different in reality to their online photos. This was different. Thom's Gaydar profile matched exactly the guy sat in front of me. He was incredibly well presented. I reached his table and Thom reached out his hand. I met it and we both greeted each other, as if we were two businessmen about to negotiate a deal. I thought it a little rude he didn't stand up initially, but I parked myself down and quickly forgot about it.

Our conversation passed by without much hesitation. It was incredible that I'd thought we'd be sat in silence for the most part. There were a couple of very notable points that I'll always remember. About halfway, Thom said that he did need to get something off his chest. He said I needed to know something about him that was very important. What was he about to say? He was born a girl? He was actually in a relationship and looking for a friend? He was dying?

'You know on my profile it says I'm eighteen...' Uh-oh, I thought. 'Well, I'm actually nearly eighteen.'

So the sneaky sod had lied about his age. If I'm honest, it didn't concern me. So what if he'd said he was three months older than he actually was? If he'd said he was ridiculously younger than eighteen, OK, we'd have had a problem.

'The thing is I don't really have any gay friends and you can't be on Gaydar if you're under eighteen!'

Panic was written all over his face. I told him it was fine and that if he'd have just said it in a message that would have been fine, too. We continued to sip our wine.

I'd thought I looked great as I was leaving Mum's house earlier that day, donned in my new blue jeans and polo shirt, but Thom was dressed impeccably. He was clad head to toe in designer labels: Ralph Lauren jumper, French Connection jeans and Gucci shoes. For a trainee hairdresser probably on less than minimum wage, Thom certainly looked the part. Maybe he was rich?

It turned out Thom didn't share a flat with somebody in town; in fact he still lived at home. I ignorantly assumed that he, too, wouldn't be 'out' to his parents and worried where we'd hang out together, if indeed we were going to meet again.

Everything he'd said so far was fine with me. I didn't care that he was still seventeen; I was only nineteen after all. I also didn't overly mind that he lived at home, usually it didn't matter anyway as I'd only really have one thing on my mind. This, of course, was different from the start.

Thom and I had certainly hit it off. To be blunt, we really liked each other. It wasn't as one-sided as I thought it might be. Although he played it cool, I could tell that he'd probably spent hours getting ready. He mentioned again and again that he'd told the girls in his salon that he was going on a date with a real soldier, so he'd clearly been excited about the whole thing. He kept making references to us meeting again: 'Oh, we'll have to go to the cinema and see it', 'Wait until you meet the girls in the salon'. This was music to my ears. I really fancied him and to hear him implying he saw us meeting again and doing things together really filled me with joy.

Our plates were cleared away and our thoughts turned to what we might do next. At this point, I had assumed we'd either go back to his flat, which now didn't exist, or head our separate ways.

'Well, we can head nearer to my place, there's a nice pub down the road from my house. Do you fancy another drink?'

I thought it incredible how this seventeen-year-old was taking charge. It could have been so different. He might have been very shy and sheepish, but he wasn't.

'What about your folks? Won't they be in?'

'Yeah, they might be. But they're fine!'

Oh my God! Thom's mum and dad knew he was gay. This was incredible! He instantly became my hero. How ironic it was that Thom had spent more than an hour telling me how much of a brave person I must be, being a soldier and all, when all along he'd clearly been a lot braver than me. He didn't live a lie with his mum and dad; he was the total opposite to me. I wanted to quiz him endlessly about how he'd told his folks. I thought that perhaps his parents were liberal hippies.

'My dad will like you. He's a soldier, too!'

Oh. My. God. 'Your dad's in the army?'

'Yes... Well, the TA anyway. He spent his life in the army, then joined the TA when he left. He's a master chef.'

Christ. Not only was I facing meeting a fellow soldier whose son I was dating, I was about to face a senior warrant officer, which I knew he'd be due to his appointment as a master chef, with a hell of a lot of service under his belt.

'My mum used to be a soldier, too. That's where they met. She was a dental nurse.'

If I'm totally honest, I didn't want to go to Thom's house, ever. I just didn't feel brave enough to meet his mum and dad and spend an hour telling them everything about me and my job. Thom's dad would know just about everything there is to know about being a soldier. He'd know everything about barrack life, about the binge drinking that occurred in the bar. He'd surely know that young soldiers, especially troopers like me, were quite a wild breed. I wondered if Thom had mentioned me to them yet.

I told Thom that I wasn't overly keen on meeting him for the first time and then a few hours later meeting his parents. Call me old-fashioned, but it was just too much for one day's stress level. He understood and insisted I joined him for another drink near his house anyway. I agreed, as it wasn't a million miles away from my own parents' house, and we headed off on the bus.

I enjoyed a few more hours with Thom in his local pub. I remember it being run by an older gay chap, who knew Thom's situation and was someone Thom would talk with and confide in. He was a role model in a sense. We all need those characters in our lives. By the end of our date we were both quite tipsy and Thom asked me again to consider going to his house with him. It was obvious what he was implying. My response was quite an achievement. I told him I'd love to see him the following day, but I didn't want to go to his house with him. This was possibly the first time I'd ever declined an invitation to return home with someone, and it wasn't just down to the whole parent thing. I didn't want to jump into bed with him straight away. In my mind, sleeping together was the last thing I did with people before never seeing them again.

'I'm playing golf tomorrow with some friends. Do you want to come?'

In my head I was screaming 'NO!' but to be honest, if Thom had asked me to jump out of a plane to see him again I would have said yes. So it was decided. I was off on a second date the following afternoon. I felt amazing.

As we said our goodbyes at the pub, Thom leaned in to kiss me on the cheek. Forgetting where I was, I complied and kissed him back. He turned away from me and as he did I noticed two familiar faces sat on a table near the exit, staring at us both. The pair were friends of Mum and Phil's. And they looked extremely surprised by what they'd just witnessed.

In the taxi heading to Mum's, I panicked that the couple were already on the phone to Phil or Mum telling them about what they'd just seen. Oddly, however, I also felt slightly relieved. What if they were? Was it all bad? It would certainly take the pressure of making the announcement away from me.

Of course it would be bad. It would be a catastrophe! Imagine my mum being told over the phone from somebody else that her baby son was gay. That's how she'd take it. It didn't matter how old I was, or what my role in life was either, I was her baby boy.

Even if the two didn't ring my mum and break the news to her, imagine if she bumped into them at the supermarket or something, and they just mentioned as a matter of fact that they'd seen me with my 'boyfriend'. That would be a complete nightmare. She'd have a heart attack.

I got home and considered how the next few days of my life might run. I turned the key to the front door and took a deep breath. What would be waiting?

In the living room, my folks were sat in relative silence while watching some Saturday-night TV. They both looked at me.

'Well? Good day?' Mum was clearly intrigued about the day's events.

'Erm... Yes. It was OK.'

'So, who's the girl?' For a second I felt a little relief. No phone call had been made from the two spies in the pub.

'I've told you, Mum... It's no one. Honestly!'

'Why are you hiding it from us? You don't hide anything from us.' She threw Phil a glance, looking for encouragement. Phil, as I'd come to expect, told her to leave me alone.

'He'll tell you when he's ready, Pauline.'

I took my cue to leave and headed upstairs. I could hear them both bickering over me downstairs. Phil was always a very laid-back chap and I just considered it normal for him to back me up on things, but nowadays I think that he knew the news Mum was pressing me for was a lot heavier than she'd be able to handle. Phil had realised some time before that some aspects of my London life were indeed very private.

When I returned downstairs some time later, Mum didn't mention my date or my new love interest for the rest of the evening. But she was clearly troubled by the situation. I hated myself for putting her in that state.

Soon enough my secret would be known. And what then?

9

'MUM... I'M GAY!'

Since coming out, I've noticed that gay people love talking about how it happened for them, discussing at length over a dinner or drink the ins and outs of people's individual circumstances leading to the very moment they finally muttered those two words: 'I'm gay.' There have been countless occasions when I've told my story to an audience and, in return, asked others how they stepped out of the closet and into the unknown. It's a rite of passage for gay people to experience, and hopefully come out the other end a stronger, more rounded person.

For me, I have a complex history surrounding coming out. I had two major coming-out experiences – work and family – but also whenever I worked somewhere new or with different soldiers. When I'm asked, when did you come out? I can't just say, 'When I was eighteen and in the Household Cavalry.' I have to say, 'Which time do you mean? Initially? To my folks? To my friends? When I arrived in Iraq? Every time I've stood up in front of a classroom of soldiers?'

But the most traumatic of all these occasions was by far the morning I told Mum that her baby boy was actually dating men and not, as I'd made out for a long time, women.

I woke up on that Sunday morning thinking about seeing Thom and our date on the golf course. I remembered that he'd said there'd be friends with him... It wasn't just going to be the two of us. I had slightly mixed feelings about this. It was pressure on top of more pressure: seeing Thom again, being introduced to his friends, being exposed as a terrible golf player, probably talking about my job to strangers for hours and then coming home, without getting any time to myself with him. Maybe I was just over-analysing everything. Maybe I should relax a little and go with the flow.

It was another bright day and as I was rising, Mum called me down for breakfast. The three of us ate away while Radio 2 played in the background.

'I'm heading out again today, Mum.' She quickly lifted her head and looked at me.

'Where are you off today? Are you seeing your new friend again?'

'Yes, we're going to play golf.' I'd already told her more than I wanted to.

'Golf! You can't play golf!' She was right, I couldn't at all.

'Well, it wasn't really my idea to be honest.' She nodded and seemed to be settled with the snippet of information I'd fed her.

About twelve months before, something happened between Mum and me that could have cleared everything up. Indeed, it's amazing it didn't. When I joined the army, we were told from the start to continue having our private mail sent home. The army's postal service isn't very well known for its efficiency, so it was generally agreed it was best to have things sent home rather than risk it getting lost in the service mail system. Everything that needed to get to me was sent to my mum's. Mum enjoyed this very much as she'd phone and tell me off for spending too much money or being overdrawn.

I used to bank with HSBC and monthly they'd send out a statement pointing out how little or, in my case, how very much I'd spent over the previous rolling thirty-day period.

One evening as I was pottering around my little room in the barracks before heading out, my phone rang. It was Mum calling me from Phil's mobile, a very normal occurrence. As soon as I answered the call I could tell she was a little anxious.

Mum began by telling me my bank statement had arrived and that I'd been spending far too much of my wages too early in the month. But this was all background information, what she really wanted to know was something else...

'You're spending a lot of money in somewhere called Gay, James.'

I couldn't believe I'd been so careless. I couldn't believe I'd been using my credit card at the bar, practically outing myself in my bank statement. How had I been so silly?

Wonderfully, HSBC had very kindly decided to take the hyphens out of G-A-Y; what Mum was now reading was line after line of the word 'GAY'.

GAY   5.99
GAY   10.99
GAY   6.50
GAY   9.00

On the spot I made up some terrible lie that Dean, whom she knew well, had recently announced his sexuality and that I was supporting him by joining him in G-A-Y every now and again. Incredibly, she bought it. I was surprised she was so accepting of my poor excuse. But she did; I was off the hook.

How very different things would have been if the news had been dealt with back then. It'd be old news. Going on a date with a guy would be quite the norm and Mum would've completely understood.

About an hour later I was putting the finishing touches to my hair before making the walk to the golf club, which was just through the country park at the bottom of the village. Phil had gone to the shop to buy his Sunday papers and Mum was beginning her ironing in the living room. As I put my jacket on, she shouted me into the living room.

'Will you tell me who this young lady is, James?' I was gutted Phil wasn't in to dampen her quizzing flames. She had a slight smile on her face and I felt more love for her that very second than I'd ever felt for her in my life. I knew the answer to her question would hurt her deeply.

'I've told you, Mum, I'll tell you when I'm ready!' In an instant the smile went off her face. She was upset. She sat down on the chair and started to cry. I'll never forget how upset she seemed at that very moment.

'As long as you've been alive, James, you've never kept a secret from me. You've never hidden something away like this!' Seeing her so upset with me was hard to deal with. I hated, as do all sons, seeing my mum cry. Why couldn't I just tell her the name of the girl I was dating? That's all she wanted to know, but because I wasn't offering that very basic bit of information, she'd concluded that the truth was something much worse.

'Is it someone I know? Is she a lot older than you? Is it your brother's ex-girlfriend, Claire?'

She was going all out; her mind had clearly been running away with her. I had to tell her she was wrong. In the commotion of it all, it happened. I told her the truth.

'I'm gay, Mum. I'm gay.'

The tears stopped and she paused. The entire house was silent. Slowly her head began to sink downwards. Then she started crying again.

'No. Please God... no!'

'His name's Thomas... I really like him.'

'And how old is he?' I found it incredible that this was the very next question she asked me. I couldn't understand what relevance Thom's age was to the news I'd just told her. She clearly expected him to be much older.

'He's seventeen, Mum. He's not some old man that's tricked me into fancying him. He's a hairdresser in town.' This final piece of information was little help.

'Oh of course he is.' She carried on crying and I considered giving her a hug, but I just couldn't. In my heart of hearts, I honestly thought my mum would have accepted the news and followed it up with 'I knew all along'. But she hadn't. She was devastated by what I'd told her. I zipped my jacket up and left to meet Thom. I left her crying in the living room, next to a pile of ironing and all alone. It was a horrible experience.

Heading down the hill I felt like a zombie. The previous year, when I'd come out to my friends in London, I'd felt exhilarated. This was wholly the opposite. I felt traumatised. I'd had the closest of relationships with Mum all my life and now I felt like it was all over. I'd ended it by telling her the truth.

My mobile phone rang. It was my sister, Liza.

'Hiya, baby! Are you OK? I've just had mother on the phone.'

As always, Mum had picked up the phone and called her daughter immediately, probably still crying, telling her about 'what I've done now'.

'James, I love you very much. And she does too, but you have to give her time. I've told her off for what she's said to you!'

Liza and I have always been close. It was Liza who used to mind me constantly as a boy. Mum was at work, Dad was cleaning windows or drinking in the pub, Liza would look after me all the time. Ten years my senior, she's acted as the natural link between me, my adolescence and my parents. In 1997 she gave birth to her daughter, Chloe, who I'm godfather to. Chloe is my most favourite person in the world.

On the phone at that very moment, I couldn't believe I'd not told Liza about who I really was. If there was anyone in the world who'd have supported me from the start, it was her. I sat on a bench beside a small walkway surrounded by trees. Liza reminded me how much she and Chloe loved me and said her goodbyes, promising to call me later in the day to see how I was feeling.

In the loneliness of my surroundings, and the stresses of the morning's events, I finally allowed myself to cry. I was crying because at no point in my life had I ever upset my mum to the extent I just had. I cried because I'd allowed myself to live a lie, digging a hole deeper and deeper every time I'd chatted with her on the phone and said I was dating a girl. I cried because, at that very moment, it felt like my own mum didn't love me or accept me for who I was.

The entire event made coming out to the boys in the army a year before a walk in the park in comparison. For a little while that day, I felt I'd lost my mum. Looking back, I am more sympathetic to my mum than I was that sunny Sunday morning. Mothers have a natural way of planning a son's life out, almost to the letter. She had envisaged me marrying the woman of my dreams at a huge military wedding. She'd planned children and grandchildren. In an instant I'd ripped all those hopes apart by saying two little words. Of course it was a shock.

I arrived at the golf club a little late and a little flustered. This was only the second time Thom and I had met and I worried that my swollen eyes would give away the events of the morning.

Thom introduced me to his friends: Jo, his lifelong best friend; Eleanor, who was also a school friend of his; and Sophie. Sophie had her boyfriend with her, who was a boy I'd been in school with – John. He'd had no idea I was gay so I was a little startled by his presence but he shook off the news almost immediately and was far more interested in my time in the army than anything else.

The company and general feel of the group was a huge contrast to how I'd left my parents' house a little while earlier. Here I was accepted, there I was not.

I was the world's worst golfer but Thom was a bit of a pro – well, compared to me anyway. As we progressed, we'd share the odd moment while he coached me over a shot. In the end I was glad to be so useless. The two hours spent on the course that afternoon were invaluable to my coping with what had gone on at home. It helped take my mind off things slightly and, by just being in the company of a guy I was really into, it made me realise that I had done the right thing in telling Mum.

At the end we all grabbed a Pepsi and chilled out at the club-house. I mentioned to Thom that I'd made a little announcement to my mum before coming along and that I'd left her alone to deal with it. He smiled and grabbed my hand. Telling me every-thing was going to be fine, I realised right then that Thom was very special. I'd never felt the way I did right then.

As we readied ourselves to leave, my phone rang again. This time it was 'Phil Mobile'. I drew a deep breath.

'James, I want you to know how much your mother and I love you!'

I don't remember much more about the conversation other than those important few words. For a man who'd entered my life quite late on, I was lucky to have a father figure like him. I was also lucky to have a man in my mum's life who could pick her up and point her in the right direction when things got on top of her. I thanked him and told him I'd be staying with Liza that night. I couldn't face going home and trying to play happy families. I called Liza back and told her I was coming over to stay.

I used to stay with Liza often while I was growing up after she'd bought her own house soon after Chloe was born. It was, for all essential purposes, my second home. I had my own things there when I was a teenager and, though I'd left home and joined the army, it still felt like a haven to me.

That night, while having a takeaway, Liza's 'coming-out treat', I fully absorbed all of the day's activities, from waking in the morning and feeling excited about seeing Thom, to leaving my mother in a state of breakdown after telling her the truth; the crazy contrast only an hour later while playing golf with Thom and feeling very relaxed in his company, to crying with my sister about the years of secrecy I'd put myself through growing up with my hidden sexuality. It was a whirlwind of a day and one I will never forget. The most notable moment of the entire day, however, was that Thom and I shared our first proper kiss at the end of our golf date. It had become clear to me what I now wanted. I wanted Thom in my life. More so, I realised that he wanted me.

The remaining days of my week off were spent mostly giving Mum as wide a berth as possible. I'd seen her on the Wednesday after my announcement for coffee at the house but hadn't stayed long. By then I could tell she'd begun to accept the news.

I saw her again the day after and agreed to spend the night at the house, but was out most of the evening with Thom. The whole process was very gradual. By the time Sunday afternoon arrived and, of course, my return to London, she'd plucked up enough courage to cook me a roast dinner and sit me down for a mother-to-son chat.

I'm not sure what exactly motivated Mum's change of heart in the short space of a week. Maybe it was our closeness and the worry of never regaining our special relationship. Maybe it was the fact that I had already left home and could quite easily exist in the army if she didn't accept who I really was. As tragic as it sounds, it wasn't as if she could kick me out.

Whatever the reason, I'm sure Phil and Liza had spoken to her constantly throughout the week; she'd turned her emotions and behaviour around completely within seven days. She gave me the tightest, longest hug that afternoon before waving me goodbye and, more surprising yet, demanded I introduce her to Thom at the very earliest opportunity. When that would be, I didn't know.

I'd said farewell to Thom the evening before. Thom had introduced me to his mum and dad, both of whom I found extremely nice and very likeable. I just hoped they thought the same about me. We spoke a lot about the army, what exactly I did and how I'd found things. It was great to share some common ground with them. We enjoyed a dinner then Thom and I headed out alone to say our goodbyes. I wasn't sure when I'd next be off work long enough to warrant a journey all the way to North Wales. I told Thom and he understood. I really didn't want to return to London and leave him behind.

After a couple of red wines, I walked him home, hand in hand. As we said our goodbyes I asked Thom if he thought we were a couple and he kissed me and said yes. I had my boyfriend. And I'd found him in the last place I ever thought I'd fall in love, the very place I'd grown up hiding who I really was.

✝

I returned to work after my week-long leave feeling refreshed and ready to take on the coming months of the summer silly season. On the first day back, I familiarised myself with the forecast of events and realised just how very busy the Blues and Royals would be leading up to summer leave; an awkward three months away. Would it be that long until I saw Thom again?

It was quite a challenge switching back on to my duties and the way of life that goes with being a ceremonial soldier. I was to go on Queen's Life Guard the following morning and I had no

kit at all prepared for the duty. Faulkner helped me out by lend-
ing me most of his kit which was, as always, immaculate. This was
quite a normal occurrence among the boys, although officially
forbidden. Throughout the day and the weeks that followed, I
was distracted by Thom almost constantly, whether it be by text
message, phone call or the memories of the things we'd got up to
over the course of our seven days together.

The first major parade of the season was usually the Major
General's Parade in Hyde Park, when the major general inspects
the regiment prior to commencing the ceremonial calendar. The
grand parade is a giant of a spectacle for any passer-by who's
lucky enough to witness the proceedings first-hand. It's also the
one occasion that 'unseats' more riders out of the saddle than
any other.

I sunk my teeth into preparing for this important parade. It
slightly took my mind off Thom, whom I was missing already. I
worried about when I'd next get to spend time with him.

As the parade drew nearer, news got around the barracks that
the colonel was allowing us a regimental stand-down once the
Major General's Parade was out of the way, before picking up
the momentum again for the Queen's Birthday Parade. It meant
that I'd get a long weekend off and therefore enough time to
visit Thom. The catch was we all had to turn out immaculately
and ride brilliantly in front of the general. We had our carrot and
everybody set about their business with conviction.

I didn't head out into Soho at all in the fortnight leading up
to Major General's. I enjoyed a few nights in the bar on camp
or across the street in the Paxton's Head pub with Faulkner and
the boys, but at no point considered returning to my old habits.
I associated unhappiness with the clubbing scene and I didn't
want to be sucked back into the pattern of late nights and early
mornings. I didn't want to be chatting to Thom on the phone

with a stinking hangover from a Soho late night, not now he was my boyfriend. I certainly didn't want to run the risk of meeting another guy while out on the scene.

I told Thom about my pending long weekend off and we hastily made plans for our time together. We spoke about going shopping in Chester, about me meeting more of his friends and us all going out for dinner and drinks. I just thought about seeing him and spending time together, perhaps at the cinema.

When I told Mum I was heading back to North Wales in a couple of weeks' time, she reminded me about meeting Thom and how important it was for her to have him over for dinner. I told her, although I'd already agreed to her wishes previously, that it might not be the best idea. What if she wasn't really ready to sit and have dinner with her gay son and his boyfriend? What if she started crying? But she was very firm. I was to bring Thom for dinner on the Friday night.

I really didn't fancy the whole thing. I was worried from the off about the meeting and more so for Thom. He'd only heard fairly bad things from me about Mum. He'd only known me for a little over two weeks and in the time we'd started to fall in love I'd come out to my mum. It's amazing he didn't run a mile.

I didn't phone home as often as I used to after my announcement. Although I knew that I was very loved, I thought it best to let the dust settle a little before reappearing and introducing my boyfriend. I didn't want to find myself answering questions over the phone about my secret life and the things I'd been doing since being in London. In work I'd answered enough questions about being gay from the other boys; I didn't fancy setting myself up for the same conversations with my folks or my brother and sister. I knew the time would come when I'd have to answer some questions, but that time wasn't yet. And it certainly wasn't over the phone.

After days of endless rehearsing in the park, the morning of the Major General's Parade dawned and we all, the entire regiment, hurried about our business. I was riding my favourite house, Quality Street, and we both looked very smart waiting for the general to ride past, looking over us as he did. The parade wasn't like any other. We'd usually sit and look pretty, or trot in front of or behind the Queen. Major General's was when we collectively showed off our equine abilities as a regiment. The culmination of the parade was an advance as a regiment in canter; basically a cavalry charge towards the major general before stopping at once and presenting him with a general salute. When pulled off correctly, there was nothing more impressive. That day we nailed it: the general was delighted with us all and naturally so was the colonel. I was heading home for the weekend! Quality Street was turned in, groomed and bedded down for the day straight after we'd dismounted; I had a train to catch.

Sat in Euston waiting to depart, I felt the stress of the previous two weeks' workload disappear. Indeed, it felt like I'd worked hard enough to warrant an entire month off, and this was only the start. The following weekend we'd be thrown deep into the first rehearsal for the Queen's Birthday Parade – the Trooping of the Colour, the most important parade of the year. I'd coped better than I had before with the crazy workload the Household Cavalry placed upon its men. I'd had a clear goal: I had to be well turned out and ride correctly with sureness, or I'd lose my weekend off with Thom. This was the first time in what seemed like ages that I could just sit down and do nothing but relax for three hours in the middle of the day.

A week before, when I'd told Thom my mum wanted to meet him on the Friday night, he'd said he was fine with it all, although I could sense the change in his voice and I realised that I was putting him into a situation he wouldn't be comfortable in. After a movie-style reunion in North Wales, we discussed the follow-ing evening's events. Thom was dreading meeting my mum, but he knew he'd have to sooner or later. I felt the same but wanted to look as if I was calm about the whole thing, hopefully instill-ing confidence in Thom.

We made a plan to meet each other on the Friday afternoon in the town centre, then make our way to my mum's for the dinner. I didn't want Thom to have to make an entrance alone. I wanted to arrive with him and, if needed, calm him a little before the big introduction. I headed home late that night, deliberately waiting for my folks to go to bed to avoid any uncomfortable conversation.

The weather on the Friday was again hot. It had been bril-liantly sunny for what seemed like months. When we met in the town centre, at the bar we'd had our very first date at a month before, I noticed Thom had glammed up for the occasion and looked very smart. I joked that he'd put more effort into meeting my mum than he'd done for me on our first date. We polished off a bottle of wine to calm our nerves and headed for the bus, neither of us chatting very much as we went. The whole thing felt very ominous.

Thom was certain he wanted to make the best impression possible, understandably, so we got off our bus a few stops short in order to buy a bottle of wine. Walking the few streets towards Mum and Phil's we chatted a little more and kept each other amused, taking our minds off the stresses of what was about to happen. I was so nervous. These days I remember how nervous we were and wonder how nervous Mum must have felt too. It was a very new thing for her to get used to.

As we walked and chatted, something ahead of us caught my eye. Soon Thom had spotted it too and made a remark. A small figure could be seen sitting on the pavement. At first I thought it was a homeless person, sipping on a bottle of whisky or something, but as we got closer, the realisation of what we were both seeing dawned upon me. I was utterly devastated to be looking at my dad sat drunkenly on the side of the road.

I couldn't believe it. I considered for a second crossing the road and passing by as if he was just a stranger to me, but I automatically hurried my step to get to him and help. Thom looked at me, a little surprised by my reaction.

'That's my dad, Thom.'

Dad was in a mess. I hated myself for not being there for him, for not preventing this from happening. Thom didn't really know what to say or do, and hovered around my father and me as I dragged him to his feet. At the back of my mind I considered just what he must have been thinking. How could my family seem so dysfunctional in comparison to his?

Dad slurred a surprised greeting to me and I noticed some of the neighbours staring out of their windows. I walked the short distance to his flat with him cuddled into my shoulder.

I didn't want Thom to come into his flat with me; I didn't know what state it would be in. I worried that he might leave while I was putting my dad to bed but when I got back he was still stood there, very patiently and wearing a warm smile. I still felt totally humiliated.

On reflection, I wish I'd have done something more. I wish I'd have picked up the phone and called Liza and told her enough was enough. It was already past the stage of danger for Dad, he was visibly close to the end, but right then, with Thom on his way to meet my mum for the first time and the stress that I was under with that, I didn't act upon the situation. I left Dad in his flat, in a highly drunken, uncontrollable state, and made my way to dinner. It's the biggest regret of my life.

As I rang the doorbell, we both drew a deep breath. Could it get any worse?

Mum answered the door with an extremely graceful and welcoming greeting and ushered us both in. I was immediately taken aback by how fabulous she looked. She looked like she was on her way to a posh restaurant or the theatre. She'd really dressed up for the occasion. It was the first time she'd ever set eyes on Thom and I could see she was surprised by how he looked. To this day I don't know what she expected, but I guess it was something quite different from what she found.

Thom acted, as you'd expect, fairly quietly and was very well mannered. Everyone was acting on the whole 'first impressions' thing. I'll never forget how it felt to be sat in the dining room at Mum and Phil's that night, the pictures of me in my uniform surrounding us on the wall, and my boyfriend beside me, me holding his hand under the table and squeezing it occasionally in reassurance.

I guess, and certainly when I think back to the whole coming out to my parents situation, the rest is pretty much history. Mum took to Thom. Thom took to Mum. The disastrous meeting of my drunk father earlier on in the day brought us closer together in a way; our first crisis, if you like. We spent the rest of the weekend in a lovers' bliss; lots of laughs and lots of hugs and kisses. By the time I had to catch my train from Chester on the Sunday afternoon, I felt that Thom and I would be together forever. I was gutted to be leaving him, but excited at the same time for the future. Life was going to be alright!

10

CHANGES

The Trooping of the Colour is one of those occasions that make Great Britain great. Marking Her Majesty's official birthday, the Queen's annual review of her personal division is viewed by thousands in the capital and millions around the world. The entire royal family comes out to celebrate this incredible tradition.

For the hour and ten minutes or so of military display seen on that second Saturday of June each year, weeks and weeks of meticulous preparation is conducted by the lucky soldiers who find themselves performing in it. Occurring two Saturdays prior to the big day, the Major General's Review of the Trooping the Colour is a complete full dress rehearsal for everyone except the few members of the royal family who aren't required until the following week's practice. The parade is so close to the real thing that they even sell tickets to the public to watch it.

Getting to work on that first Monday back after my long weekend in North Wales was, again, a shock to the system. The dates and times for every rehearsal, every horse exercise and every inspection were published for us all to look over; it made grim reading. Life was busy indeed, but before I could worry too much about it all I was pulled into the office by the troop leader.

The soldier who was currently looking after our troop leader, someone I didn't really know as they'd always be working over in the mess, had apparently pushed his luck a little too far and was being sacked. The job was now being offered to me.

Although I've painted the job as quite ridiculous, it was a million times better than working in the yard with the other lads and the horses. For a start, you didn't have to do duties – ever. No Queen's Life Guards, no state escorts, nothing. Your sole responsibility was the officer you were charged to look after. Nothing else mattered, but if you did fail at this primary task you'd be sacked and returned to the harshness of the troops, and made to wear it somewhat due to being absent for so long. I bit his hand off. I remember him asking with a look on his face that suggested I'd be offended, but he'd barely finished his sentence before I accepted the job offer. I was to be 2 Troop leader's orderly. The best part of the job was the fact that you had every weekend off, unless, of course, your officer was needed on duty.

The orderlies were pretty much considered the most organised soldiers within the regiment. The guys who'd completely sorted out their own lives and responsibilities would naturally be the best to sort out the officers' lives and responsibilities in a similar fashion. As well as being wholly accountable for security, cleanliness and usability of all the relevant kit an officer needed to execute his duties, the orderlies also ran the mess in which the officers lived. The orderlies would set the dinner table, chase up officers for their dinner orders, iron the napkins and even prepare the drinks, usually wine, for the daily lunch with the commanding officer. Sometimes an important guest would be booked in for the lunch. On one occasion, Princess Anne was in for lunch after riding a Blues horse in the park. I served her lunch like I would anybody.

Every officer had his place at the dinner table. The commanding officer would sit in the centre; opposite him, the adjutant. Heading out either side of both men would be the remaining officers; the further away from the centre they were sat, the less important they were within the regiment. Stood behind everyone were a handful of orderlies dressed formally in Blues who were waiting on the lunch.

We'd stand around for an hour, clearing each course and offering wine as the business of the regiment was discussed. Orderlies were very useful to the corporals of horse who ran the troops at the other side of the barracks, where we all kept loyalties. If something quite important was overheard at the dining table, an orderly, out of respect, would pick up the phone and pass the sensitive information on accordingly; if there was going to be a surprise spot inspection, for instance. It was very beneficial being such an early-warning system at such a very junior level.

I knew I'd enjoy the pace of life in the mess but, more importantly, it offered me much more stability than I'd been used to in the troops, constantly going on Queen's Life Guard and the like. And it was a very fortunate turn of events now that Thom was on the scene. I was able to plan my life – once I'd planned that of the officer I was now responsible for.

My first major tasking was this first rehearsal of the Trooping the Colour – the Major General's Review. I spent the remaining days of the week preparing my officer's kit, his boots and brasses. I found this a doddle, going through all his uniform at a good pace without the distraction of a horse to wash down or a yard to sweep. Before I knew it, the Saturday morning arrived.

As always, the regiment was formed up on the square ready for the colonel's inspection prior to setting off down the Mall towards Horse Guards. After the colonel had walked the two lines of the regiment, he made his way to the officers, with me and the other orderlies stood to attention next to our bosses. I considered how ridiculous it was that the colonel would tell his officers off for having poor boots or something, give them quite a dressing down and then, once he'd walked off to the next, the orderly would get it in the neck from the officer. I couldn't figure out why the colonel just didn't address his bollocking to the orderlies in the first place.

For that first rehearsal my officer was fine. I'd turned him out to a high standard, the same standard I intended to turn him out to on the big day itself. Once the regiment departed, the other orderlies and I headed up to the bar for coffee to pass the time; we couldn't knock off because we were needed to help the officers get undressed after the parade.

A soldier in the Household Division, whether he be in the cavalry like me or in one of the five Foot Guard regiments, looks forward to his first Trooping of the Colour. The Queen's Official Birthday Parade is the highlight of any ceremonial season, unless there's something unique planned like a jubilee or a wedding; to not be a part of it is a very tough pill to swallow. I realised on that Saturday afternoon that in a fortnight's time the lads would be riding out of the gate to the main event, beaming with pride at being the Sovereign's personal escort in front of the entire world. I wouldn't be one of those lucky men. I'd missed the previous year because I was doing Escort Guards, something junior members of the regiment found themselves doing for the initial stages of their careers within the regiment. I'd shrugged it off the previous year, assuming there'd always be next year; next year had arrived and again I wasn't sat in the saddle. Though I was disappointed, I wasn't envious of the boys stuck right in the middle of this hectic period; their lives were simply put on hold while they prepared for the state ceremonial. Besides, I was involved, although not on the front line, and was still enjoying some normality. The chaps were quite envious of us orderly guys. Everyone wanted to be an orderly.

After the first rehearsal, the regiment returned and the dismount was carried out. Away the horses were put and the men broke down into skeleton crews before knocking it on the head for a well-earned 36-hour rest. The Blues and Royals headed out en masse to unwind in the West End and, in keeping with my recent lifestyle changes, I stayed behind and had a movie night in the barracks, alone. The nightlife just didn't appeal to me any more after meeting Thom.

On the Sunday afternoon, after a well-deserved lie-in and roast dinner, I sat at my desk and began to write Thom a letter. I didn't usually write letters, but it felt like a nice thing to do, so I took pen to paper and began expressing myself on the page.

I wanted to tell Thom how, in the space of a short time, he'd affected me and how it felt like he'd changed my life. I decided to write him a short story entitled 'The Most Beautiful Boy in the World'. I wrote about a boy who had completely lost his way in the world, who had been thrown from the steadiness of the countryside into the energy and busyness of city life. I described how dark a place he'd found it to be and how he'd considered life was just going to be miserable for ever. Then, out of nowhere, he meets another country boy who helps him realise that there is something else out there. I ended it by saying that 'although the most beautiful boy in the world would never realise it, he'd saved somebody's life'.

It was true. Thom had saved my life. The dark nights of my appalling recent past, sooner or later, would have been the end of me, I'm sure. That was all now behind me.

The letter was well received and Thom still has it today. I noticed in the weeks and months that followed that he carried it on his person almost constantly, or had it in his bag at work.

The week leading up to the second rehearsal flew by, and Thom and I made plans for him to come and stay with me the weekend after the Trooping. He'd been to London before with his family and loved the place. I was delighted he'd be coming to stay.

The second rehearsal, the Colonel's Review, during which the Duke of Edinburgh would give his nod of approval, went swimmingly and the regiment entered the final week leading up to the big day. Everyone was working at full steam, including us boys in the mess.

I finished the troop leader's kit off on the Friday afternoon and spent the rest of the day relaxing before the big event. I wished I was going to experience the parade first-hand on top of Quality Street with the rest of the boys instead of watching it on television.

The excitement of riding on a state escort is immeasurable. Everyone working together to keep covered off in perfect order, the centre NCO barking commands left and right of the line telling people to either kick on or rein back. The panic in everyone's stomach when the royal carriage speeds off and the entire regiment is forced to ride faster and faster, all while maintaining smartness and discipline. The banter between the lads in the middle of all this excitement is incredible. I remember laughing along with Faulkner as we both rode only a few dozen metres behind the Queen, with one of the other boys losing his stirrups and sliding off his saddle as the carriage opened up on the Mall. Tears literally rolling down our cheeks, we cheered as he finally gave up and accepted that he was falling off. Watching the Trooping on TV was a stressful experience in itself. I knew my whole family were watching back home and from the text messages I was getting from some relatives, news that I wasn't on parade obviously hadn't been passed around like I'd asked. It was a beautiful day – the second Saturdays of June usually are – and the entire regiment looked magnificent. I was jealous. Well, there was always next year, I thought.

I dismounted my troop leader from his horse and walked with him to his dressing room. He was full of adrenalin after the success of the parade and was looking forward to dinner at some venue in town. The other orderlies and I, however, weren't able to knock off in earnest like the officers. Monday was another important day on the ceremonial calendar: the Garter Ceremony at Windsor Castle. All the officers' kit needed to be prepared fully for the Monday afternoon ceremony. The boys in the troops were in the same position too; they had to be turned out immaculately. The celebrations were put on hold and the regiment, less its officers, carried on with endless kit cleaning. One final push!

Thom and I continued our daily chats over the phone, and excitement began to build between us over his impending visit to London. The three weeks were flying past. I was to finish work on the Friday and have the entire weekend off and spend it exclusively with my boyfriend.

In mid-2006 a rule had been introduced in Knightsbridge that allowed soldiers to have their partners stay over at the weekend, as long as permission had been granted from the squadron leader. Simply, you had to submit a form and a decision would be made by the major commanding the Blues and Royals. He'd sign the piece of paper and it would then be held in the guard room so that the regiment would know exactly who was in the barracks over the weekend. It wasn't that long since the front-page scandals of 2005, so the hierarchy was quite particular about the process and the boys were made to follow the rule to the letter.

I gained a form from the squadron office and filled it in with the dates of the forthcoming weekend and Thom's details. It was all straightforward but very personal. It asked the name of the guest and the guest's relation to the host soldier. I had no problem filling it in accurately, but considered whether it would be met further up the chain of command with ignorance.

About a day later I was called into the clerk's office to pick up the consent form and was horrified to see that it had been rejected. I asked the clerk why and he simply said they didn't give a reason. They didn't need to. I considered for a moment storming into the squadron leader's office and demanding an explanation, but what was the point? The squadron leader might not have known anything about it. The form might have been rejected further down the chain before landing on his desk. Anyway, imagine a trooper pushing his way into a major's office. I'd have been in serious trouble.

Quite simply, the army just wasn't ready for a gay soldier to have his partner stay over on base yet. I felt let down but didn't know who to turn to. Where on earth would we stay? Fortunately a civilian pal offered us his place while he was out of town, but it didn't remove the sting from the army's blatant unfairness.

I was given a tasking for the remaining days of that week after the Garter Service at Royal Ascot. The officers of the Household Division have their own enclosure at the upmarket event, run by the orderlies who work in the mess. I was to drive there on the Tuesday morning and set up a wine bar for the officers of the regiment to enjoy before they headed into the main enclosure for the afternoon's racing. It sounded like a brilliant little job after the fairly mundane ordeal of cleaning kit for parades. My line manager accompanied me on the first day to ensure I was doing the job properly; a senior NCO, he spent the day wandering around the many different enclosures of Royal Ascot, dropping in on me to check if I was OK. Once the officers had gone off to enjoy the racing, he approached me with a bizarre request.

The enclosure we'd been placed in to look after our officers was being shared with another corporate hospitality group. You'd never think it possible that another group of individuals at Royal Ascot could outdo the Household Cavalry in terms of extravagance, but they did. The group who were rubbing shoulders with our lot had much fancier silver on their tables and even a premium brand of champagne, as opposed to our fairly average sparkling wine. The boss had been eyeing them up all afternoon.

It turned out he'd had his eye on the silver champagne buckets that our co-hosts had littered around their tables. He wanted one or two to take home and the task was handed to me to execute.

'I'll give you a day off for every bucket you get me.'

A day off! Days off were few and very far between. This offer was quite an incentive. The following day I watched the movements of the champagne buckets very closely, noting where they were being kept, when they were being replenished with ice and where the actual source of the ice was. By the end of the second day, I'd drawn up a plan and had managed to bag myself two buckets. I informed my boss of my progress and asked him when I'd be entitled to my two days off. He told me it was completely up to me, so I told him I intended to take the Friday and Monday flanking my weekend with Thom off, just two days away.

I very much enjoyed my extra two days off with Thom that weekend. I could achieve results if the correct incentives were placed in front of me, it appeared.

Thom and I spent the weekend acting like a pair of tourists visiting London for the first time. Incredibly, I'd visited very little of the renowned sights the city has to offer, and that weekend many an hour was passed by in a gallery or museum. It almost felt like a mini-holiday. I loved every minute of it. Thom wanted to visit Soho and the bars he'd only read about on the internet or in the gay press. I desperately wanted to keep him away from the place. All I associated with those streets and bars was depression and pain. I didn't want to expose him to that. I wanted him the way he was.

But I gave in to his wishes and took him to a few of the bars, and I introduced him to some of my friends. I constantly noticed other men eyeing up my pretty boyfriend. Some were like vultures circling some unsuspecting prey. He headed away from London after his stay feeling revitalised. Our relationship was going from strength to strength.

Before summer leave was finally on our doorstep, the regiment went off to Norfolk for its annual three-week jolly in the countryside, and the majority of the horses went along too. It was a great time of the year for everyone to unwind after the business of the harsh ceremonial season. In all my time at the ceremonial regiment I never heard anyone say a bad word about the three-week break in the east of England.

Later starts, earlier knock-offs, plenty of chance to have a bit of fun away from the greyness of London, and with it all, one thing: drinking. Every troop went out nightly, usually en masse, to either Norwich, Ipswich, King's Lynn or simply the nearby small town of Watton. The local economy must rocket every July when the Household Cavalry circus turns up – as must the local crime figures.

Earlier in the year, *Loaded* magazine had ranked the Blues and Royals squadron as the No. 1 bad lads of Britain, topping a list that included the Russian mafia, the Triads in Chinatown and the elusive gangsters of the East End. Her Majesty's personal guard was not to be fucked with, it reported.

Within three days of being at summer camp that year, the entire regiment was gated and barred from leaving the perimeter of the small camp of Bodney, our home every July. There had been two car accidents, one involving a drunk driver; numerous violent clashes with locals at one of the larger towns in the region; and a thief was doing the rounds of the lads' belongings, mostly while everyone was out having a good time. It happens every year: the boys go out and cause trouble, the local police boss rocks up at camp demanding to talk to the colonel and, the next thing you know, everyone is imprisoned on camp. You could almost set your watch by it.

Since finding Dad drunk on the side of the street, I'd been making more of an effort to check up on him. The only way I could really do that was to call him every few days and make small talk over the phone, assessing what state he was in by how conversational he was. Since leaving for summer camp and arriving in Norfolk, I'd tried dialling him a handful of times, but was getting nowhere. After the third or fourth time over the course of three days I conceded that he must have lost his phone in some drunken state. I was sure if something had happened to him someone would have phoned my sister or even Mum. The village of Gwersyllt is a very small place.

Today, I wish I'd made more of an effort to reach him.

While working in the mess at summer camp, cleaning my officer's riding boots, I was distracted by my phone ringing. When I looked I saw it was Liza and, before I'd even answered the call, I knew something was wrong and that it was something to do with Dad.

He'd been found unconscious in his flat by the landlady of the local pub. Worried after not seeing him for days, she'd sent a few of his drinking buddies the short distance to where he lived and they'd broken the door down to find him face down on the living room floor. He wasn't dead but, from what Liza was telling me, he was as good as.

I didn't cry. That's the main thing I remember. To this day I don't know why, but right then I just knew I was needed back home to sort him out and maybe even arrange a funeral. The lack of tears didn't mean I wasn't upset. I was mortified. How had we failed him? Why hadn't we forced him through treatment?

The regiment sent me back to London in a car straight away. If there's one thing the army does well, it's welfare. Within an hour I was shooting down the motorway, London bound. The regiment bought me a train ticket and promised to call me every day to check I was OK. I felt very supported by my army family.

I spoke with Mum while travelling home on the train and she told me to prepare to turn Dad's machine off. This was just too much stress for one person to deal with. I wanted to pass it all on to my sister. She was ten years older than me, a mother and far more settled in life. She was far more equipped to deal with crisis; but I couldn't do it. I was Dad's only legal next-of-kin. Nineteen years old, I was suddenly faced with making big decisions.

Thom, who wasn't expecting to see me for some weeks, was very concerned, but I guess he must have seen it coming after the whole situation on the street. I know on reflection I did. To just have someone to talk to about Dad's situation was brilliant. Of course I had Mum and Liza, but Thom and I were at a stage where we were opening up to each other. His support really helped me through such a difficult time.

I got to the hospital where Liza and some people I didn't know were waiting. I struggled to think straight in all the commotion. There was no way I'd be able to think clearly and make life-changing decisions on my dad's behalf in the state I was in.

When I saw him for the first time, the tears finally arrived. Liza and I were left alone in privacy with him. The man who was once the life and soul of the party, a pillar in the community, someone everyone knew, all of a sudden looked very old and unwell. I cried with Liza for what seemed like for ever. Liza told me that she thought Dad was going to die, and I think she was more upset for me than she was for herself.

Dad had not been conscious for four days. He was in a coma. At that point he was being kept alive by what seemed like hundreds of machines, all doing some crucial job to keep him with us. Looking at him and thinking about the journey from here on, I considered whether or not the machines should just be turned off now to save him from a wretched existence and everybody else the pain of seeing him like this for what could be for ever.

Liza and I spent about an hour alone with him, not really talking, not really doing anything. Then some people came to talk to us, a doctor and two women from what turned out to be social services. I looked at Liza to see if she was going to sort out whatever it was they needed, but she couldn't. He was my dad and they'd come to talk to me.

The doctor told me the prognosis was bleak. He said that Dad, if he did wake up, would have brain damage of some sort. It was too early to know to what extent exactly but his life was going to be very different from now on.

The woman from social services had some forms for me to fill in, mostly to do with Dad's background and other personal data. The other lady asked me if I had right of attorney over my dad, to which I responded with a very blank expression. I'd never heard those words before.

The process seemed endless and after about an hour talking through what exactly had happened to Dad, the three left Liza and me in a state of shock.

When my boss rang the following morning for an update on me and Dad, they told me that I had as much time as I needed They didn't need me back at summer camp and again they underlined their support. How many jobs offer backing like that?

Not a lot happened with Dad for about a week but the doctors stressed that it was excellent news that he hadn't deteriorated at all while in his coma. His organs were improving constantly and slowly the colour started to reappear in his face.

Thom had offered to come and sit with me in hospital with Dad, but I didn't want him to. Dad didn't know who Thom was; he didn't even know I was gay. To be sat there with my boyfriend that he'd had no clue about just seemed wrong. We had our first row that week.

I spoke with work and told them what was going on. They suggested I might want to return to work in London for a little while to try and get my life back to some sort of normality. I agreed and, after the following weekend, I left Thom and my family in North Wales and returned to the capital for a week.

Liza called me every few hours to see how I was coping and to tell me about Dad's progress; quite simply there wasn't any. The week dragged and I put little, if any, effort into the menial tasks I was given in camp. They'd put me on barrack guard as the regiment was still away in Norfolk. I just sat in the guard room looking at CCTV cameras for twelve hours a day, thinking of nothing other than Dad. I was still battling a huge guilt that I felt about the situation. I was sure I'd failed my own father.

Back in North Wales, out of nowhere, Dad woke up. Liza was there at the time and she called me within minutes. I was zooming home on a train within an hour.

In the 1990s, Dad was involved in a pretty horrific incident. While busy on his window-cleaning round in the village, he noticed a husband and his wife arguing in their bedroom while he was cleaning their windows. He interrupted them briefly to collect his fee and carried on up the street with his round. Later that evening, as we were all settled in front of the TV, there was a loud knock at the door. Dad looked out of the window and was alarmed to see two police officers waiting. They needed to talk to Dad.

The woman he'd seen arguing with her husband earlier in the day had ended up dead. Dad had been seen cleaning the windows of her home before she'd come to her end and was therefore needed by the police.

I can't imagine how he must have felt being taken to the police station that night. We thought Dad might be a murderer.

The whole thing was cleared up in a matter of days. The husband was found and confessed to strangling the woman after rowing with her all morning. It's the most infamous thing that's ever happened in my home village to date.

When Dad woke up in his hospital bed after being in a coma for a week-and-a-half, ten years of his life had disappeared. His memory was wiped and he'd woken up in a panic over being accused of murdering this poor woman.

I thought he'd gone bonkers and it wasn't until Mum reminded me about that traumatic night that everything made sense.

He had no idea who I was. He looked at me with some familiarity and kept calling me Graham. Maybe he did know I was gay after all. He still calls me Graham by accident sometimes.

We had a starting point. His brain had taken quite a bashing and it was obvious that we had a long way to go before the more familiar Dad of the past was back with us.

As it would turn out, the Dad of the past would never rejoin us. Dad was diagnosed with something called Korsakoff's psychosis and has never been himself since. The improvement he has made is quite spectacular but today he lives with a very short-term memory in a care home that does incredible work keeping him busy and constantly improving his health.

The only positive to take out of it all is that I now have a dad in some context, which, if I'm honest, is more than I had before that July in 2006.

It was some time before I went back to work. The regiment had gone on three weeks' summer leave and no one was needed back in London until the beginning of September, when preparations for the winter ceremonial season would begin at once.

During this break from work I had a phone call from the squadron corporal major informing me that my time on ceremonial duties was coming to an end. I was to return to

Knightsbridge after leave, but to pack up and move to the operational side of the regiment in Windsor. Almost two years to the day since I'd started my ceremonial training, I was to say my goodbyes to Faulkner and the boys and begin my new role as an armoured soldier.

The words Afghanistan and Iraq were mentioned often on my last day and the realism of leaving the sanctuary and relative safety of ceremonial duties sank in. What was waiting around the corner? Soon, I'd be off to war.

11

WISH ME LUCK AS YOU WAVE ME GOODBYE...

On a chilly autumn morning in September 2006, I turned up at my new posting at Combermere barracks in the Berkshire town of Windsor.

Having already served three years in the army, I considered myself a fairly well-rounded and established soldier. I thought, while making the short journey along the M4 motorway, that I'd be placed into a troop with a lot of younger, less experienced soldiers and I'd retain some sort of seniority from Knightsbridge, but I was to find quite the opposite.

I'd been dropped to the bottom of the pile. My two years of ceremonial experience in London was to count for nothing. I was what is affectionately termed the 'crow' and right at the bottom of the heap in the eyes of the squadron chain of command. It was a tough pill to swallow, being further down the pipeline than lads who'd barely left basic training, and I was very irritated by my new-found unimportant status. The fact was I had no 'green' experience.

Before I was of any use to anybody and at level pegging with my fellow soldiers in Windsor, I needed to learn how to drive the armoured vehicles the regiment used on operations in the likes of Afghanistan and Iraq. Combat Vehicle Reconnaissance

(Tracked), or CVRTs, had many variants, the most notable being a Scimitar, which I needed to know how to drive and maintain. The regiment sent me to Bovington in Dorset, the home of the Royal Armoured Corps and School of Driving. After the six-week course in Dorset I was a fully fledged tank driver.

Back at Windsor I fitted into 1 Troop, A Squadron, which was a large body of men totalling about 130. A Squadron had a fleet of CVRTs which we maintained when we weren't deployed on exercise somewhere in the countryside. I'd spend many days and weeks tinkering away at a vehicle in the middle of the hangar with the boys. There was never a moment when something couldn't be repaired or replaced; vehicles approaching forty years of age need a lot of time and care.

There were a lot of new faces to get used to and niggling away at the back of my mind throughout my first week was that it was likely we'd all find ourselves fighting a war in the very near future. It was extremely frustrating not knowing exactly where we'd end up being deployed in the year that would follow, but what we all knew was that it would be somewhere east or west of Iran, somewhere very far away and very, very hot.

I was, by then, used to friends coming and going, with the army moving its people around almost constantly. Faulkner and Dean had by then been posted to Windsor too, but were working in different squadrons. I rarely saw them. Josh had remained back in Knightsbridge to train to become a riding instructor like Tim, something he took to extremely well. Nobody followed me to A Squadron and I certainly felt quite alone for the opening weeks of my time there.

I made an early ally in these initial stages of regimental life in Windsor, another lad of about the same age who'd not been in the army as long as me but had spent longer at the regiment and was higher up the pecking order. Matt was a London lad by birth and we clicked well and became good pals. 1 Troop was quite a mix of men. There was Hodges, an entertaining guy originally from Zimbabwe who was never short of a tale; Kirky, a quiet lad from Nottingham who'd also been at Knightsbridge at the same time as me but was a Life Guard; and Smudge, a lance corporal a little older than us. Sometimes I found Smudge a little difficult to get along with but he was very good at his job as a gunner in one of the Scimitars. The final lad I found myself working alongside was Scoffy, who was Cumbrian by birth and very experienced in the regiment as a driver and gunner. Scoffy was a completely different person to me and on the first day I dreaded the prospect of getting on the wrong side of him. He was a tall, stocky guy who knew exactly what he wanted and wasn't afraid to tell us other troopers what he needed from us. He was the senior trooper and pretty much carried the authority of a corporal of horse.

But I shouldn't have worried about him. Scoffy was a hard worker and I really admired him. If something needed to be done, Scoffy would set the rest of us to task and, unlike many others, he'd stick around and help until the job was done. He'd been a trooper at the regiment for so long he knew more about the vehicles than some corporals of horse. I learned from working closely with him that the reason he hadn't shot through the ranks as someone of his calibre should was because he was never afraid to tell people, particularly senior ranks, exactly what he thought – and often a little too bluntly. We became good mates and he took me under his wing. Commanding Scoffy's Scimitar was a chap called Danny, who was just about the coolest guy I'd ever meet in the entire army. He was an expert Household Cavalryman who, in the early stages of his cavalry career, was a riding instructor in Knightsbridge before crossing over to the operational side and becoming an excellent 'green' soldier. I would learn a lot from

Danny, and worked closely with both him and Scoffy the following year on operations.

Running 1 Troop was an officer and a corporal of horse. Lieutenant Olver (not 'Oliver', as he'd constantly remind people) and a chap called Corporal of Horse Gibson, known as Gibbo if nobody important was around.

Mr Olver was quite a character. A graduate of Bristol, he became a junior officer in the Household Cavalry Regiment by the time he was in his early twenties. He was the polar opposite of everyone else in the troop and had a very proper middle-class accent. The lads in the troop gave him a hard time for being 'posh'. I quite liked him, although there'd be times over the course of the following year when I'd have to take a deep breath before carrying out his orders. Mr Olver was to command us all throughout whatever was waiting around the corner.

Supporting Mr Olver, Gibbo was a very experienced soldier who very much acted like a father to us boys. Although Olver officially commanded us, it was really Gibbo who we'd all listen to and respect most.

Settling in to this big family of men, once again I found myself talking a lot about my sexuality. Going through the whole coming-out situation again, something I'd get used to, answering the same fairly mundane questions about who I was, I realised that the subject of sexuality was still a very taboo area of military life. Even Mr Olver was fascinated by me and my background and would spend a lot of time chatting with me, intrigued by my apparently different lifestyle.

I was struck, early on, by how different Windsor was to Knightsbridge. The obvious difference was the lack of horses constantly needing care; once we'd finished working on the vehicles, we could just close the hangar doors and knock off. Over the course of those first two or three weeks, I noticed that soldiers were generally happier at the armoured regiment. There were no stories knocking around about troopers trying to hang themselves or throw themselves out of windows. The boys would start work at 8 a.m., as opposed to the 6 a.m. start endured in London, and finish for the weekend on a Friday lunchtime and not be needed again until the Monday morning. The entire lifestyle of a Windsor cavalryman was a million miles away from that of his London cousin.

My general happiness improved considerably, too, because I could head back to North Wales every Friday afternoon and spend time with Thom or my dad. Life would be much better away from London, even with the threat of deployment and conflict. I even got a little excited about the prospect. It's what we all joined the army for, after all.

A few weeks after I'd arrived and settled into the troop, the squadron received three new officers fresh from their training who were to become troop leaders at the regiment. The week before they were to arrive, we were all called together by the corporal major for an announcement.

About a year before, to the great excitement of everybody in the regiment, Prince Harry had announced he'd chosen to become an officer in the Household Cavalry, choosing my very own cap badge, the Blues and Royals. The news went down with much trepidation both within the regiment and among the many families who count themselves as part of the wider regimental family. I remember how jubilant Mum was when she got the news.

As his training progressed, we'd read in the papers that he was almost ready to join the men of the regiment and take command of a troop somewhere, but none of us really ever considered that he'd actually turn up and do a job. A lot of us thought he'd do his time in Sandhurst then retire back to the palace, occasionally donning a nice uniform for a state occasion. As it turned out, he was actually coming to the regiment, and not just the regiment, but to A Squadron to work with us. There was much excitement, although the boys did a good job of not showing it.

On the following Monday morning at first parade the squadron formed up as normal, with the officers lining up behind us while the roll was called; a fairly shy-looking 22-year-old prince attempted to blend into the crowd. It was very surreal. He was to assume command of 2 Troop and was, as far as we were concerned, to be treated like any other troop leader in the regiment. I hoped the boys would give him a little bit more respect than that.

I'd had a straightforward couple of years on ceremonial duties, always knowing what was on the horizon and when I was on duty. I'd always had the comfort of knowing that I wouldn't be out in the middle of Salisbury Plain in the pouring rain, running around with a rifle practising manoeuvres or the like. In Windsor, that would certainly change.

The entire regiment was to carry out generic training at locations around the UK for three weeks in the late autumn of 2006. The exercise, called Wessex Warrior, would see A Squadron deployed to the south-eastern corner of Scotland to conduct training before moving to a training area known as Otterburn in Northumbria and then finally moving en masse to Salisbury Plain for the last week of the three-week operation. It would be a very difficult routine to get used to, as I'd only been on exercise for a maximum of five days at the end of basic training.

I was the driver of call sign 1.3, commanded by a chap called Shagger and gunned by Smudge. We were known as the junior call sign, simply because of how junior we were in our relevant roles. I was by far the junior driver of the troop: Smudge hadn't long qualified as a gunner and Shagger was a junior commander.

He had a hell of a lot of operational experience and had even started out on ceremonial duties like me some years before, but this was a fairly new role to him as a vehicle commander. The pressure was piled quite high on his shoulders and I tried to make myself as useful to him as possible, but I'd find soon that I could, on occasion, be quite a hindrance, too.

Apprehensive about the three weeks that lay in front of me, I boarded the coach to Scotland very early that late October morning, hoping that I wouldn't be an utter failure at being a real soldier; the Brasso tins and Kiwi polish were long gone now.

As exercises go, Wessex Warrior was bloody good fun. In later exercises, I'd find myself mind-bogglingly bored, but this one was pretty full-on from the start. The learning curve was severe and I found myself really concentrating to keep up with the other lads. One thing was clear, though: my time in Knightsbridge had made me more disciplined. If it started raining, I'd put my water-proofs on without a second's thought; if my vehicle needed more oil, I'd fill it at the earliest chance; and if my rifle needed cleaning or oiling, I'd sort it out. It was the subtle differences between us 'dual-trained' Household Cavalrymen and the lads who'd found themselves straight at the armoured regiment after basic training.

During the final week of exercise, known as the 'test phase', increasingly we found ourselves operating on our feet in a more infantry-based role, rather than in our vehicles driving to loca-tions and causing havoc with the larger weaponry. We threw flash-bangs, which are imitation grenades, into buildings then cleared them with machine guns; we put in 'observation posts' and spied on enemy movement; and, finally, we conducted full-on infantry-style squadron assaults, all on foot! This involved a lot of running and a lot of crawling through swamps and the like.

On the final night we had to conduct an insertion move, a quick walk carrying all our fighting equipment, of about ten miles, carrying everything we needed to then go on and assault a village in a dawn attack. It was pretty gruelling for me but not so much for the others, who'd done similar moves time and time again. This was the most physically demanding thing I'd ever been tasked to do since joining.

In basic training, when you stop and look around during exercise, you see other young trainees all trying hard to become soldiers; when you join the regiment and then go on exercise, you see an array of ages, all with different experiences, going about their business in a professional way. In contrast to basic training, when everyone's trying to impress the instructors, nobody's trying to show off. This was a different world. It was the professional field army and it was my first insight to it.

After the assault, and once the two words every soldier dreamed about, 'end-ex', were called over the radio, we unloaded our rifles and made our way slowly and tiredly to the muster point to discuss how the attack had gone.

Our troop and Prince Harry's troop had worked together throughout the night and indeed throughout the three weeks leading up to the final attack. He'd been slumming it in the dirt with the rest of us, tabbing the endless miles to fight through battles in the pouring rain and commanding his men throughout everything just like the other officers. I respected him anyway, but I had a new-found admiration for him after the exercise.

Gibbo, our corporal of horse, was delighted with how we'd all worked, not only during the final assault but for the entire three weeks. He kept saying how he was sure we'd be good enough 'next year on ops', signifying his satisfaction in our progress before our departure to war, which was being talked about almost hourly.

'And you, Ronald... For a poof, you've got some fucking aggression!'

Ronald had become my nickname somehow. It is my middle

name, of course, but during one of Mr Olver's intense interroga-
tions he'd discovered it and decided to apply it as my name. It
stuck. Everyone now called me Ronald – even Prince Harry.

I didn't take any offence at all at what Gibbo had said. In fact,
I took it completely the opposite way. It was like a dad telling his
youngest son that he was proud of him. In the exhaustion of that
final day of exercise, hearing those words made me feel accepted.

That night, we weren't to return to Windsor; instead we had
to stay put in the middle of Salisbury Plain. We were all gutted
about the extra night of inconvenience and especially frustrated
once somebody realised it was Bonfire Night. In the distance we
could see the occasional flurry of fireworks and the odd whizz
and crack in the air. It didn't do much for morale.

Prince Harry, probably as frustrated as the rest of us at being
made to stay out on exercise for a pointless extra night, decided
to do something that would cheer us all right up. Hearing the
distant noise of fireworks and feeling the general mood among
the lads, he and his close-protection officer drove to the nearby
town of Salisbury to buy a stockpile of fireworks.

An hour later they returned and the entire squadron gathered
with hot tea and coffee to watch the most exclusive fireworks
display in the world: Prince Harry's personal fireworks party.
It was fabulous. If anybody had anything against the prince
before that gesture, I'm sure they changed their minds sat in the
cold that night in the middle of Salisbury Plain.

The remaining weeks of the year were spent conducting fairly
low-level training at the barracks in Windsor, with the occasional
day out somewhere, either firing our weapons on a range or practising how to react in NBC (nuclear, biological and chemical)
situations. Soon we were celebrating the Christmas period, my
favourite time of the year.

At the beginning of the final week before Christmas leave, a rumour began to circulate that an announcement was coming about what the regiment would face in 2007. We knew we were going somewhere, but the question was where? Were we off to Iraq? Were we off to Afghanistan? Nobody really knew for sure, and nobody really had a preference. They were both pretty awful places at the time. I was being asked constantly by Mum and Thom what was going on. It was as nerve-racking for them as it was for us.

The day before leave, a Wednesday, the entire regiment gathered in the gym to enjoy a Christmas lunch served by the seniors and officers, as always. We donned our colourful paper crowns from the inside of Christmas crackers, and the RCM, the most senior NCO in the regiment, told us all to be quiet and to sit up while the colonel said a few words.

After telling us to relax, the colonel took his beret off and looked very sombre.

'In the spring of next year, A Squadron will deploy to Iraq on Operation Telic 10.' This was the news we'd been waiting for. We were off to the Middle East. Every day of my life since I had joined the army cadets had been in preparation for this very moment. We were getting our marching orders. The feeling was difficult to explain and the half-bottle of wine I'd drunk with dinner didn't help as I tried to process this historic announcement.

The colonel told us what to expect but made it clear that there was still 'great uncertainty' about what would actually happen. He did tell us, however, that we'd be preventing smugglers from getting into Iraq across the Iranian border. B Squadron would be deployed at the same time but operating in a different part of the country – Faulkner would be in Iraq at the same time as me. Training would start once we returned from leave.

We celebrated our Christmas dinner even more vigorously after the announcement and afterwards 1 Troop went out as one large family to drink the news away. Led by Mr Olver and Gibbo, we'd all be heading abroad on operations. Me, Scoffy, Danny, Matt, Smudge, Shagger, Kirky... We were about to become brothers-in-arms and the challenges that lay ahead would test us all as soldiers, as comrades and as human beings.

†

Christmas was a bit odd that year. It was my first Christmas with Thom and, though I was swept up in the whole romance of being with him, I couldn't help but think it might be our last.

Mum, by then, had completely got over my sexuality and had become a bit of a gay rights spokeswoman in the local community, especially in the social club where she played darts on a Thursday. If she overheard anybody saying anything remotely homophobic, she'd immediately ask them to explain themselves. I found this quite hilarious. She was also wholly supportive of Thom and me, and treated him like everybody else.

That Christmas, Dad was just settling into his new living environment at a care home that specialised in support for people who had suffered some kind of brain injury, just across the border in Shropshire. It was a huge relief when he moved into his new surroundings and they looked after him brilliantly.

Thom was always quite out of place in the countryside of North Wales. It was obvious to me from the start that he needed so much more out of life than the rural setting of Wrexham could offer. He wasn't hugely different from me in that respect and over the course of the three weeks I spent with him that Christmas, he told me that he really wanted to leave the town and be nearer to me.

He'd thought through his plans quite thoroughly before letting me know of his wishes, and had looked into work near Windsor.

He was entering his last few months as a trainee hairdresser and I worried that he was about to throw away all that training and skill he'd worked hard for in Wales, but it seemed he'd already made up his mind. He wanted to move to Windsor with me.

If I'm honest, I loved the idea. I'd lived in barracks my entire army career – and indeed my whole adult life. I envied those soldiers who were married or living off base with their girl-friends. I hated that I didn't go anywhere once work was done, just sat around in my room watching DVDs or playing on my Xbox. But I was worried. I was going away, possibly never return-ing. I worried that he'd need support. I worried he'd get fed up waiting for me. Life was pretty stressful as it was without this new development.

He'd found an airline advertising for new talent to work on long-distance flights around the world. Thom had said in the past that it was his dream job to work for a company like British Airways or Virgin Atlantic. Nobody could stop him from chas-ing his dreams and sending off his application – so we didn't. Everyone who knew him encouraged him. He sent the applica-tion off just before Christmas Day and began his wait to find out if his future lay in the airline industry.

I enjoyed every minute of that Christmas. I spent the actual day with my mum and Phil, visiting my dad in his care home in the morning, rushing home to visit friends in the village pub and standing up in front of the television to watch the Queen's Speech. Mum always served dinner at 3.15 p.m. so that the family could all group around the TV and listen to Her Majesty's message.

Christmas passed in a flash, as did my twentieth birthday, which I spent with Thom and my parents. Enjoying the occasion, and in the slightly intoxicated state I found myself in, I thought again about this being my last Christmas and birthday. I honestly thought it was more than a possibility. Every time I switched on the news or opened a newspaper, there was someone else dead in Iraq. Since learning that I'd certainly be there from May onwards, it was almost an obsession to scour the media trying to find news of another fatality in the Middle East. I would watch on the news as a distraught wife or girlfriend cried over her dead lover's coffin. I worried that when it happened to me, people would focus on Thom being another man and him being the first gay guy to lose his partner in the war.

Once leave was over, I drove back to Windsor in the car Mum and Phil had helped me buy to save money on expensive trains week in, week out. I went to work the following morning, depressed that leave had passed by in a flash. As expected, the first three months of 2007 were non-stop. The squadron had become very strong and very close as a team. Prince Harry was still very much part of our life. He'd taken a natural approach to commanding men and had taken it upon himself, as had Mr Olver, to learn more about the men he'd be going to war with. The best officers I've ever dealt with have always been the ones that have taken a real interest in the men they are commanding. Olver and Harry were both very interpersonal men who placed high importance on knowing just exactly who was serving under them.

Our training, which had included everything from learning to use different kinds of weapons, like AK-47s, and handling large crowds in riot training to understanding basic Arabic (particularly phrases like 'STOP OR WE'LL OPEN FIRE!') and learning how to administer battlefield first aid finally came to an end. A Squadron was ready to fly to Kuwait, before crossing the border into Iraq.

Three weeks' leave was granted to every member of the squadron to say their goodbyes and make whatever arrangements were necessary before leaving the country. The time had nearly come.

Thom had been successful in getting his dream job in the airline industry. Everyone was happy for him. Supported by his parents and me, he moved to Windsor, moving in with a friend of mine before beginning his training with the airline at Gatwick. This meant we weren't able to spend the entire three weeks together but we still saw each other a lot. I valued our time and it was a struggle to think how long it could be until we were back together.

Leaving Thom for a few days, I returned to North Wales to spend time with my family and say a few goodbyes to some friends. The day I arrived in Wrexham to start these goodbyes, something on the news had caught the attention of my family, and indeed the whole town. A Wrexham man, serving in the Royal Navy, was part of a group of sailors that had been captured by the Iranians while on patrol in so-called international waters off the coast off southern Iraq and Iran. The sailors had been captured and arrested and were being held inside Iran while, understandably, the world's media made a meal out of the entire situation.

I watched the events unfold in the news quite obsessively. I was off to patrol the Iranian border. The last thing I needed was an escalation of conflict between us and Iran.

Apart from being glued to the news and constantly checking my phone for missed calls from Windsor, I attempted to sort out the one or two pieces of business soldiers find themselves faced with before deploying to hostile places. I sat myself down in a small coffee shop in the town and wrote my goodbye letters that were only to be opened in the event of my death.

Sitting in the tranquillity of the small Welsh town, it was difficult to imagine events that would lead to these letters being opened by my heartbroken mum or my beautiful boyfriend.

I wrote Thom's first, which brought me to tears. It was very

short and sweet. I told him how much he'd changed my life and
how much I wished we'd be spending forever together. I then
wrote Mum's, which was equally difficult. I told her that she was
the most amazing woman ever and that I loved her very much.
Again, sealing the envelope, I felt a great shiver run down my
spine at the thought that it would only be opened if I were killed.
My brother and sister got a letter between them, detailing how
great they'd been to grow up with. Dad had one too, to be read
by his carer if the worst occurred. I knew that Dad's would be the
one that would be read again daily, possibly for the rest of his life.
The final letter was for my wonderful niece, who I loved dearly. It
wasn't to be opened until she was eighteen, but it was just a small
note to wish her all the best as she entered adulthood.

The afternoon's writing was a traumatic experience, but I felt
better for it. I knew that some of my fellow soldiers weren't both-
ering to write such letters and I was troubled by the thought of
their loved ones not getting a final goodbye. I almost wanted to
write letters for them. As my time in North Wales drew to a
close, I visited my dad at his care home and spent some hours
chatting away with him. I didn't mind having to repeat everything I told him every five minutes or so, it was just who Dad
was now; what I valued was simply the father–son time we were
enjoying together.

The night before I was to head back to Windsor, Mum
arranged a leaving party for me at the local club, which was
attended by just about everyone who knew me in the small
village of Gwersyllt. Thom flew home from Gatwick and arrived
with his parents just as the party was getting underway, which
was a massive relief as at one point I thought he wouldn't make it.

I hadn't seen so many of my friends in the same room since
leaving school or the army cadets and I was seconds away from
tears all through the night, wishing it would never end. Most of

my schoolmates and the friends of my parents had never met Thom before, so I was delighted when he was given such a nice reception by everyone.

Both Liza and Paul made speeches telling me how proud everyone was of me and, with tears rolling down their faces, they both wished me all the luck in the world. I couldn't believe that the event I'd been thinking about since I was just thirteen years old – when I'd enrolled as an army cadet in the building next door to the social club I was now having my goodbye party in – was actually about to happen. I was heading away with the British Army to a conflict far, far away. There were lots of laughs and lots of tears as I said my goodbyes. Thom held my hand throughout.

Thom and I were to drive back to Windsor the following day to enjoy the last few days of leave before my deployment. Instead of staying together after the party, I decided I wanted to spend one last night alone in my old room, in the bed I'd grown up in before becoming a soldier. I wanted to wake up and enjoy a cooked breakfast made by my mum. I also knew it would make her very happy knowing that I wasn't spending my last night at home in somebody else's house. It felt proper to spend it with them.

I knew that saying goodbye to Mum and Phil would be one of the hardest things I'd ever have to do. Mum's MS couldn't stand too much stress and I feared I was putting her in a position where she'd end up very poorly. I also knew that Liza wouldn't tell me over the phone or by letter if that was the case. It was a day Mum had been dreading since I came home from cadets as a kid telling her I wanted to be a soldier, and boy, was it hard.

As she squeezed me, tears pouring from her eyes, she told me that I meant the world to her and I was very special. She told me she'd write every week and that she wouldn't stop thinking about me at all. She promised me she'd phone Thom and make

My granddad, James Crumlin, in 1938. He was seventeen years old and serving in the Royal Navy.

With my dad, Ronnie, on a snow-covered Christmas morning in Gwersyllt, 1995.

Mum and I on our annual holiday to Butlins, Pwllheli, 1996. Not sure about the jumpers.

Playing the side drum with the 4th Cadet Battalion, Corps of Drums in Wrexham town centre. I'm on the left-hand side, third from the front.

Aged sixteen, on my second day in the army, September 2003. Alongside me are Junior Soldiers Reucker and Perryman; Reucker would go on to receive the Military Cross.

Basic training: boys will be boys!

4 Section, 6 Platoon in 2004. Back row: Shickle, Warren, Cpl Hayhurst (Section Commander), Rutter and McDonald. Front row: Abraham, Vella, Wharton and Williams.

LEFT Liza, me, Mum, Paul and Nan at my passing out, 13 August 2004.

BELOW Drill ride with the boys at Hyde Park barracks, October 2004. From left: Smith, Elliot, Hendy, Whitehead, Wharton, Warren, Perryman, Evans, Johnstone, Reid, McAllen, Tate and Ibbetson.

Kit ride, March 2005. I'd 'come out' to the boys two days before this photo was taken.

Nan tries on the kit for size at my passing-out parade, St Patrick's Day 2005. There would never have been a more loyal guard!

The one that got away. Steven was the first guy to ever take a real interest in me.

Regimental barbecue at Hyde Park barracks, spring 2006. The regiment often enjoyed moments of relaxation during the preparations for state ceremonies.

Me and Thom on our second date. I'd told Mum I was gay only hours before.

With my sister Liza on her wedding day, October 2006. She looked every bit a princess.

Basra, 2007. At the COB awaiting a helicopter for our first trip to Maysan. Trooper Hodges and I try to get used to the overwhelming heat. © Byron Kirk

On the general-purpose machine gun, with Scoffy driving and Lance Corporal of Horse Danny Abbott commanding. The three of us were extremely close during our months in Iraq. © David Penny

Making the most of the hot weather.

Posing with Kirky and looking a little grumpy. © Byron Kirk

Ibbo and I attempt to entertain some of the local kids, who were all too used to seeing soldiers and guns.

Driving the battered WMIKs across the open desert was great fun though not without risk.

At Mum and Phil's wedding in May 2008. I was honoured when Phil asked me to be his best man.

A Squadron in Canada, September 2008. HRH Prince Harry stands at the far right.

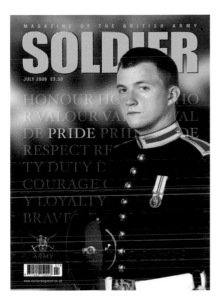

On the front cover of *Soldier* magazine in 2009. The response would alter my course in the military. © *Soldier*

With Thom in New York, Christmas 2009.

The happiest day of our lives. Thom and I enter a civil partnership in March 2010. © David Sanderson

Thom and I meet Prime Minister David Cameron at a Downing Street garden party, July 2010.

Moments before the regimental dismount of the Sovereign's Escort at the royal wedding, 2011. It would be the last time I ever escorted Her Majesty the Queen.

With Sir Ian McKellen and Daniel Winterfeldt at the Inter-Law Diversity Forum Winter Carnival. © Inter-Law Diversity Forum

The divisive *Attitude* front cover, which called for equal marriage in the United Kingdom, May 2012. © *Attitude*

sure he was OK, too. The final thing she did was hand me a small envelope with a letter inside. Handing it to me, she made me promise not to open it until I'd taken off and was surely on my way to Kuwait. The letter was a bit of a surprise but deep down I had kind of expected it. I took the letter, which I would guard with my life, and placed it in my pocket. It was a part of Mum I was taking to Iraq with me. It became sacred the moment she handed it to me.

Thom drove me away, the neighbours from up and down the street waving to us from their driveways as he did, and we began our long journey back to Windsor. We hardly spoke the entire way.

The timings changed almost hourly for our flight out, something we deploying troops would identify as an all too familiar trait of the RAF. We were stood down from work but had to remain within three hours of the barracks, just in case our flight was moved forward – there was no more training to be done and everyone wanted to get as much time with their loved ones as possible.

Thom completed his airline training and I celebrated with him and his new friends at their training base near Gatwick. It was such a contrast of new beginnings for us both. We were both about to start something we'd wanted to do all our lives, the only difference being that I considered my challenge as a possible ending. I was sure Thom would be waiting for me upon my return, but the closer to deployment I got, the more I was thinking about meeting a nasty end. I became so obsessed with the prospect of death that I planned my funeral to meticulous detail: who I wanted there, what I wanted to be read, the music I wanted played. It was a very eerie state to be in and I'd occasionally find myself spontaneously bursting into tears.

After his training, Thom had some time off before carrying out his first flight the following Friday, the very day that I was due to leave the UK. Thom was off to Orlando; I was off to Iraq. The contrast was unreal.

The final few days flew by, like I knew they would. It was a relaxed time spent with Thom at Thorpe Park or in Windsor eating out with our friends. He was thrilled about his first trip with work to Orlando, where he'd be staying for about two days before returning. I was a little jealous about his dream job, but I didn't really say so. He tried to keep his excitement fairly low-key so as not to upset me too much, but who could blame him?

Prince Harry's troop was told that they wouldn't be flying out with the bulk of A Squadron and would remain in the UK for a further two weeks acting as a rear party. Nobody could quite understand why, but the boys who found themselves in 2 Troop were obviously delighted they were getting extended leave. Why on earth couldn't they just deploy at the same time as us?

Friday 4 May dawned, the day we'd finally be flying off to war, and Thom and I woke to face two very different journeys.

I spent the early morning helping him get ready in his nice new uniform. I helped him throw his last few essentials in his suitcase and checked and double-checked he had his passport and air pass. He looked smart in his three-piece suit that morning. When he was all ready and fully packed, he gave me a big hug and kissed me goodbye. There was no big ceremony like with Mum. He told me he loved me and that he'd miss me, before turning away and leaving me in the hallway. He'd gone.

I dressed myself in desert combats, put on my new boots specially designed for the hot climates of Iraq, finished my cornflakes and walked the short distance to the barracks. Life for the next six months was on hold.

We drew our rifles out of the armoury, boarded the coach and travelled through the streets of Windsor towards the M4, then away to Brize Norton to board our plane.

I looked at the streets of Windsor as we pulled away, at the majestic setting of the castle overlooking the town below. I imagined the Queen looking out of her window back at us all, sending her best wishes with us as she did. I tried to keep the image of Windsor Castle fresh in my mind as I wondered if I'd ever see it again.

Three hours later, having spoken to Mum and Thom before he'd taken off in his 747 bound for Orlando, I boarded the battleship-grey TriStar aircraft that would take us the many thousands of miles to Kuwait, pausing to touch the ground with my hands one last time before climbing the steps into the plane. Would I ever touch England again?

As the plane took off over Oxfordshire, I looked down at the green fields and hills below and for the first time in my life, I realised just how beautiful England really was.

As the plane flew into the distance, I clutched the letter Mum gave me and braced myself for what was in it. The contents were very private but very special.

Great Britain, our past, our training and our loved ones were behind us. We faced the uncertainty of the most hostile environment in the world, united as soldiers.

12

UNDER PRESSURE

We arrived in Kuwait a little after 4 a.m. As soon as the door of the plane opened, I was immediately struck by the intensity of the heat. It was barely light, but the temperature was far higher than the UK would enjoy at noon in the middle of August.

Desert. There was nothing but desert. We were all initially stationed at an American base called Camp Virginia, complete with its very own McDonald's. I could get used to working with Americans – they certainly didn't do anything by halves. Camp Virginia felt about the size of Wales, though in actual fact it was about as big as Hyde Park. It had everything a fighting soldier would ever need. The American troops could even buy their next Ford car, tax-free, and have it delivered to their home upon their return. As well as the McDonald's, the camp had endless shops for troops to spend all their hard-earned wages in. A British soldier is used to having his three square meals a day; the Americans had four and the option to just turn up as and when they felt like just in case they were still hungry. We'd never seen so much food. Of course, it was all free! The place was just incredible – it was like a big holiday camp.

Our first morning in Kuwait was spent sorting out our belongings and trying to track down our weapons. We had all been placed in huge white canvas tents for our week of training.

There were about a hundred small camp beds in neat rows for us to sleep in. There were no plugs, no TVs, nothing. Just the occasional heavy-duty refrigerator packed with bottles of water. I was starting a fresh bottle the moment I'd finished the last. Once settled, we were shown around the base by the team who would be taking us through our 'acclimatisation' package.

Kempy, a guy in the squadron whom I knew well and was close to after serving with him in Knightsbridge, and I wandered the vastness of Camp Virginia. We both felt incredibly dwarfed by the sheer size of the place and by the huge American presence in the region. Later on I spoke to my mum and was surprised to hear that Phil, Nan, Liza and Chloe were all with her at the house. She obviously needed the family around her but I was glad that she seemed to be coping alright.

We spent our time in camp receiving lectures and training for our forthcoming mission. The lectures were endless and generally repeated what we already knew: there were lots of Iraqis up north who wanted to kill us. In the central operating base (COB) in Basra, we could expect to be rocketed at any moment. The bad guys normally sent their rockets at dawn, at lunch and as the sun set in the evening. But you couldn't rely on there being no other attacks throughout the day.

Though we were well informed about these rockets, for some reason everyone seemed so blasé about the whole thing. Everyone was quite matter-of-fact about it all. 'When the rocket attack alarm goes off, take cover straight away and hope for the best' seemed to be all the advice that was needed. It wouldn't be until I was on the receiving end of rocket attacks in the near future that I'd fully understand how deadly and terrifying they were.

The other thing that was quite clear about the Iraqis was that they liked their roadside bombs, and as we were constantly reminded, there were plenty of unexploded mines and other munitions lying around from the Iraq–Iran war to fund their methods. Weirdly, the only thing I wasn't too worried about was being shot. The information we were getting was that the bad guys north of the border were pretty dreadful shots. I almost piped up and said 'wait until you see our shooting before you judge theirs', but thought better of it.

Preparations in Kuwait continued, mostly surrounding physical exertion in the thick heat. Body armour, my helmet and the endless bits of kit attached to my person made life tough. I looked forward to getting a vehicle on the ground so I could at least offload some of my kit. Before I knew it, my time was almost up. After a week at Camp Virginia, we flew up to Basra in a Hercules. In a weird way, I was looking forward to it.

✝

On 11 May 2007, in the middle of the night, I sat anxiously, yet silently, in a very loud RAF Hercules aircraft as I passed over the border of Kuwait into Iraq. Approaching the border, the crew completely dimmed all lights, making us as invisible as possible from the ground below. Within fifteen minutes we made the steep dive towards Basra International Airport.

'If the siren goes off while you're disembarking ... run for cover as quickly as possible! We'll close the door and take off. Make sure you're out the way of us!'

On receipt of that information, I wondered what the hell was about to happen. Would we be met with attack? Would I be just leaving the ramp at the back of the plane as it was trying to take off to avoid rocket damage? I tightened the strap to my helmet as I prepared to disembark, and took a deep breath.

The central operating base built around what was Basra International Airport before the invasion was a huge base that

most of the servicemen and women in southern Iraq operated out
of. It was made up of a number of camps, all individually named
and home to a particular set of units or regiments. There was a
large offering of welfare facilities, internet cafes, fast-food joints
etc., and, of course, the airport, which had been transformed
into an Anglo-American airbase. Surrounding all of this were a
number of perimeter fences and blockades, constantly patrolled
by 'force protection'.

Walking out of the airport and towards the transport to our
camp, passing by signs that had been left at the roadside from its
time as a busy international travel hub, it was easy to forget that
this was all captured and safe ground. Once in camp, however, I
had to keep reminding myself that just on the other side of the
perimeter fence was a deadly war zone – the camp was just so big.

The safety blanket wasn't secure enough for us to walk around
without some crucial pieces of equipment. Everywhere I went I
had either my rifle or my 9mm pistol; I needed my body armour
and helmet constantly in case of rocket attack from above and,
as a team medic, I always carried my medic pack and morphine
pens in case somebody around me needed them.

A Squadron's job in Iraq was to patrol the Iran–Iraq border in
a province known as Maysan, north of Basra by about a hundred
miles. Maysan was a large province of mostly desert, running
parallel to the border with a large settlement in its centre called
Al Amarah. The squadron would be flown out to relieve the guys
who'd been on the ground through the winter months, who were
extremely keen to get home to loved ones. Not much information was available about how successful they'd been in the area,
but we all knew that two of their guys had been killed by a roadside bomb a couple of weeks before our arrival. There was clearly
activity out there.

On heading out to Iraq I had begun a diary to detail all of

the things that happened while I was away. I wanted to keep something that would remind me of my emotions and instant reactions as I faced the biggest challenge of my life.

12 May 2007
Basra

About an hour ago the 'incoming' alarm sounded and for the first time I experienced what it felt like to be on the receiving end of an aerial attack. I dived to the ground the moment the horrible screeching sound of the siren wailed out of the hundreds of speakers around the COB. Lying on the ground fixing my helmet secure, I awaited the impacts, hoping they weren't landing on me. The sound of the explosions quickly eased my worry; the distant sound of them falling short of the perimeter fence. There were about five impacts over the course of the forty-second attack, none of which landed close enough to cause any concern. The 'all clear' sounded and everybody just carried on with their business, as if nothing had even happened. Kempy and I gave each other an excited glance. We've had our first incoming. We really are at war.

Initially I was only having a couple of days in the COB before flying out to the desert to relieve some of the Queen's Royal Lancers. I spent those two days, apart from constantly diving for cover and dodging incoming enemy rockets, prepping maps and other kit we'd be taking north with us on the helicopter. The night before our very early-morning flight to Maysan I spoke to Thom for one last time before beginning the job I'd travelled so far to do. He excitedly talked about his new job and the new friends he'd made on his first two trips. I sensed lots of partying and late nights while he'd been away and although I was jealous a little, deep down I was glad he had something to occupy his mind. I finished the call, re-checked my kit and bedded myself down for the few hours of sleep before flying to the desert.

15 May 2007
Maysan

I never found chance to write yesterday, it was non-stop from the moment we woke up to catch our helicopter flight up here. We travelled on a Merlin, which was very exciting. My first trip on a helicopter, ever. When we arrived at the FOB [forward operating base] we were greeted with a huge task. Our chopper was two hours late picking us up from the COB and the whole battle group were sat in their vehicles waiting for us to get off the Merlin and jump straight into crew positions. We then had the most painful 27 km move in the blistering heat. The CVRT I was driving had no cooling fan in the driver's cab and I had to endure the drive with the intense heat from the sun alongside the enormous heat off the engine next to me. I decided to chin off my body armour. It was just too hot. I thought I was going man down at one point. Just as I was forcing myself into settling and getting on with the job, my vehicle broke down. First day on operations and my fucking tank breaks down!

We eventually got to the new FOB location and 1 Troop took watch for the night. I did a two-hour stag [sentry duty] with Mr Olver and we just chatted about our various backgrounds. He seems a little more chilled out than normal out here. Our vehicle is off the road and has to be towed everywhere by the REME [Royal Electrical and Mechanical Engineers] until a new gear box is flown out from Basra. They reckon this will be a few days yet. Today we sat around mostly under the cover of our Israeli cam nets. It just gets too hot to do anything.

Everywhere I look there are naked soldiers pouring bottles of water over themselves to cool down. I'm going on a foot patrol tonight at 0200 hrs, just to see if there's anything around. Could be interesting.

The plan was to relieve the Queen's Royal Lancers fully over the course of about five days. We had come out on our own initially but were soon followed by the remainder of A Squadron. The final phase was to be the joining of 2 Troop, who were still held back in Windsor. They were due out in about a week's time, led by Prince Harry. The task, as I saw it, was to be a very overt and visible show of force in the region, thus preventing or restricting enemy action. We were close to Iran and we knew we'd have many roles watching the border for suspicious activity. But in those first few days in the desert, I found it difficult to accurately describe what our day-to-day job was. It felt like we were just out there to exist in the blistering heat.

By the time the rest of the squadron flew out and we'd said our goodbyes to the QRL boys, nothing much had changed. We'd travel around the desert, like a large circus in convoy, pick somewhere to pitch our tents, or in this case Israeli cam nets, and then simply be. It was a caveman existence really. Everything we needed, we carried in our vehicles. There were no sanitary facilities, there was no catering tent or section of chefs. Our entire survival hinged on how well disciplined we each were as soldiers.

Every five days or so there'd be an air drop out of the back of a low-flying Herc, a resupply with rations and water, which would then be collected and shared among the troops. Within the FOB group there was a refrigerated container on the back of a truck, but that often didn't work and would keep water only slightly cooler than the outside temperature. Soldiers became amateur scientists when it came to inventing ingenious ways of keeping water cool. The same is true about cooking. I've never seen so many soldiers, especially Mr Olver, think up amazing ideas to change the monotony of eating boil-in-the-bag rations. A few weeks into the tour, Olver had a parcel sent out to him from his friends back in Fulham, full of different spices and herbs. I remember him pulling out ingredients like chorizo sausage and fresh garlic while the rest of us looked on in utter bewilderment.

Occasionally, a couple of guys or even an entire troop would be flown back to Basra for some downtime, if you can call constantly being rocketed from above 'downtime'. We'd look forward to it massively. It was a chance to grab a shower, a milkshake, phone home or even do a bit of shopping in one of the many shops inside the COB. The whole issue of having to constantly dive for cover was pushed aside somewhat by the thought of those few luxuries. It was something everybody looked forward to.

17 May 2007

Maysan

Last night at about 2000 hrs the squadron leader called us together suddenly. We all thought it was bad news. I personally thought something had happened back at the COB to one of our many men still down there. He pulled us all close and told us the news that, sadly, 2 Troop would be deploying to Iraq without their leader. Prince Harry will not be joining us after all out here in the desert. The news was met with mixed emotions; some lads weren't bothered either way. Me, I'm a little disappointed. I was looking forward to fighting alongside him. I doubt now that A SQN will have any real action. It's terrible to say, but with Harry here we'd have certainly had some interesting moments. Now I guess it's all about sunbathing and trying to survive the IED [improvised explosive device] threat.

I'm heading back to Basra at some point in the next twenty-four hours, there are people waiting to come out here and they are rotating people around. I'm so looking forward to having a shower and not having to dig a hole to have a shit. Oh, and another thing... I've never seen a thunderstorm like I saw last night. It was AMAZING! Mum would have had a heart attack though.

When we were just passing time I'd lie on my camp bed outside of the cam net and look up at the stars. I was awestruck by them in the desert. You could see millions and millions. Gibbo, who was a bit of an expert when it came to astronomy, spent hours pointing out various constellations and planets to the rest of us. We could even see satellites orbiting the earth. It was hard to put into perspective what we were doing on this tiny little planet when looking up at the vastness above. Boredom never struck after dark; it was impossible looking up at such a sight.

Once back in Basra, for various reasons (mostly helicopter-related), the guys I'd come back with and I found ourselves stuck in the COB for about a week. It was obviously great for us, but I couldn't help but think it was unfair on the guys out in the desert. Some hadn't showered in two weeks. I managed to talk with family lots over this time, and even made one or two calls to Thom in between his busy schedule. I was missing him so badly. I'd never been homesick in my four years in the army, but that week back in the COB I really struggled thinking about him and our life, currently on hold, back in the UK. The constant rocket assaults from downtown Basra only fuelled this stress and by the time my week was up, I was pretty much running for the chopper back to Maysan.

21 May 2007

Basra

At 1310 hrs, the incoming siren sounded. I was in bed at the time catching up on some sleep. There isn't much else to do in the peak of the heat. Suddenly a huge explosion outside went off and I was a bit slow reaching for my helmet and body armour. It was the most deafening noise I've ever experienced. The rocket had landed VERY close. With the room shaking, the reality of what was going on struck me. It was terrifying. No 'all clear' was given but me and a few others made our way outside the tent to see what the damage was. The rocket had landed about 200 metres away, on the concrete tank park next to our camp. It looked like nobody was hurt but a great dust cloud had been created and the daylight turned to night. Suddenly the incoming sounded again and a split second later another rocket landed, this time even closer. It was a direct hit on our camp and as we all dived for cover, rubble and debris covered us in the explosion. It was the most awful noise I've ever heard, like a huge high-pitched screech followed immediately by the sound of thunder, only a hundred times louder. My ears are still ringing now as I write this. I honestly think I now have some understanding as to what it might have been like during the Blitz.

On a separate note, I think someone has died today as all the phones and internet have been cut off for most of the day. They do this when someone dies until their loved ones have been told. The last thing someone needs is to find out their husband's been killed from another soldier's wife who's read it on Facebook or something. Makes you think.

It turned out somebody had died. It was announced on the British Forces Broadcasting Service (BFBS) radio later that night. It was the first death of our tour and it drove home the fact that our enemies weren't to be thought of lightly. They meant business alright. To make matters worse, towards the end of my week at the base, added stress was heaped upon us when it was thought a soldier had been kidnapped from within the COB. The news created anarchy as every single person had to be accounted for. Nobody was allowed to move until everyone was confirmed to be in the right place. The whole thing turned out to be a mistake and I'm not too sure what exactly had caused the panic, but it was enough for me and Kempy to want to prepare ourselves against any such eventuality.

There was a little shop in the middle of our camp run by a local Iraqi man who sold pieces of equipment that a soldier might find useful while serving in Iraq. It was basically a weapons shop that sold pretty much anything you wanted except actual machine guns and other firearms.

When we got to the little shop, set up in a disused large metal container, we found that we weren't the only ones interested in added protection. There was a small queue going out of the door. The local Iraqi man was enjoying a boom in business from the widespread panic after the false kidnapping alarm. In front of us, two infantrymen from the Royal Welsh were debating which electric taser to buy. They were going for about US $100 and they seemed to be quite a popular choice to protect oneself from being bundled into the back of a van. Without warning, and to the great shock of Kempy and me, one of the two infantrymen, in a moment of curious madness, pressed the button on the hand taser, exposing its nasty blue pulse and stinging his mate in his side. I'd never seen someone collapse to the ground so quickly in my life. Kempy pointed out that the lad had pissed himself while falling to the ground. I have no idea what went through the guy's mind but the lad recovered shortly afterwards and calmly punched the other to the ground. Neither of them bought one, nor did Kempy or I. I did buy a cosh though, a sort of metal bar used by the police that extended by flicking the device away from you, and Kempy bought himself some mace spray. Everywhere I went after that I had either my rifle or pistol, my helmet and body armour, and in my pocket my new cosh. No fucker was kidnapping me.

The bombing continued and I patiently watched the clock tick until I was flying to the relative safety of the open desert.

26 May 2007
Basra

At dinner tonight I was caught without my helmet and body armour as the COB came under rocket attack. I'd left my kit by the entrance to the tent while eating my dinner. The siren sounded and while everyone climbed under the tables I was faced with having to run over to the exit to grab my kit. Instead, Corporal of Horse Parker lay on top of me protecting my head with his body and his armour. The impact landed quite far off and the all clear sounded soon after, but I was silently moved by this incredible act. Instead of leaving me exposed, scrambling to my protection, the corporal of horse put himself in danger to shield me.

One of the rockets that landed yesterday near our camp failed to detonate. It just dug itself far into the ground and then didn't explode. The Royal Engineers have been today and have decided to just fill the hole up with concrete. Hope nobody builds a house there in fifty years' time.

Once back in Maysan, our life of contradictions, at once both simple and difficult, continued. We would set up an FOB, stay for twenty-four hours or so, move to another location, carry out some obvious patrols so people could see us, sleep in the heat, sunbathe and do the whole thing again. It was becoming frustrating not really having anything to do. We weren't getting any action and we were also starting to lose people through heat-induced illnesses and the like. At one point, one person a day was being evacuated out of the desert because of the heat or the harsh desert conditions. Even Mr Olver got airlifted out after being stung by a scorpion. A lad in 4 Troop practically blew himself up after throwing empty fuel cans on a fire one morning. He set most of his upper body on fire after not realising that one of the cans still had fuel in it. Kirky fell ill on his twenty-first birthday and was evacuated out of the desert to Baghdad by two Black Hawk helicopters.

With a lot of bored soldiers trying to pass the time in the middle of nowhere, gambling soon became the norm. Most afternoons in the desert, under the cover of our cam nets, we'd all sit around in a circle and play poker. Nobody had brought cash out into the desert for obvious reasons, so we'd play with IOU notes. Scoffy was the king of the poker table and Danny wasn't far behind him. Often, I'd get the feeling the two were working as a pair and splitting the winnings. The whole troop would play and would each pay $20 into the table. The winner would get the lot, usually over $100. Scoffy won for about five days in a row and when we were eventually back in Basra, he'd collect his winnings. It was a lot of fun and passed the time; morale was always high and we'd sit around and drink water as if it were beer. I miss those days, but I don't miss having to cough the money up afterwards.

One evening, and quite out of the blue, we were pulled together for a briefing from the squadron leader. 1 Troop was finally getting a tasking. And a real one at that, not some comedy foot patrol in the middle of the night.

Op Charge was a four-day task which would see 1 Troop

covertly observing a key crossing point on the border with Iran. Under the cover of darkness, we were to move up to the border and find a location to secretly observe the crossing point over the course of the few days. Mr Olver and Gibbo fully knew what to look out for, but all I really understood was that they thought the officials at the border forts on both sides were corrupt and letting people smuggle stuff to and fro. We went en masse and quite heavily armed. Gibbo and even Danny kept saying that this was probably going to be 'it'. Action at last.

1 June 2007

3 km off Iranian Border

Within the last hour, we have enjoyed a very refreshing thunderstorm. It's the closest we're getting to a shower for the foreseeable future. We're currently hiding in a big ditch with our Land Rover WMIKs [Weapons Mounted Installation Kits] hidden under some cover. Gibbo reckons we won't have any more rain for months now. I'm not sure how he knows this, but he's usually right about stuff like that. Before we came out on Op Charge this afternoon, we sat down in a circle to listen to Mr Olver talk about how he hopes the next few days will go. This involved a long chat about the Iranians and what he expected us to do if we somehow got captured, like those navy people did a couple of months ago. His wishes were that if we were to be captured, we were to remain tight-lipped and quite conservative about the whole thing. He said he didn't want anybody to be on the news looking friendly with our captors. Gibbo, a family man at heart, quite disagreed with Olver, and something that doesn't happen often actually did. The boss and Gibbo had a full-scale fallout over it. Gibbo's line was that he'd personally do anything it took to see his wife and kids again, and Olver was having none of it. The whole thing got quite irate but finished soon afterwards. The rest of us just sat there and watched the 'grown-ups' argue it out. I think Gibbo was right, to be fair, though. He ended the argument by saying, 'Who the fuck are you to tell me how to see my daughters again?' Olver backed down somewhat. Before leaving the FOB, I spoke to Thom on the satellite phone and told him I loved him very much. He told me he missed me. We're moving up to the border shortly by foot, hopefully as covertly as possible. It's all very James Bond.

Our first night on the border wasn't overly exciting. We didn't get captured and we didn't really see anything very suspicious. I'm not sure what we were expecting. President Ahmadinejad walking up the road with a big rocket under his arm? But we returned to where our vehicles had been stashed, and slept through the daylight hours, taking it in turns to keep a watch-out with the machine gun. Night descended and we repeated our task again that night, this time in a different position.

3 June 2007
Iranian Border

Same as yesterday, not a lot to report really. Progress is quite slow and I'm finding it hard to survive with a very limited supply of water. We didn't have room to bring as much as we needed, so we're taking on about half as much as we should be. We've moved up to the border and are observing the two forts again, the one in Iraq called Al Fakka and the one up the road in Iran. There's a road connecting the two forts that's about 800m long. It's kind of like no man's land in between these two forts. There's a lot of mines lying around from some war in the past. The Iranian fort has a huge Iranian flag draped over the wall that faces Iraq. We're clearly not being as quiet as we should be; a couple of young Iraqi boys brought us some bread earlier as a gesture of goodwill. I gave them what sweets I had left. The bread tasted awful! Far worse than my sweets would have tasted. I guess I lost out there!

On the final day of our mission we made an overt move to the Iraqi border fort in broad daylight making as much noise as we could so everybody could see we were there. Scoffy drove Danny and me there; I was on the general-purpose machine gun at the top of the vehicle. Once there, Gibbo and the boss spoke with the Iraqi officials while the rest of us kept our wits about us at the border crossing. Much to Danny and Scoffy's entertainment, one of the officials at the border point had taken a liking to me and was waving quite bizarrely in my direction. This set the boys off and then the guy came over to our vehicle and gave me a can of freezing cold Coca-Cola... he even blew me a kiss as he handed it over. Incredible.

'Fucking hell, Ronald! You've pulled on the Iranian border,' said Scoffy in his deep Cumbrian accent. The whole situation was very creepy, but quite hilarious, too.

After Op Charge, 1 Troop adopted a few days of quietness where it was hoped we'd either be flown back to Basra if helicopters were available or, failing that, enjoy some quiet time without tasking in the desert as part of the FOB. But that wasn't to be the case.

6 June 2007
Maysan

After I wrote in here yesterday, we carried on playing a few hands of poker. I also wrote a letter to Dad. Out here, we burn our rubbish daily in a pit dug just next to our cam net. Sometimes, and we're getting quite used to this now, people throw dead batteries in their fire pits, which explode making a noise similar to distant gunfire. This happened a few times yesterday and nobody really raised an eyebrow. Suddenly there was a distant bang which made the whole troop, and probably the whole battle group, take notice. It sounded just like a mortar being fired off in the distance. And guess what, a few seconds later the eerie whistle of a falling mortar shell filled the air, getting louder and louder as the shell fell closer towards us. We were being attacked. Widespread panic set in and everyone dived for cover in the few seconds we had before impact. I was topless with just my shorts and flip-flops on; four or five of the lads were playing poker and one of the guys was even doing some weightlifting in the shade. It was a little after 6 p.m. and throughout the attack, David Bowie's 'Under Pressure' played on the stereo in the background. Whenever I hear that song in the future, I'll always be reminded of the sheer panic and adrenalin that kicked in within a second or two from hearing that dreadful whistle.

I'd dived under one of the WMIKs, hugging on to Shagger's leg like he was my mum. I was still topless and listening to the explosions, each getting louder and closer. All I wanted was my helmet and body armour. After about the tenth explosion it seemed to all go quiet. Danny threw over a helmet and Scoffy slung me some body armour, which I chucked on still under the WMIK. We now needed to move. Instinctively, we all started to pack everything away. The poker game was well and truly over, but at this point good old-fashioned British humour started to kick in. Scoffy was telling people how gutted he was coz he had 'two aces in that hand'. Later, we heard that Craig from 4 Troop was actually having a shit at the time. He was joking around, telling people he'd finished his poo watching the first few impacts before calmly taking cover. Nobody was hurt during the attack, we were lucky, but needless to say the battle group moved location pretty sharpish to prevent another attack and possible casualties. Really looking forward to getting back to Basra now, even though they have rockets incoming constantly. Trying to relax best I can, but I know for sure... I don't want to hear David fucking Bowie again.

I enjoyed being part of 1 Troop, but in the days that followed us being attacked in the desert, I was becoming increasingly stressed and agitated. Our return to Basra was delayed day after day which really took its toll on everyone. During this time, I was extra glad to be with Danny and Scoffy, as the pair really worked hard to cheer me up and keep me happy. I woke up after one afternoon's sleep to Danny saying, 'Look what I've named our vehicle...'

On the side of our WMIK, Danny had painted in pink letters 'Killer Queen!' and was really delighted with himself. I too thought it was brilliant and just the simple gesture of it all really cheered me up.

Eventually, 1 Troop was back in Basra and enjoying some days of rest and downtime from the harshness of desert existence, and although we were diving for cover almost constantly, the promise of a hot shower and some privacy seemed to block out all of the negative factors.

Back in Basra, I didn't have Kempy to keep me entertained: he'd caught chicken pox from somewhere and was bedded down in isolation. I spent most of the time with Danny and Scoffy, sipping on milkshakes and putting away a lot of food; the Pizza Hut that had been opened in the middle of the COB sure took some money off the three of us. I also attended a few repatriation services throughout the week. I felt it important to pay a final respect to a fallen soldier before them being flown out of Iraq and released back to their families for burial. I'd try to imagine how it must feel for the loved ones who'd be greeting the aircraft when it arrived back in England.

Faulkner, and the guys he served with in B Squadron, had been working hard in the centre of Basra, operating from a remote building that was constantly being battered by insurgents. While we were getting hardly any action at all, our brothers in B Squadron were enduring a pretty hard time at the hands of the Iraqis.

It was Danny who told me the bad news.

Faulkner, while dodging stray bullets and continuous incoming mortar rounds in the centre of Basra, had found himself in the wrong place at the wrong time. While diving for cover from incoming shells landing all around him, he exposed himself at just the wrong time to the full blast of a landing mortar. He'd been blown up. I thought I was being told my old pal had been killed. Panicking, I fell to the ground, not wanting to hear another word. How had this happened? I'd barely seen him throughout our time in Iraq. And now I'd lost him. Danny picked me up and told me he was still alive. He was still alive! 'But you can't see him, he's being flown home.'

Faulkner had taken a lot of the blast to his front. The damage to his stomach was serious and he was sent out of the country on a medical flight extremely quickly, eventually waking up in Queen Elizabeth Hospital, Birmingham. Poor Faulkner had a long road to recovery and his fighting days were put behind him. He has some magnificent scars from that blast but when I consider how close he came to death – possibly less than a foot away – I think he'll accept those scars as a lucky escape. Almost twelve months later, he was back on duty in London with the ceremonial regiment.

On the Friday night, 1 Troop headed to Pizza Hut to enjoy a collective bite to eat and a milkshake or two. Mr Olver footed the bill and it was a chance for us all to chill out a little in the company of each other. It was good fun and much needed after the news about Faulkner. Gibbo presented the idea that we should have 1 Troop T-shirts made to remember our time together in southern Iraq. It was a great idea and everyone agreed, but what followed was an hour-long debate about what the T-shirts should have printed on them.

The biggest debate was over what nicknames we each were going to have on the reverse of the shirt. Gibbo insisted that the names should be chosen collectively by the troop for each man, which was a great chance to really throw around some good-quality banter.

Gibbo was handed 'Mr Burns' in reference to him looking like the *Simpsons* character. He took it well. Hodges was given 'Token': he was the only black guy in the troop. Again, he received this well. Danny got 'Hollywood Dan' because of the relatively calm and cool way he operated as a soldier and Scoffy was affectionately allowed to retain 'Scoffy'. I was handed the title 'Camp Freddy'. I think he was originally some East End gangster back in the day, but I was very happy with it – it could have been much worse. The final name to be decided was quite an event.

Mr Olver wanted to have the word 'Boss' printed on the back of his T-shirt, but Gibbo outright refused to allow it. Olver's second offering was to have 'Troopy' but again this was overruled.

'What you should go for, sir, is "Glass Eye"!' said Scoffy with enthusiasm.

'Really?' returned Mr Olver with interest.

'Yeah... as in the "All-Seeing Eye" doesn't miss a trick and is in complete control of all that's going on around him.'

Scoffy was doing well, as were we all, to keep a straight face. Danny and Gibbo backed him up and told him it was a great idea.

'That's perfect, guys. Thank you so much.'

To this day I still chuckle, but feel a little sorry for Olver because he was genuinely delighted with what Scoffy and the rest of us had insisted he adopted as a nickname. The reality was that 'Glass Eye' was in no way any relation to him being a great leader and a man who didn't miss a trick. In fact, it was totally the opposite. It was in reference to the saying 'to make a glass eye cry', used to describe something that is either very boring or incredibly unexciting. A little harsh really – deep down Mr Olver wasn't that bad at all – but right then, he had become the butt of the joke and astonishingly hadn't even realised. The boys were in creases for days.

One of the final notable points of our week-long rest in Basra was finding out when exactly we'd be returning to the UK to our loved ones for our two weeks of rest and recuperation: 2 August. I immediately began to make plans for Thom and me.

13

THE ENDLESS COUNTDOWN TO REST AND RECUPERATION

15 June 2007

Basra

Twenty-five years ago, the Falkland Islands were liberated. White flags flew over Stanley, victory belonged to us! I've just watched a programme on BFBS showing the commemorations taking place in the South Atlantic, UK and Germany. It's inspiring to be out here and able to see the veterans from twenty-five years ago, which in my opinion was the greatest victory in our recent past. Very important to remember the 255 lives that were lost though. Tomorrow is the Trooping of the Colour back in London and we've been invited to watch the event on TV with the Irish Guards at their camp in the middle of the COB. Apparently they're giving us two cans of lager each too... I can't even remember the last time I had a drink. Well, I do... It was the night before leaving the UK, which seems like a lifetime ago.

I can't stop thinking about how different my life is now from last year's Trooping when I was turning out the troop leader. Incredible!

16 June 2007

Basra

Our BBQ and drinks with the Irish Guards was cancelled due to them having a fatality in their battle group late last night. A soldier from the Royal Tank Regiment died when his vehicle, a Warrior, overturned, causing him to drown in his driver's cab. It's dreadful news and it's really shook my inner nerves. I'm a driver in an armoured vehicle... It could easily happen to me.

Tomorrow some general is walking around our camp so we've been really busy making the place look nice. Ridiculous! We're supposed to be at war. If he asks me what I think, I'm going to tell him how pointless I think this whole thing is.

Only one rocket today. It's been strangely quiet.

We returned to the desert the following morning extremely early, all of us pretty much gutted to be doing so. I, and I'm sure I wasn't alone, had developed a new fear of drowning in the cab of my armoured vehicle because the utterly rubbish hatches wouldn't open very easily. The poor lad from the Royal Tank Regiment hadn't died due to enemy action; he'd died because they'd accidentally rolled their Warrior over into a river. He was trapped and nobody could help him. It must have been a horrific ending. I really wanted to get home and never even think about returning to the Middle East again. I wanted to be with Thom.

20 June 2007

Maysan

Not written for a few days. I haven't stopped. Already longing for a rest in Basra with the rockets again. As soon as we got out here on Monday, we jumped into our vehicles and participated in an FOB move. This was an outrageous 35 km, which took 6.5 hours. And, shockingly, our Scimitar broke down 10 km in. This is the third time my CVRT has broken down out here and we're pretty typical of a lot of the battle group. They're just so unreliable and completely not suitable for this dusty desert terrain. When we got to the new FOB, me and Shagger had to go to the REME and work on our broken wagon. This took five hours and included stripping all the top armour, stripping the fittings that held the fan and generator belts, identifying the problem, which turned out to be a coolant flow one, and then putting everything back together again. It's a FUCKING JOKE! We were done for about 21.30. Long day! But not to bed yet...

I then went on stag for an hour and a half, finally slept for about two hours, then was awoken and put back on stag for another hour. After all this, another FOB move. The move was another 30 km and took seven hours to complete. Six hours in, just as I was about to black out in the intense heat in my driver's cab, Scoffy swapped places with me and took the controls for the last hour. I was about to become seriously ill, ill enough to be flown out of the desert, if I stayed in that cab any longer. Scoffy measured the temperature at 61 degrees in my driver's seat.

Finally, at the new FOB location we were able to rest for some hours after the endless running around of the previous forty-eight. I've had eight hours' sleep in two whole days!

I've got burns all up my arm from the engine wall that runs next to my driver's. They're really painful! I might go see a medic about them.

The reality and harshness of desert life was soon returned to us after our week-long break in Basra. The constant moving around the vast open space of Maysan was taking its toll; vehicles and soldiers were dropping like flies. The huge operation of keeping us sustained was costing millions. Every time someone collapsed in the heat, a helicopter would have to fly the 150 miles or so to evacuate him. Every time a gear box blew, which was quite regularly in those conditions, one would have to be carried beneath another helicopter and flown out to our location. Every three to four days a Herc would have to resupply us with water and rations just so we could survive. What was the benefit? I really struggled to put into words what we were actually achieving out there in Maysan. We hadn't spotted a single person carrying anything they shouldn't have been. Our jaunt to the Iranian border, although a little interesting, failed to achieve anything of any real importance. Rather soon, right across the spectrum of rank, the men began to question why we were being put through such harsh conditions.

Things were about to get a whole lot rougher for us in the final weeks before our R&R break back in the UK.

23 June 2007

Maysan

A SQN have been handed a tasking: Op Octavia.

Octavia is a large convoy heading up to us from Basra. We've been tasked to greet it about ten miles away and escort it in to our FOB. There's a lot of worry something is going to kick off as it approaches. I don't feel right about it at all. Yesterday we'd been mortared again by some unknown group who'd disappeared sharpish. Olver has moved the troop around and me, Scoffy and Shagger are now the lead call sign for this operation. The drama with being lead call sign is that we'll be greeted by any IEDs that are placed on the route. Scoffy isn't happy about this and he's told Olver just what he thinks of him. With Scoffy being so open about his fears, I have to say he's made me more panicky than normal.

The start of the op has been delayed due to them encountering a number of planted IEDs on its way which have taken some time to be dealt with.

Later:
Eventually we moved to a location near to where we would be meeting with the convoy, just behind some large mounds and quite out of sight, but news came through on the radio that the convoy was being attacked by mortar fire and was delayed once again. Two hours later we moved out on to the road, operationally named 'Falkland', and slowly crawled along. My eyes were searching every inch of road in front of me for disturbed ground. When we got to a bridge crossing a large river, we moved right up close to some civilians who were also crossing the bridge. We know insurgents won't kill civilians to get at us.

Once over, Shagger, Scoffy and I carried on our slow crawl along Falkland and finally came to a halt at a small roundabout. The last thing we now needed was yet another delay. We were completely exposed. And guess what? The convoy had struck a roadside bomb which had caused casualties who now needed to be air evacuated off the ground and back to Basra. This kept us waiting at the roundabout for about an hour. My arse was twitching throughout! How many problems does one convoy need? After what seemed like an eternity, finally Octavia arrived and with Shagger in command, Scoffy on the gun and me in the driver's seat, we led the biggest convoy in the whole of Iraq home to our FOB in the middle of the desert. I would rather have been anywhere else on the entire planet than at the front of that convoy which had been battered since leaving

Basra twenty-four hours before. I'm holding it as one of the most stressful days ever. The convoy is due to return to Basra tonight having delivered the various pieces of equipment we need out here, including an armoured petrol tanker to fuel us for the next few weeks. Poor Shagger is the lead call sign again, but me and Scoffy are now back working with Danny in the much more pleasant vehicle of a WMIK. Danny is FACing [forward air controlling] the mission so he'll call in air support from fighter jets if the convoy, or us, comes under any attack. It's a pretty cool job.

Once Octavia was out of the way, everyone thought that we'd just return to our normal boring lifestyle of desert existence ... but in the days that would follow, Danny, Scoffy and I would find ourselves pulled together, faced with the reality of how delicate life truly is.

26 June 2007
Maysan

Today 1 Troop had a slight lie-in. Danny, who is acting as the corporal of horse due to Gibbo falling unwell and having to return to Basra, left us to carry out some menial troop tasks while he pottered around the FOB on various errands. At about lunchtime, a runner from HQ came over to tell us to pack our things away as we'd been given a tasking. Danny returned and told us all what was going on. Some intel had been received from the brigade that insurgents were planning to attack us later tonight with rockets. So as a result, a few of us have been on patrols in and around our FOB location. I'm on one now actually. We're sat looking over an area from a piece of cover. Nothing exciting has happened and, to be honest, nothing exciting will, I'm sure.

Later:

As I put my pen down earlier, a call came over the radio that there had been an RTA [road traffic accident] involving a vehicle from within our battle group at a location not too far away from where we'd been observing under cover. We raced to the scene and the three of us rushed off our WMIK to help with the casualties. We were the first soldiers on scene. What greeted us was sheer devastation. A WMIK had flipped and rolled off the side of a road and everyone on board was seriously hurt. There was also an Iraqi interpreter travelling on board who I could tell immediately was dead. I checked for a pulse but it was completely pointless as his head had been squashed between the vehicle rolling over him and the desert floor. His brains had come out of the major damage to his head. I covered him over with some sheeting. It was the first dead person and major trauma I'd ever seen in my life.

Scoffy and Danny had begun treating the other crew members, during which some more battle group call signs arrived. The real medics came and took over and we crewed our vehicle, giving cover to the medics as they gave their treatment. About forty or so minutes later, a helicopter came in and took the injured soldiers away, but left behind the dead Iraqi due to there being no room on board and him being already dead.

He was then taken back to our FOB location and placed in the field ambulance overnight. He's in there right now, about fifty metres away from where I'm writing this.

The events of that day will stay with me forever. Incredibly, the three of us instinctively knew what we had to do to save the lives of the three crew members. Two of them were T1 (priority one) with spinal and neck injuries; the other was a T2 (priority two) with what looked like a broken arm and other superficial injuries. The poor Iraqi interpreter had died instantly when the vehicle rolled; he wasn't wearing a seat belt or a helmet and found himself squashed between the weight of the vehicle and the tough rocky floor of the desert. The sight and the smell were beyond words. Incredibly, once the medics arrived from the FOB and while we provided security from our vehicle, closing the road either side of the incident, the three of us pulled together by having a little laugh and a joke about life while the sun went down and the helicopter arrived. Danny really came into his own where the well-being of the men under his command was concerned. He knew that the sight of the dead man had knocked me, and he was able to distract me and Scoffy from what we'd just witnessed. He rustled around in his rucksack and set up his iPod and speakers and the three of us listened to Elvis Presley while the three seriously injured guys were evacuated back to Basra and the dead interpreter's body was scraped off the floor and bagged up before being placed in the back of a wagon and taken to the FOB. I couldn't help but think how easily the whole thing might have been prevented. It turned out in the days that followed that the tyres of the Land Rover WMIK were under-inflated and it was probably that which caused the vehicle to roll off the road. Also, we all knew that if the guy had been seat-belted and simply wearing a helmet, he would have likely survived. The tragedy could have been avoided. It was a tough pill to swallow.

Worse, in the hours that followed, we became aware that they'd got the identity of the dead Iraqi wrong, causing the wrong next of kin to be informed of his death. It just didn't seem to me that anybody had shown much respect to this poor guy who'd bravely volunteered as an interpreter for the British Army and had now paid the ultimate price. They stuck him in the back of a wagon overnight instead of flying his body back to Basra, where it should have been tidied up with respect before being released back to his family. What's sadder yet is that I don't even know his name. I'd like to have known more about him.

As things would go, the death of the interpreter and the serious injuries of the soldiers in the crash were some of the last nails in the coffin, sealing the fate of our existence in the desert. A decision was made back in London that our 'aggressive camping' in the desert must come to an end. They were pulling us out. When the announcement was made by our squadron leader that our role in the desert was going to soon be over, 1 Troop was back in Basra enjoying some downtime after our turbulent stretch in the desert.

Scoffy, Danny and I were put on trauma management once back in the COB, after our recent experiences in the north. We had to sit with a padre and talk about what had happened. I thought the whole thing was pretty pointless. I considered how cold I'd become. Yes, what had happened was awful, and I wouldn't wish it on anybody, but I had totally accepted that the government had put us fully in this situation... and what could we really expect? It was a very tough game we'd all chosen to play. This was what being a soldier was all about. We'd pause with respect, but ultimately we had to continue.

Personally, my longing for my boyfriend back home in the UK and the opportunity to call my family without being under pressure to get off the phone and give someone else the chance to use it was increasing by the hour. As the days decreased until our flights out of Iraq, the tension among us increased. It seemed to me that every time a rocket came into the COB, they'd each get nearer and nearer to where I was taking cover. I thought my luck was slowly running out and that I may never get to see Thom and my family again.

There was one significant task left to complete before heading back to the UK for R&R: the withdrawal from the desert.

Unfortunately it wouldn't be as simple as just getting on a chopper and flying everyone out of there. We had millions of pounds' worth of equipment sitting up in the desert that all needed careful extraction. A huge plan was drawn up and the entire squadron was flown out to the desert to ensure maximum effectiveness.

8 July 2007

Maysan

The final push starts this evening. We are setting off at 1700 hrs and moving initially to a new location. I hear it's going to be close to the river Tigris. I'm looking forward to setting off and finally finishing this job. There are rumours going around that we will be sent home from Iraq by September after this major pull-out. I'm optimistic. Just spoke to Mum on the satellite phone. She's in a bad way with her MS at the moment, which is an added worry for me before this big move. I'm thinking about her lots at the moment.

So the next few days aren't set to be too easy. I'm slightly concerned that it won't go well at all. Thom's off to Washington DC tonight, hoping he keeps safe while he's over there. He told me it was the British Grand Prix today and the Wimbledon final. He also said it hasn't stopped raining for weeks. I'd love some rain right now!

The plan was to move the battle group south-west towards the large town of Nasiriyah, where the Australian forces had an airbase. Our equipment was to be left there to be collected at a later date and we were to be flown back to Basra on a Hercules. The task was huge and as our large convoy slowly meandered its way through the dusty roads of southern Iraq, problem after problem hindered our painful move until we came grinding to a great halt. The endless hours of driving coupled with the dry dusty environment we were ploughing our vehicles through just proved too much of a match for our efforts. People were having accidents due to their fatigue and trucks were breaking down constantly. The move seemed to take forever and, at one point, I thought the task was just too much to ask, but in great British style we eventually turned up at the finishing line with the Australian Army greeting us with open arms. Our time in the desert was over. And for the most part, we'd escaped unharmed.

Once back in the COB, 1 Troop just needed to plain sail until R&R, which was a little over a fortnight away. We weren't to be given any major taskings before then apart from the usual array of duties that befalls any unit within a camp environment – guard and the like. We almost felt like the family relative that had been forgotten about. Other soldiers from other regiments were having a very tasty time in downtown Basra while we Household Cavalry boys were just left festering away in our camp within the COB. I wasn't complaining too much, however: the desert had taken its toll on us. I felt like we'd done our bit.

But just as me and the other boys in 1 Troop began to unwind slightly from the stresses of the desert, looking forward to our break, the Iraqis threw a stick in the works. The final two weeks before our flight out of Basra would be jam-packed with stress.

20 July 2007
Basra

Flags are flying at half-mast all over the COB today. The events of the past twenty-four hours have left us all very shaken. I found myself on guard yesterday from 08.00 for a day-long duty, during which we endured rocket attacks throughout. It was the rocket attack that came at 14.30 that was to cause the most devastation ever caused within the COB since the army got here in 2003. The rocket landed on a part of the COB occupied by the RAF, hitting a tent in their compound, killing three people – two of them pretty much instantly, the third dying some hours later in the hospital. Two of them were RAF regiment, the other was an RAF reserve. The incident has left me in shock. I spoke with Mum this morning and she told me that the incident was all over the news back in the UK and that she'd been worried sick. She was relieved to hear from me but I can't stop thinking about those poor three men who've lost their lives. Later in the day there was another rocket attack which injured a few guys from the King's Royal Hussars – the chaps we'd pulled out of the desert with last weekend. They've really turned the heat up on us over the past two days. Fear is rife amongst us all.

Twelve days until R&R...

I was in a tall watchtower next to the main entrance to the COB sat behind a machine gun when that awful attack came in. I felt more exposed than usual being so far off the ground, reacting to the screeching noise of the incoming alarm. I heard the rockets scream overhead and impact shortly afterwards towards the centre of the base. I could see they'd had a direct hit on a large object of some sort; there was a huge plume of fire initially, followed by thick black clouds of smoke. Rockets were still landing so I returned my attention to the perimeter fence and main entry point to the base, cocking my weapon ready in case the rockets were followed up by a ground attack of some sort. I wanted to close my eyes and curl up into a ball, but I had a responsibility to remain alert overlooking the gates with my machine gun as the ground security took cover. It was some time before the all clear was given, by which time it was obvious to everyone that the four or five rockets that had landed centrally in the COB had caused serious damage. About an hour later we were informed at the main security point in and out of camp that two members of the Royal Air Force had been killed instantly in the strikes and a third member was fighting for his life at the field hospital. It was crushing news and it struck us all deeply. Rockets could land on anybody. They're so indiscriminate.

By the time the news had broken about the third casualty dying from his injuries, the COB had been rocketed about six further times, each rocket having a deeper psychological impact than the last. The bad guys in town had done a good job of securing fear in our hearts and minds, and they'd done it in the space of an hour or two.

When guard finished for me the following morning at 8 a.m., I wasted no time in getting to a phone and calling Thom. I knew it would wake him, but I needed to hear his voice. I broke down to him with tears of genuine fear. I was more terrified in the COB counting down the days to safety than I'd been at any point in the desert near the Iranian border. I just felt that a rocket was sat somewhere in Basra with my name on it, waiting to land on me. Thom tried his best to talk me around on the phone but it was to no avail. I was very, very scared.

I wasn't alone. Mentally, many soldiers were struggling to cope with the relentless aerial bombardment we all found ourselves on the receiving end of. The toll it was taking on almost everyone was incredible. The padre was very busy over those two weeks counselling soldiers over their grief and fear, as were the other welfare teams that were dotted around the many camps that made up the COB.

Kempy and I didn't really buy into the whole religion thing and found ourselves coping by talking through everything and usually having a bit of laugh. We'd never think of it as counselling but it certainly was, on reflection. Our bed spaces, which had gradually become more and more bombproof as the weeks and months passed by, were side by side and we'd spend many hours talking and giggling about the situations we found ourselves in. I'd joke with him that there was nothing faster in the world than Kempy taking cover when the incoming alarm sounded. And it was true to an extent. We could be watching a movie or playing a hand of poker with some of the other guys, perhaps even a board game, but as soon as the dreadful screeching sound of the incoming alarm sounded, everyone would dive for cover, closing their eyes and hoping for the best. Often the impacts were far off and we'd react accordingly with relief, other times they'd be nearer and someone would shout 'Fuck, it's close!' but on every occasion we always ran like the wind and dived for cover.

Over the course of a few days, I'd become closer to a lad in the squadron who I'd never really worked with in my time at the regiment due to us being in different troops. He lived in the tent next to ours and had become generally more chatty and keen towards me in the days that led up to that afternoon. He was someone I quite liked and I was fairly pleased to be making a new friend while serving abroad.

One afternoon I was in my bed space, which was now surrounded by large concrete bricks to help with cover from the rockets, reading a copy of *Attitude* magazine. I'd emailed the team at *Attitude* and told them there was nowhere to access any gay-related media in the middle of Iraq and they'd kindly sent me a copy. The lad came into my tent to see what I was up to and ended up climbing over the little wall and reading the magazine with me on my bed. The whole situation felt strange and I wondered initially if he was trying to find a way to tell me something. He kept looking around to see if anybody else was in the tent, which nobody was, and then he'd tell me who he thought was hot in the magazine and then the squadron. He reminded me that he wasn't gay, but deep down I'd decided that he was and was just struggling to accept the fact. I felt excited by the revelation. This guy was a popular lad, very well liked and good at his job. I also found him very sexy, but I was simply too in love and very much missing my Thom to do anything about it. I knew that the guy was trying to get his end away with me that afternoon in the tent and the whole situation was, although slightly awkward, a very close and personal moment between two soldiers, both individually struggling with various aspects of fighting a war. I hurried off to use the internet and the phones soon after, not wanting to do something I knew I'd regret.

The guy and I carried on talking in the days that followed, though neither of us mentioned much about the situation that we'd found ourselves in. The truth was I had been dangerously close to indulging in something that would have been totally wrong and, in a way, the whole thing made me long for Thom even more. I was on a desperate countdown to the moment I'd see him, which would be within five days.

The rockets continued to fall, our stresses and worries raised each time one hurled in. Finally, as the clock ticked slowly by in the blistering Middle Eastern heat, the morning of our flight to safety dawned and 1 Troop excitedly began the long process of getting home.

Right up to the moment of boarding the plane the rockets continued to land closer and closer. It felt like they knew we were moments away from returning to the West, to our homes – and to safety.

Three months almost to the day since we left England, we headed home in our desert uniforms stained with blood, sweat and tears, back to the land where our families and loved ones awaited us. We'd made it, and I intended to enjoy every single moment of my two weeks off with my beautiful boyfriend, Thom.

14

MY LIFE IN PIECES

The moment our wheels touched down in Brize Norton on the morning of 4 August 2007, the most unimaginable relief was felt by everyone. We'd made it back to the peace and tranquillity of Oxfordshire and were about to embark on two weeks of rest and recuperation. Thom and I were going to make it count. I had imagined spending every moment of our precious time together and, before I'd even set eyes on him, I already feared the moment I'd be saying goodbye again.

He was waiting for me in the small arrivals lounge at the Oxfordshire airbase. Dressed perfectly in his usual splendour, he highlighted just how very rough and tired I looked in my desert attire. I hugged him without a care in the world, tears rolling down my face. It was perfect.

The first thing that struck me about Thom was that he looked like he'd grown up while we'd been apart. As he drove me away from the airbase, I looked at his beautiful sun-kissed skin and floppy brown hair. He moved much more elegantly than before. I put it down to his new career in the airline industry and always having to be well turned out. He spoke with a certain level of confidence I'd never noticed before as he told me tale after tale of his work antics in various foreign countries with his many new friends. I enjoyed just listening to him as we drove towards

Windsor. He didn't ask much about me, only about the flight and the airline we'd travelled from the Middle East on and how the service was. I could tell he was stepping around the whole Iraq thing and the fact I looked so worn out and tired.

That night, we were both going to be in Liverpool to surprise my nan on her eightieth birthday. I was delighted to have the chance to surprise her on her special day and even happier that Thom would be right there with me. Already, we were starting to look more like a regular family. It was so important for me to have him there that night; I wanted everyone in my family to see Thom again and get to know him more. It was the man I was spending the rest of my life with, and the pain of our separation over the previous three months had cemented that fact. After a long drive to the north-west, we arrived at the party, surprising my dear nan and causing many cheers and claps of happiness.

Since the death of my granddad in 2002, Nan, as a widow, had become the figurehead of our family, and everyone respected and loved her dearly. She'd had a bit of a rough ride with my granddad after the Second World War and was a classic example of true British resilience. A week after I told Mum I was gay, we let Nan know, too. She passed a judgement that, I think it's fair to say, is typical of people in their eighties who have lived through a generation where homosexuality was illegal for the most part. As expected, she'd rejected the news, citing that it was more than likely a phase. She wasn't ready to accept the fact that her youngest grandson was gay. I didn't let her opinion or comments get in the way of the huge amount of affection I held for her; I count her as one of the most important people in the world to me. I admire her deeply, but in the months and early years after I came out to the family, she couldn't accept that I was gay.

This made me want to bring Thom into the family fold even more. I hoped that she would soon see him for his true colours and accept him, as she had done with every other person brought into the clan. In the two weeks that followed, however, it seemed that Nan was more right than wrong about not wanting to get to know Thom.

Thom had warned me that he had to work a flight to Barbados midway through my time off. He was sorry about it but didn't really have much choice. After spending four days in North Wales with my parents, we were back in the car heading to Windsor for Thom to get ready for his work trip to Barbados. I was a little annoyed about the whole thing, but I accepted it as a matter of fact. I'd be alone for the three days he was away, but as soon as he returned, I figured we could just make up for lost time before my departure back to Iraq.

Eventually back in Windsor, Thom got himself sorted before departing for the airport. He went to work looking like a different person. Three-piece suit, nice black shoes, smartly done hair and a face plucked and made up to death. He looked incredibly sexy in his uniform and as he pecked me goodbye as I dropped him at the airport, I wondered how many heads he'd be turning as he walked through the terminal to his aircraft, pulling his black suitcase along as he went. I sighed as he walked away and drove myself back to the house.

Three days later, Thom was due to land back at Gatwick. It was his nineteenth birthday and I'd made secret plans to surprise him on his big day. Firstly, I was going to pick him up from the airport without him knowing. He'd said he would get the shuttle bus from Gatwick to Heathrow and then just use public transport to get home. I thought it would be nice to turn up and surprise him as he walked through the arrivals gate. Secondly, Thom had organised a party to celebrate his birthday that night, inviting our friends and apparently some new faces that I didn't know. I spent the three days helping Thom's housemate Nicole prepare the place for the big event. I bought Thom a fairly extravagant present, more so because I could afford to, but also because I really, really loved him and I wanted to spoil him. My sister was also travelling to Windsor to enjoy the party, it being the last time she'd see me before I headed back to Iraq a few days after. All was ready by the day of Thom's arrival.

I was at Gatwick early, so I bought myself a coffee and waited for his plane to land, keeping an eye on the arrivals board. Soon his flight landed and, holding a 'Happy Birthday' balloon I'd bought especially, I stood patiently with a huge grin on my face ready for the moment he appeared through the swinging doors.

I was still waiting an hour later. Initially I put it down to passengers taking their time to get off the aircraft. It was annoying but I continued to wait. By the time another half an hour had passed, I started to wonder if Thom had even caught the flight. I went over to the help desk for his airline and asked the lady at the counter about him and his flight.

'He landed over an hour ago. Yes, I can see here he collected his bags some time ago, too.'

How strange, I thought. Why hadn't he come through the gate? Why wasn't his phone switched back on by now? Where on earth was he?

I sat back down at the coffee shop and thought about what to do. I was still in sight of the arrivals gate just in case he came through, but I began to realise that it wasn't going to happen. I wondered if he'd left the airport through a different exit and caught his shuttle bus to Heathrow. I continued to try his mobile. Nothing. A flat battery, perhaps?

I rang the house and Nicole confirmed he hadn't come home or made contact. I tried his dad's mobile to see if he knew anything. Again, nothing. I was really starting to get worked up over the whole thing.

Defeated, and taking the advice of Thom's dad, I decided to drive back to Windsor and wait for news there. Where was Thom? What was he up to?

Some time later, as I neared Windsor, my mobile phone rang and I saw it was Thom trying to get through to me.

'Hey! I've just landed. How are you?'

I knew he was lying. I knew he'd landed about three hours before and he'd had his phone turned off since. I told him I'd arrived at the airport to surprise him and that he was nowhere to be seen. I expected him to be quite defensive about the morning's events. Instead, he simply said: 'We need to talk when I get home.'

We need to talk when I get home? What the hell did that mean? What did we need to talk about? We loved each other. Nothing was ever going to break us apart. Surely we weren't going to be...

I sat myself down in the living room waiting for Thom to get home. I had so many questions I needed answering. Where had he been? An hour later, the key turned in the door and in walked Thom, topped up with suntan and looking fairly tired from his long flight. He didn't say a word to me, just sat down on the couch opposite and looked at me. Immediately tears filled his eyes.

'I've met somebody while you've been away.'

Seven words and my entire life was ruined.

'I didn't mean to. It happened while I was away on a trip and I just met somebody. I'm sorry but you just weren't here.'

The tears were now flooding from his eyes, and indeed mine. This had happened because of things completely out of my control. I'd been away fighting a war, for God's sake. All the phone calls, all the letters I'd sent him, all those moments I was terrified but coping because I knew soon enough I'd be back with Thom, and all along he'd met somebody else.

What did that even mean, anyway? 'I've met somebody else'?
I could only think of one thing to say: 'Happy birthday.'

Thom took himself and his suitcase upstairs and I stayed on
the couch trying to make sense of everything that had gone on.
I still didn't know where he'd been all morning. I didn't know
who this 'new' person was or why Thom had decided he was a
better choice than me. I'd never experienced the thoughts and
feelings that were flooding my body in the moments after those
awful words. I absolutely hated everything about the job that had
driven us apart. The army! This was all the army's fault. If I hadn't
have been sent to Iraq, I'd never have found myself in this situation. If I'd been there for Thom, he'd never have needed to 'meet'
somebody else at all. We'd be just great.

We didn't speak for some hours but as Thom's party edged
closer, and guests started to arrive – like my sister who'd spent
four hours travelling to be there – we forced ourselves to answer
each other with single words and agreed to attempt to put on a
unified front. This, of course, wouldn't last.

The party started and I avoided most conversations, drinking
far too quickly, far too soon. Liza told me to pack it in at one
point, but she had no clue what had gone on earlier in the day. I
saw some people look at me and assume that Iraq had put me in
this state, but that wasn't it at all. All my sudden problems were
down to Thom meeting someone else. About Thom falling out of
love with me. I was falling into a hole.

At about midnight I took myself away from the party. I sat on a
deckchair in the garage with a drink in one hand, staring into the
darkness. I was drunk, and the feelings I'd suppressed for most of
the day surfaced. I was in a bad way and I wanted answers.

And as chance would have it, into the garage walked Thom,
looking for something. I pounced on him with my many questions. Thom had met a guy on a trip who also worked for the

airline, called Johnny. He was older and completely different from me. He had long blond hair, was tanned like Thom and seemed a bit of a hippy. Thom told me he was a vegan. I also discovered, although deep down I had known all along, that earlier that morning, when Thom should have been surprised by me in the Gatwick arrivals terminal, he was actually in a hotel next to the airport with his new lover, trying to get some last-minute precious time together before their next meeting.

I'd been completely cheated. This wasn't just a one-off fling that could be worked out; Thom had met somebody else and fallen in love with him. And he was a bloody hippy of all things. Thom wasn't like that at all. How had these two fallen in love?

It didn't matter. I asked Thom if he still loved me and he told me he didn't. That was it. We were over.

The boy who'd rescued me from my old ways on the scene in London; the boy who'd fallen in love with me the previous summer, and had moved to London to be with me, had found another fish in the sea. It was just too much to accept. I stormed out of the garage and into the house where the party was still in full swing. People tried to talk to me as I struggled through the kitchen. I saw Liza talking to a group of people who were Thom's friends and felt embarrassed to see her. I didn't want her to know my life had fallen to pieces. I didn't want her to be upset and see me in that state but, as I headed to the front door, I slammed the living room door shut, smashing the window pane as I went. The music stopped and everyone looked. I left the house and headed off into the night.

The following morning I woke up in the guard room at Combermere barracks. I wasn't in trouble; they just hadn't known what to do with me when I turned up at half-past one in the morning in a drunken state. The easiest thing was to just put me in a cell for the night. I woke up with a huge headache and soon remembered what had happened. I had created a massive scene. I sorted myself out and went back to the house. I wanted to talk with Thom in the hope that I might be able to salvage our relationship, but he had already left to be with his new lover for a few days until I'd returned to Iraq and was out of the way. That was it, then. We had certainly come to our end. He didn't even want to see me before I went back to war. What if I died? He'd never see me again. Maybe that's what he wanted.

I told my sister everything and she, as you'd expect, completely sided with me and comforted me in my state of shock. Heartbreak was a completely new experience for me. I'd never been through anything like it. It felt as if someone had ripped my beating heart clean out of my chest. The pain was unbearable.

I packed my things and returned to the barracks. I always liked the safety net soldiers are afforded when things go wrong. There was always a roof over your head if you needed it. There was always somewhere you could hide. I said my goodbyes to Liza and locked myself away in my little room in the base to think about my life. I'd never felt so bad before and I struggled to make sense of it all. I'm sure I'd have coped better if he'd written to me weeks before, explaining the situation. I'd have had a job to focus on and lots of people around me to help me through. Right then, I was alone. Alone with lots of problems and no shoulder to cry on.

After a day or so of lying around and feeling sorry for myself, I realised that I needed to do something. I resented the army and Iraq for costing me my relationship. 'The most beautiful boy in the world' had slipped through my fingers and it was because I hadn't been around. I took myself off to see the doctor. I didn't feel I was in a state to return to Iraq and just carry on my duties; armed to the teeth, I didn't trust myself. I told the doctor everything and he agreed that I needed more time off to sort myself

out and awarded me ten extra days in the UK. I realised that
we were fighting a war, although I hadn't yet come face to face
with an enemy, and that I had to go back eventually, but an extra
ten days was very much welcomed. I rang Gibbo and told him I
wouldn't be on the flight back to Basra with him and the other
boys of 1 Troop. He accepted it and told me to stay safe. In hind-
sight, I wish I'd just boarded that plane and moved my life on
straight away.

It's true that no matter what, regardless of how much time
passes, your friends stick with you and drop everything to help
you in an hour of need. In the hour that followed my meeting
with the doctor, I rang an old friend from London, Donna, and
told her everything that had gone on. Donna was a civilian groom
within the Blues and Royals when I'd been based in London, and
we'd enjoyed many a late adventure in Soho. We hadn't seen each
other in twelve months, but she dropped everything and came to
my help. I would never have got through that week without her.

It was a messy week. Donna and I had always been big drink-
ers and the way in which she helped me forget about Thom, and
indeed Iraq, was by picking me up and taking me out, distracting
me from everything in the process. She helped me pack a few
things and took me back to London. I checked into a hotel – I
could afford to after my three months in Iraq – and we hit the
scene. I wasn't at all interested in men. There wasn't a man in
the world that could get me over Thom; I was just there for the
company and the drinking. I'm ashamed about how much money
we just threw away in the days that followed, and about the state
I was walking around in. I was in a complete daze, buying new
clothes daily and living out of a hotel room. Donna would return
home and sleep and I'd just go back to my hotel room and slip
into a drunken coma, waking the next morning to try and piece
together what had happened.

Mum went mad worrying about me over those few days, so much so that she decided to travel down to see me. Mum didn't usually travel anywhere to see people, people always travelled to her; she was clearly very concerned about me. I had one last full day partying with Donna on the scene and returned to Windsor for the arrival of Mum and Phil the following day. They were even bringing Nan, who was also very worried about me and had insisted on joining them. I worried I was in for it, and that they were travelling to tell me off and put me back on the straight and narrow. I was happy with the medication I was getting from Donna and London; I'd even messed around with a random guy in my hotel room on our last night out. I must have been getting over Thom. It must have been working.

When the three of them arrived they didn't start telling me off and giving me grief about how I'd been behaving. Nan took charge from the start and they were all very compassionate about my situation. Mum was worried I was in the process of throwing away my career and Nan kept saying how much of a 'slut' Thom was. I'd never heard an eighty-year-old use words like that before.

'During the war, people who did that while their soldiers were away fighting had their heads shaved off in the street!' It was great seeing the family, but I was still in a complete daze. I'm so glad they came to see me. The weather throughout my time back in the UK had been great. It was sunny, very hot and not a drop of rain had fallen. Before my family returned to North Wales, the four of us had a day out in Brighton, on the beach. Mum told me that she was desperate for me to go back to Iraq. Bizarrely, she felt I was safer away, having a job to do and something to focus on. Back in the UK she could see what was happening to me. I was blowing all of my hard-earned cash on drinking and partying and soon I'd pay a big price for my actions. I promised her I'd go back, although I really didn't want to. My life was just stress followed by stress. I hated that my time off had been completely ruined and that I was heading back to the rocket attacks without having had a proper chance to forget about them. I hated Thom and everything he'd done to me and, although I'd never met the lad, I hated with a huge passion the hippy, veggie-loving idiot Thom had left me for.

With my flight back to Basra delayed, there was time for one final go at London with Donna. I checked into a hotel, and we hit the scene for one last session – a session that lasted forty-eight hours and involved a lot of partying. It was two days of trying to forget my recent past and also my impending future.

I said my farewells to Donna and thanked her for helping me through everything. I'd had a great time, albeit in a state of depression and sorrow, and she'd really prevented me from falling into a complete hole of despair. I'll be eternally grateful to Donna for being a true friend over that difficult period.

15

MILKSHAKE CONVERSATIONS

In the three weeks I'd been out of the country, Iraq had changed considerably for us A Squadron boys. A battle group had pulled out of Basra Palace, a previous home to Saddam, which had in turn reduced the number of rocket attacks everyone else was suffering at the COB. This was all part of the gradual reduction in strength the British Army was moving towards in southern Iraq, eventually leading up to us withdrawing in 2009. A SQN was being re-rolled to the port of Umm Qasr in the extreme south to act as port security and a local show of force.

The SQN was totally reorganised over the course of three days before moving via helicopter to Umm. The five-troop-sized squadron was reordered to three 'super' troops and one HQ troop. Soldiers found themselves working with lads they weren't used to working alongside, myself included. There was a lot to get used to and not a lot of time to do so.

I returned to A SQN after my extended break. The boys were all brilliant, as were the seniors, but I could tell people were walking on eggshells around me. A senior NCO called Warren was the first to really approach the subject of Thom. He told me that I should feel able to talk with him or the others and that just because I was in a gay relationship it didn't make the circumstances any less real. I appreciated his words of encouragement, even if they were a little to the point. He was from a generation of soldiers who'd lived through homosexuality being outlawed in the forces. Warren would later tell me that as a young corporal, instructing new recruits in basic training, he was forced to terminate a young recruit's career because he'd told Warren he was gay. He said it was the hardest thing he'd ever had to do because the lad was the best recruit in his platoon, but the army was very strict about homosexuality and Warren was risking his own career by not informing the chain of command.

'People did used to lie about it too, Spicy.' Spicy had become Warren's nickname of choice for me. 'People would say they were gay if they didn't want to be in the army any longer, especially in basic training. It was a very quick and easy way out of the military. But this lad was different. He was an excellent soldier and I knew he loved his job; it broke my heart reporting him.'

The corporal major was, characteristically, less compassionate. He welcomed me back but then immediately told me he wasn't ready to give me all my weapons. He didn't trust me alone with a rifle and 120 rounds. I was outraged by this but there was little I could do. This meant I was exempt from guard duty and the like. Kempy also had to accompany me to the welfare village if I fancied a pizza or something; he was more than happy with the responsibility.

In the reshuffle, I was moved out of 1 Troop and placed in squadron headquarters for the remaining three months of our time in Iraq. I was to be a radio operator, communicating with the troops on the ground and plotting their positions on a huge map for the squadron leader. It would be quite a change from what I was used to. I was taking a back seat, and at that point, before stepping foot into Umm Qasr, and not knowing what kind of environment we'd be faced with, I worried I was going to miss out on lots of action.

My new boss was Corporal of Horse Parker, the chap who'd laid on top of me when I was caught without my body armour in the cookhouse that day, and working alongside me were two other lads, Wilko and Cardiff, the latter an obvious nickname for a Welshman. The three of us would share the day manning radios. I'd never worked in a busy operations room before and the thought of the task both excited me and worried me in equal measure. I feared something awful would happen and it would all be my fault for directing a troop down the wrong road or something.

We closed down our business in Basra and over the course of forty-eight hours moved our operation to the port of Umm Qasr, quite unsure what state we'd find it in.

It was a fairly quick trip down to Iraq's only maritime asset on the British fleet of Merlins; the same Merlins that had ferried us back and forth to the desert much further north. The buzz of activity helped me take my mind off Thom a little, who was moving on with his life back in the UK. I was still, however, unarmed. We landed in a market area of Umm and were picked up by the soldiers we had come to relieve. They were heading back to Basra to end their three months on tour.

I got to the operations room, where I would be spending eight hours of every day, and familiarised myself with the new surroundings. I'd never seen so many radios all set up on different frequencies and networks. In just two days I'd be responsible for operating them all. I was shown to my new living quarters, which were quite an upgrade from what I'd been used to in Basra. It was the Ritz compared to roughing it in the desert, too. Wilko and I were sharing; Cardiff managed to bag his own room somewhere else in the compound.

Our new base, Umm Qasr North, was a brick building surrounded by a large perimeter wall dotted with tall watchtowers every hundred metres. The towers were known as sangers and had to be manned twenty-four hours a day by members of the squadron. Each sanger had a radio to the operations room. It was quite a well-defended little fort but on our first day in Umm, the local Iraqi police commander came to the operations room to tell us they had heard the local militia were planning to over-throw us while our busy handover commenced. Immediate panic set in as everyone prepared for an imminent attack. Warnings couldn't be taken lightly, especially from senior Iraqi officials. I told the corporal major that I wanted my 'fucking guns' back at once. I was the only person, it seemed, in the whole of Iraq who wasn't carrying a gun and that had to change immediately if we were to be attacked.

An extremely anxious evening of waiting and hoping that the police commander was wrong followed. The mixture of being in a completely alien environment and under the threat of imminent attack didn't go well. Widespread panic set in across the squad-ron as I sat in the operations room with the squadron command element, waiting to see how the night would unfold, but, as would become normal, the threat was just a threat. There was no attack, but it made everyone wake up to the fact that in Umm we were pretty much alone. Our only support would be from an American base a few miles away called Camp Bucca.

A week later, A SQN had completely settled in. The task was different from everything we'd done before and, actually, anything we'd trained for. One troop would be constantly on sanger duties, providing security to our compound; another troop would be 'stood by' ready for anything to kick off – this would turn out to be the task of preference for the majority, as it mostly involved playing on a Nintendo Wii, waiting for a call that seldom came. The final group would be the 'tasking' troop, who had to carry out menial tasks in the AO (area of operations) – mostly admin runs to Camp Bucca or to a large hill some thirty miles away to make contact with the soldiers based there. There wasn't much threat of rocket attack at Umm North due to us being a relatively small compound right next to a mosque and a number of other settlements; it would be too easy to miss and destroy something they liked.

I was satisfied with my new job. I'd either be on duty from midnight until 8 a.m., 8 a.m. until 4 p.m. or 4 p.m. until midnight. The three of us rotated for the remaining three months of our tour, swapping shifts weekly. I also had the added job of exchanging all the faulty radio equipment every ten days or so, giving me a regular helicopter trip back to Basra on a two-day stopover. The occasional trip back to Basra would be a pleasant break in the daily routine of the operations room, and I felt sorry for the boys who had to spend hour after hour with a machine gun in the sangers.

Two weeks later, during a day shift, I was first introduced to Sammy. Sammy was an American soldier who was doing the same job as me in an operations room in Camp Bucca and who had to travel to us at Umm Qasr North once a week to update the American radio in our ops room, enabling us to listen in to their movements. He'd travel up in a small convoy of Hummer vehicles and he'd work away at his radio while the other soldiers in his team would grab a coffee or a milkshake at our NAAFI (the camp shop). Sammy was, like me, twenty years old but slightly shorter with a shaved head (his hair, I could tell, was blond), and had an athletic slim build. I'd later find out he was from New York.

He walked into our ops room and saw me marking something on the map. I looked over and I guess my eyes widened or something; Sammy stopped dead and, for a second or two, we stood in silence.

'Can I help you?' I eventually said.

'I'm here to change our radio, that one there.' The American pointed and I nodded. I moved out of his way, though I really didn't want to, wishing he'd squeeze past me, and stood admiring him from a few feet back. He turned back and asked if I was OK.

'Would you like a coffee?'

I watched over him working away at his radio while I made us and my senior, Rich, a coffee. The tension in the air was notably different since the guy had entered the room. I felt a lot of the communication between us both was unspoken. I handed him the coffee and introduced myself.

'Hey, I'm Sammy,' he said in response.

Sammy! Sammy was perfect and I immediately fell in lust. We continued with the small talk. He noted that he'd never seen me before and I explained that we'd only just taken over the job at Umm and this was the first shift I'd done with the American radio visit. He told me that it was his job to come weekly and it was his only opportunity to get out of his own ops room. I told him I had the excitement of flying to Basra just over once a week with broken radios and he looked thrilled for me. I noticed Rich's eyes raise from behind his book and scout over the two of us nattering away. We'd both stopped working and continued to make conversation. I asked him where he was from and he told me. I told him I was from Wales and he laughed.

'I've heard of that place.'

I asked him how long he'd been in Iraq. He told me and I returned the same information. The Americans served a lot longer than us on tour. The usual would be an eighteen-month posting. In Sammy's case, he'd already been in the country for six months but still faced another year from home. Unaware of this fact until then, I used it as a chance to pry more into Sammy's backstory...

'Jesus, that's a hell of a long time to be away from home. I bet your family really miss you. Do you have a girlfriend waiting for you?' Sammy hesitated and then looked at the ground. The question was probably a little too direct.

'No... I don't have a girlfriend.'

Inside I was screaming 'DO YOU HAVE A BOYFRIEND?' but even in the buzz of meeting Sammy I had better judgement than to just come out with it. I also knew that though Rich had his head in his book he was really listening to our conversation.

After my abrupt question, his focus returned to the task in hand: the American radio. A few moments later he finished his effort and returned the station to how it was. For the final five minutes of our meeting there was an awkward silence while he finished his coffee, more out of politeness than thirst. Maybe my questioning was a little too near the bone. What if he did have someone waiting for him back at home and he was trying to put it out of his mind? Eighteen months was a hell of a long time to be separated from a loved one. Thom couldn't even manage three months waiting for me.

He told me he'd be back the following Thursday at about 1 p.m. and Rich made a note of it in the occurrence book. I walked Sammy to the door and offered my hand as he bade farewell.

'It was really refreshing seeing a new face, Sammy. Maybe I'll see you next week?'

'Yeah... I hope so!' And off he went.

I hope so. What did that mean?

All week I thought about our meeting and those final words. He hoped to see me again. He must have liked me. Then I considered the American situation and remembered that being gay in the military wasn't allowed. Crazy. But I still wondered.

Our meeting drew many similarities to a random hook-up in a West End bar. I'm sure he looked me up and down as I did exactly the same thing to him. The flow of conversation between us in the short time we'd spent together was more than I'd spoken to some of the lads in 1 Troop for the entire three months we'd been in the desert; there was certainly some chemistry – even if I had put my foot in it.

As soon as the door was shut, Rich put his book down and looked at me with a huge grin on his face.

'I saw what happened then! Got a little friend, have we?' Rich, who was a warrant officer, was a large chap who spoke with a very thick cockney accent. We got on well and I really admired his calm approach to the job. He was right. Sammy and I had made friends and we'd flirted our way through twenty minutes of time. I smiled to Rich and insisted I didn't know what he was talking about. From the second I closed the door on Sammy, though, I started counting down until he'd next be playing with his radio in the ops room and we could carry on our little chats.

With Wilko taking the day shift the following Thursday, I told him I was getting increasingly bored during my sixteen-hour rest time every day and offered to cover him for an hour or so while he worked out in the makeshift gym that had been assembled. Wilko jumped at the chance to get out of the ops room for an hour. I'd got myself in for the arrival of Sammy.

The following day I sat and awaited Sammy's arrival. Wilko had told me that the Yanks had been in touch on their radio to say they were on their way and due to arrive at any moment. On the desk in full view I planted a copy of *Attitude* which had a semi-naked actor from the TV show *Skins* on its front cover. *Attitude* had continued to send me a copy of their latest magazine while I was away, ensuring I was kept current on all things gay. I'd showered and even smartened my hair a little. I was ready!

As Sammy walked in he sounded genuinely happy to see me. I wondered if he'd thought of me as much as I'd thought of him.

His eyes lit up and I jumped out of my chair to greet him. I had to tone it down somewhat as the squadron leader was pottering around the room. Sammy walked over to his radio and, like the previous week, I offered him a coffee.

'Would you like one as well, sir?' The squadron leader declined and left the room. It was just me and Sammy now.

As I busied myself with the two coffees, I looked over to see Sammy staring interestedly at the magazine I'd cleverly placed on the desk next to his radio. He didn't look turned off by it. He was fidgeting with his equipment throughout. I coughed and he looked over; I just stood there smiling away waiting for the kettle to boil.

'Have you been busy, Sammy?'

'No, not really. Just carrying on as normal. How about you?'

Our conversation didn't really go anywhere in particular and I could see Sammy's eyes occasionally darting to the magazine.

'Counting down the weeks 'til home now, hey?' I adored the way he spoke. I'd never really been a huge fan of the American accent, but Sammy spoke so beautifully. He didn't rush his words, unlike me. It was particularly warm in the ops room that day and Sammy took his shirt off and carried out his maintenance in just his light green, and very well-fitting, T-shirt. He had beautiful arms and I could see through his shirt just how very ripped he was. He must have seen me checking him out. I barely looked him in the eye but I could tell he was becoming more and more relaxed. And then, the moment I was hoping for.

'Is this yours?' he asked, touching the magazine.

'Yeah. They send it to me every month. Not many magazines like that out here.'

'No, there's not.'

'You can have it, if you like?' I pushed it to him thinking he'd accept it, but of course he couldn't. If he was found reading it back at Bucca, he'd be on the first flight back to America, facing a dishonourable discharge. He declined the offer immediately.

'You're just allowed to have that, yeah?'

'Yeah, nobody's bothered here.'

'That's crazy. Are there any others?'

'No, not here. Just me. But there are one or two who pretend they're not, but I know are.'

'We have "Don't Ask, Don't Tell".' He'd lowered his voice to a whisper.

'I know. Are you—' Right then, the door flung open and in walked my boss, Stevie.

'What you doing here, James? Thought you were on at four?'

'I'm just covering for Wilko while he goes to the gym. Everything OK?'

Stevie nodded towards Sammy, who looked startled by Steve's sudden entrance.

'I'm almost done here. I think next week I need to bring some more tools with me. There's a fault with it.'

Stevie had sat down and began typing away at his computer. It was the end of our conversation. I was just about to ask Sammy if he was like me. I was sure he was about to tell me, but I didn't get to finish my sentence. I was gutted.

Later that night, while on my own shift in the ops room, our conversation circled my mind. The tone of his voice throughout our chat was low. He was talking to me and saying things that he wasn't at all comfortable in saying, things he'd obviously not been able to say in his own unit. I couldn't get his beautiful face out of my mind and I wondered if he was thinking of me. He must have been gay. I was sure of it.

I pondered how difficult it must be for him. I had completely taken for granted the environment I was operating in. Sure, I'd had my problems, but they were few and far between. If somebody didn't like me, I simply kept myself out of their way. Sammy, if he was gay, had probably never told any of his fellow soldiers. He hadn't had the chance to be his true self in the military simply because it wasn't allowed. In my small room, I'd put posters on the wall of semi-clad popstars, my favourite footballers and casually left my gay lifestyle magazine lying around for anybody to read if they wished. I had nobody rooting through my mail, listening in to my phone calls or quizzing me about which internet sites I liked to use. I enjoyed a persecution-free working environment. Sammy, on the other hand, had to deal with the possibility of being interrogated like a criminal and then dishonoured for simply being the person he was. How could the US, the apparent leaders of the free world, do this to their own people? I felt very sorry for Sammy.

The following day I caught a flight to the COB to exchange a few broken radios and managed to catch up with Kempy, who'd remained back in Basra as a link man for us in the south. I told him about Sammy and, as always, he gave me his honest opinion over a milkshake. He told me I should go for it and forget about Thom. I wasn't too sure what 'it' was, but I decided he was right. Time was ticking and I only had a precious hour a week with Sammy. I needed to make the time count.

If he hadn't have been so gorgeous I would have let him be, but without even knowing it, Sammy was helping me out hugely after Thom. I hadn't thought about him and his hippy boyfriend at all since Sammy had entered my life the week before.

I had some mail waiting for me upon my return to Umm that was a little bit surprising. Incredibly, Thom's parents had decided to continue to write to me even after the break-up between me and their son. They mentioned the break-up in their letter but wanted to make it clear that they continued to wish me well while serving abroad. It was a wonderful gesture and it really cheered me up after a horrible ride back from Basra.

I'd looked in the occurrence book to see when Sammy was next due in camp and pondered how I might be able to talk with him more about his personal situation. I needed to establish the facts, whether or not Sammy was indeed gay and how he was finding serving in Iraq. I decided not to place myself on duty in the ops room for his arrival but, instead, I'd just turn up unannounced and offer him a milkshake at the shop in the compound.

I walked in a little after he was due to arrive but was surprised to see Cardiff sat alone in front of the radios. The Americans had cancelled; fortunately they had only put it back a day.

The following day I arrived at the ops room to find an American soldier busily unscrewing the back of a radio set. It was Sammy. We said our hellos and I messed around with the computer, making myself look busy. About ten minutes later, and after a few glances between us, I piped up and offered him a milkshake.

'Sure! I'd love to. I was going to grab one after this anyway.'

We walked together to the other side of the compound and bought milkshakes. Sammy's colleagues were sporadically dotted around our base either using the internet or waiting in the TV room. Two were even having a milkshake a few tables away from us, but we didn't look out of place, just two soldiers sharing a drink and having a chat. It was quite a usual sight.

'Are you gay, Sammy … like me?'

There was a long pause and, very quietly, Sammy said, 'I've never talked about it.'

'You can't?'

'I'd be thrown out. Sent home. My dad would never understand.'

I had no idea what to say to fill the silence. It wasn't as if I could say, 'Oh, just come out, it'll all be fine', because it wouldn't be. Sammy's situation was completely different to mine. I could stand on the table and scream to the whole of Umm Qasr I was gay and proud, and not a thing could be said, whereas Sammy couldn't even comprehend the same freedom. It was complete inequality. I was safe, he was not.

'I wish there was something I could do, Sammy. I'm really sorry.'

'Sucks!' He managed a slight grin.

'All I know is that, soon, it will change for you. It has to. And you don't even know, but you've really helped me.'

'I have?'

'I hate it out here. I absolutely hate being in Iraq. I had a boyfriend but he gave up waiting for me.'

'Holy shit. That really sucks!'

'This is the last place I thought I'd meet someone like me – in the middle of Iraq! You've helped me forget about him a little.'

If we'd been anywhere but in the middle of an armed compound in the middle of Umm Qasr, I'd have grabbed him and given him a big hug. Our conversation was the most surreal but heartfelt chat between two gay men ever imaginable. Two soldiers, different armies, different times; equality for one, inequality for the other.

For six weeks or so we continued with our milkshake conversations. He'd ask me about London and about my coming out, I'd ask him about New York, his family life and his hopes for the future. After every meeting there was an air of regret that we'd have to wait a whole week or so before carrying on our chat. We'd become close over the space of just seven hours and I considered where our friendship would lead. There was no way in the world Sammy and I would ever have met if it hadn't have been for Iraq and, in a way, I changed my opinion on the circumstances that had led to me being sat in my operations room at the southern tip of the country. I'd spent months mourning the demise of my relationship. Thom was now officially out of my life. Fate, I'd decided, had traded him in for a much more pleasant human being. I'd moved on.

16

HOMECOMING

The routine of life at Umm Qasr quickened the final part of our seven-month tour of Iraq, and before we knew it we were counting down the weeks and days until our return home to the UK.

As the final weeks ticked away, I felt deeply anxious about returning to a normal way of life. While away, I didn't have any of the mundane day-to-day hassle that goes with a complex life in a busy city environment: no bills to pay, none of the hustle and bustle of having to shop, queuing for goods, paying for expensive fuel to sit in traffic for endless hours in London. Yes, I had become used to stress of a different nature, but as the time approached for us to return to the real world, the reality of normal life really played on my mind, especially as the library in Windsor was trying to take me to court for something as petty as failing to return a book before departing for Iraq.

There were a few moments of excitement throughout our final weeks at Umm. The highlight of every week was naturally the visit of Sammy from Camp Bucca, which I'd use to recharge my enthusiasm batteries. Sammy brought some happiness with him despite the repression he was faced with as a gay man in the American military.

One afternoon near the end of our time in Iraq, 1 Troop, my

old troop, were on the ground carrying out a patrol along the Kuwaiti border. I spoke with Gibbo and the other commanders over the radio as they went, plotting their positions regularly on the map. It was all very normal when all of a sudden something happened that grabbed my attention.

'One, One, contact wait out...' The dreaded words of hostile engagement. It was Gibbo. I shouted for the squadron leader.

'Hello Zero, this is One, One. Contact at seventeen thirty-four, American call sign. BLUE ON BLUE!' Everyone in the ops room looked at each other with horror. Gibbo had been shot at by American troops. The leader instantly picked up the American radio handset and screamed down it for attention. In the three months we'd been in Umm Qasr, I'd hardly seen the leader excited about anything; right then he was livid.

'HELLO! THIS IS UMM QASR NORTH... HELLO! ANSWER THE FUCKING RADIO!'

Soon a voice could be heard over the crackly Yank radio. It was a voice I recognised instantly.

'You have a call sign firing on British soldiers. Cease fire immediately!'

'Erm... Can you confirm what grid this is at?' The leader's face went bright red. How could their ops room not know which one of their call signs was firing? The first thing we'd do if we'd started a firefight with someone is report back to base; even asking for permission to engage was pretty run-of-the-mill.

Gibbo came back over the network to say the shooting from the vehicle had stopped and they were now approaching them. I imagined, knowing Gibbo as I did, him strangling the commander of the US call sign in blind rage, but later he'd tell us how very gentleman-like the two commanders were with each other. Our regiment had had its unfair share of Blue-on-Blue incidents over the years, especially in Iraq. Thankfully this incident ended without any bloodshed, but it could have been a very different outcome.

With our time in Iraq nearly up, we learned that our roles were to be taken over by members of the Royal Mercian Regiment and the squadron was to fly home in two movements. Stevie decided to put me and Cardiff on the first flight, which after a 24-hour stop-off in Cyprus would get me home on 6 December. The remaining members of A SQN would return two days later.

Sammy knew our weekly chats were coming to an end and as somebody who's never been a fan of or any good at saying goodbye, I dreaded our final farewell. Sammy still had twelve months left to serve in Iraq before he'd be going home, so I played down my feelings towards leaving so as not to cause him unnecessary stress.

As our final week in the Middle East began, the heavier items of our belongings were shipped home by sea and, slowly, unfamiliar faces started to appear and begin settling in ahead of their six or seven months at Umm North. Wilko and I remained in our secluded room, while the remainder of the squadron had to make do with sharing accommodation with the new boys. Wilko and I had become good mates over the three months we'd shared the room. I hadn't mentioned my relationship with Sammy to him directly but I knew he was aware of it; when I asked him if it was possible to have the room to myself for an hour or so one afternoon just a handful of days before flying home, he pretty much knew exactly what I was asking.

It wasn't anything crude I had in mind; more than anything I wanted a hug and a cry. Every week we'd had some very stressful and heartbreaking conversations and each time we held back our tears to save a scene. I needed to give Sammy a huge hug and tell him how glad I was to have met him. I was already thinking about visiting him upon his return the following year. I needed to get his postal address, his email, perhaps a phone number. But our last time together never happened. As I opened the door to the ops room expecting to find Sammy messing around with the radio, I saw the figure of a young American woman, dressed neatly in her combats and carrying out the tasks I'd been used to seeing Sammy do. Sammy hadn't come.

The girl told me that Sammy had reported sick earlier that morning and had been sent to rest in Camp Bucca. Of course, that might have been the case, but inside I was heartbroken. To this day, I believe that Sammy couldn't face the goodbye and had taken the easy option not to come. I didn't know his surname, his postal address, his email address or his telephone number. Sammy was completely gone. I returned to my empty, windowless room, sat on my metal-framed bed and started to cry. I was gutted.

Two days later a helicopter came into Umm and took me and a bunch of the other soldiers to an American airbase in Qatar. My time in Iraq was over. As the chopper took off from Umm Qasr North, I could see in the distance the large site of Camp Bucca towards the Kuwaiti border and wondered whether Sammy was thinking about me.

I'd been in touch with my parents frequently towards my return to the UK so they knew when I'd be off the ground and out of any possible danger. I could hear how excited and pleased Mum had become the closer the day of my return came. I'd missed them terribly, of course, and I couldn't wait to see them at the earliest chance.

The plane touched down in Cyprus for our customary de-climatisation period: twenty-four hours of drinking, eating and lounging on a gorgeous beach before continuing on to England. Nobody had had access to alcohol while away so the army diluted us with booze to limit the shock of returning home and drinking ourselves stupid. Naturally there was trouble and towards the end of the night the Household Cavalry boys got into a fight with some Royal Engineers after trying to outdo each other with their behaviour. This meant lots of stripping and nakedness before upping the game with more naughtiness and finally all-out fighting. I avoided most of the trouble, leaving it to the bigger lads, and the following morning we headed to the waiting aircraft to carry on our journey home, with nothing more than a few black eyes and bruised egos. A SQN was in one piece.

We slept our hangovers away as the plane made its way back to Oxfordshire. Finally we touched down in the land we'd spent seven months serving; we were back in England.

A coach collected us and someone had kindly put a few crates of lager on board for us to enjoy on the drive back to Combermere barracks. It was almost time for tea and medals as they say, but I was just looking forward to taking off the desert fatigues and not having to put them back on again. They'd become so old-looking and worn; soon we'd be back in greens.

We pulled into camp and saw a huge blanket hanging, painted with the words 'Welcome Home A SQN'. The gates of camp were decorated with union flags and through the windows of the coach in the darkness, the married guys waved at their wives who were crying outside. The coach halted outside the mess and we were directed inside to have a drink with the waiting commanding officer. As I entered the room, keen to get a pint from the bar, I was surprised to see so many families waiting for a glimpse of their returning sons. I didn't consider for a moment that Mum would have made the journey down but as my eyes circled the room, I noticed a very familiar figure sat in the corner with tears rolling down her cheeks. Mum had come to greet me. I ran over to her and Phil and hugged them both. It was the greatest surprise. I'd had no idea they were planning to be there. Relief was felt by everyone in the room; we'd all come home together. The worries and stresses of an entire year, the training, deployment and role changes we'd been through since early January, were put away as we all squeezed and cherished the time with our nearest and dearest.

We stayed at Aunt Audrey's house in Sussex and spent the night chatting and drinking wine into the early hours. A Squadron had been stood down for the weekend and told to be in work in fresh desert combats (much to my annoyance) the following Monday to prepare for our forthcoming medal parade. We were to receive our campaign medals from Lord Guthrie, who was also the colonel of the Life Guards and held the title 'Gold Stick in Waiting to HM the Queen'.

After a pleasant weekend with the family catching up and unwinding from my recent adventures, I said my farewells and returned to Windsor to begin the rehearsals for the medal parade which was scheduled for the Thursday. My family would be returning to Windsor and bringing my dear nan with them for the occasion. It was great seeing the other A SQN boys back at work on the Monday morning, most of whom had arrived two days after us. The squadron was back together again for the last task of the year.

The corporal major drilled us around the barracks endlessly for the three days before the medal presentation; we'd let our personal drill go a little while abroad and found ourselves out of step or turning the wrong way on command. It started off as a laugh, but as the parade edged near, the corporal major lost his patience with us and kept us practising our drill movements until late Wednesday evening. Early on Thursday morning, he had the entire squadron out running in Windsor Great Park to 'blow out the cobwebs' before our big day. We were embarking on seven weeks' leave following the medal parade and we'd have run all day if it meant getting the best part of two months off in return.

As Lord Guthrie made his way along the line, pinning the

shiny medals with the Queen's head engraved to the front on each man's chest, I could see Mum, along with the many other mothers who'd travelled to Windsor to witness the occasion, with tears rolling down her face. It was a cold December morning, but not even the chilly weather could get in the way of our parents' pride. After the ceremonial part of the medal presentation had passed, A SQN exercised its right of Freedom of Windsor and marched to the Garrison Church, stopping the traffic as we went. The band played along the way and the memories of the events of the previous twelve months filled my mind. The following day would mark a year since the start of my Iraq diary, the day we'd initially learned of our fate, and almost everything in my life had changed since then. I'd completely grown up: I'd seen some awful things and I'd had my heart broken, twice. I wondered about the first heartbreak. Where was Thom now? Was he stood at the side of a street applauding us as we marched by? Was he with his new lover, possibly abroad? My mind quickly changed to Sammy, who was still in southern Iraq. I wondered if he thought about me every time he travelled to Umm Qasr North to maintain his radio. I hoped he was OK, but of course there was never a way to find out.

At the church service we gave poignant thought and remembrance to the twenty-six servicemen and women who hadn't made it back from Operation Telic 10.

PTE Kevin Thompson	21 yrs	06/05/2007
Cpl Jeremy Brookes	28 yrs	21/05/2007
Cpl Rodney Wilson	30 yrs	07/06/2007
LCpl James Cartwright	21 yrs	16/06/2007
Maj Paul Harding	48 yrs	20/06/2007
Cpl John Rigby	24 yrs	22/06/2007
PTE James Kerr	20 yrs	28/06/2007

PTE Scott Kennedy	20 yrs	28/06/2007
Cpl Paul Joszko	28 yrs	28/06/2007
Rfn Edward Vakabua	23 yrs	06/07/2007
LCpl Ryan Francis	23 yrs	07/07/2007
Cpl Christopher Read	22 yrs	07/07/2007
SAC Matthew Caulwell	22 yrs	19/07/2007
SAC Christopher Dunsmore	29 yrs	19/07/2007
SAC Peter McFerren	24 yrs	19/07/2007
LCpl Timothy Flowers	25 yrs	21/07/2007
Cpl Steve Edwards	35 yrs	31/07/2007
PTE Craig Baker	20 yrs	06/08/2007
LAC Martin Beard	20 yrs	07/08/2007
LSgt Chris Casey	27 yrs	09/08/2007
LCpl Kirk Redpath	22 yrs	09/08/2007
Sgt Eddie Collins	Unknown	05/09/2007
Sgt Mark Stansfield	32 yrs	21/09/2007
LCpl Sarah Holmes	26 yrs	14/10/2007
Cpl Lee Fitzsimmons	26 yrs	20/11/2007
Sgt John Battersby	31 yrs	20/11/2007

Rest in peace.

17

PRIDE

Six months had passed since our return from southern Iraq and life within A Squadron was somewhat different from the style we'd been used to over the previous two years. Much like other units that had returned from tour, the soldiers in our unit were dispersed to concentrate on other duties, sometimes in other bases. I was remaining in A SQN with a handful of original lads, working with and alongside a fresh breed of recruits. Some of the guys had been posted to Knightsbridge on ceremonial duties, others had been promoted and sent to work in another squadron. It was a sad affair and a strange environment to get used to; the team that had endured seven months of the blistering Iraqi heat was no more. The corporal major had retired from the army and Warren, the senior NCO who'd offered me an ear upon my return to Iraq the previous year, had taken his place, something that would pay dividends for me in the upcoming months.

After our relentless tour build-up and the operations that followed, the pressure was removed from us somewhat. Our fitness, although kept at a respectable level, didn't have to meet the constant battle-ready standard deploying troops need to have. We'd take leisurely runs along the Thames in Windsor, through the grounds of Windsor Castle and out into the vast Great Park two or three times a week. Warren's emphasis on fitness was through sport, something everyone preferred to tough battle-style physical training.

With no clear goal or objective, the squadron existed in a strange bubble that saw us playing on our Xboxes most of the time or playing football in the gym. Our vehicles had returned from Iraq and were given to another squadron to use for their own forthcoming operations, leaving A Squadron with nothing to do in our working hours. Glad of the rest initially, soon the boredom settled in, steadily replaced by general unhappiness among the boys in the squadron. We needed a job. Suddenly we got one.

'Who's ever been to Canada?' Warren asked the squadron. Not many of the lads' hands were up, but a few of the more senior guys had been.

'OK. Let me put it this way: who wants to go to Canada?' Instantly, the whole squadron sprang to attention and placed their arms in the air, me included.

'Right, I can only send half of you, so, Wharton, you're first: squadron leader's driver!'

Warren looked down at his notepad and scribbled my name. I was delighted I was going but I knew none of the details of the trip. How long would we be going for? What were we going to be doing? None of it really mattered though. I was so bored sitting around an empty tank park anything would have been better.

Squadron leader's driver was a good job, but I'd recently qualified as a gunner and operator. I'd hoped my time in the driver's seat was long gone and had been waiting patiently to be placed in the turret with an experienced commander, to practise my new skills.

Becoming a gunner had meant a six-week-long course in gunnery, in the classroom and simulator at Windsor and then live firing on the range in South Wales. The course had been much fun, but it was marred by a large incident.

I was in the middle of a smoke-grenade lecture with my instructor, Rich, the chap who'd overheard my conversation that day with Sammy back in Umm Qasr. Everything was going fine until we practised the firing-off of grenades. We were, of course, supposed to be in a safe environment and handling duds. I wish we'd spent longer checking they weren't real smoke grenades.

'OK, James. You've loaded them in. I want you to pretend now that you've gotten into some trouble and you need to fire them off.'

I dropped down onto my gunner's seat and went through my checks before confirming to the commander that they were ready to be fired. On my nod, he went through the actions and very much to our dismay, two grenades fired off.

Horrified, the instructor and I looked at each other. How had this happened? Why were there live grenades in the gunnery wing? As the grenades fired off and bounced around the small gunnery wing hangar, Rich pulled himself out of the turret and made a run for the door. I was so shocked that the grenades had fired off that I decided to stay put, dropping to the bottom of the turret awaiting their explosion. Outside of the vehicle I could hear the other lads legging it out of the building, leaving me alone in the vehicle hoping for the best. Another instructor screamed for me to get out and run before it 'blew', so I did and climbed out of the tank. When I made it outside, everyone looked bewildered by what had gone on and fire alarms sounded all over the barracks. Thankfully, the grenades were just filled with smoke and not phosphorus, so once they'd been detonated from the side of the vehicle they just bounced around filling the air with thick white smoke. Nobody was really hurt, except one of the guys who'd jumped out of a window to safety and sprained an ankle.

A full investigation was launched immediately. I'd handled real smoke grenades in Iraq and should have noticed them when

I was loading the grenade banks up, but I hadn't even considered the possibility that those used in an instruction would be 'live'. It was a stressful episode but I came through without much trouble from the regiment. My gunnery instructor, on the other hand, was punished quite severely for the incident and was soon posted away from Windsor to finish off his time in the army. There were also questions raised about the handling and secure stowage of ammunition in general. What a day! Kempy thought the whole thing hilarious.

Despite having secured my gunnery training, I wasn't too disappointed I wouldn't have a chance to use my new skills. I just wondered when I would get the chance and who I might be working under as a gunner for the first time. Little did I know it would turn out to be Prince Harry.

We were going to Canada to act as an enemy force to a series of battle groups made up of British regiments training for deployment to either Afghanistan or Iraq. As a smaller, self-contained body, we'd give the 'good guys' a run for their money and hopefully allow them the chance to hone their battle skills. Everyone liked the sound of the job, which also promised plenty of free time while in Canada to travel and partake of some adventurous training. Preparations began immediately.

In May, news hit the regiment of a tragic incident involving a vehicle crewed by members of D Squadron, who were, at the time, serving in Afghanistan. Kempy rang me from the guardroom to tell me there had been a fatality. All around the regiment, dread settled in. It was awful. We'd lost a soldier. Trooper Babakobau, one of the two Fijian men we'd gone through riding school with years earlier, had died after his vehicle struck a mine. It was a massive blow. Every death is tragic, but Babs was someone I knew well and I mourned long over the death of my friend. There it was. One of the people I'd bonded with over the course of those winter months while learning to ride was gone. The Fijian community within the Household Cavalry went into deep sorrow and I felt for each and every one of them. His closest friend, Torou, who'd followed him from his homeland to join the British Army, walked away from his career very soon after. It was a sad state of affairs, and I'll always keep the photograph of us both, dressed in our ceremonial attire in 2004, extremely safe.

✝

Arriving into work a few days later, a casual remark about 'gay pride' caught me off guard. To my amazement, someone, some-where in the army, was trying to collect lesbian and gay soldiers to march proudly in uniform at London Pride. Incredibly, a padre was organising the effort to coincide with the navy and the Royal Air Force LGBT presence, which, by the sound of things, was slightly more developed than the army's.

I decided not to make a big fuss about the whole thing in work, but Warren secured me the day off and I was able to attend. I got on the train to Waterloo that Saturday morning very appre-hensive about how the day might unfold. Carrying my uniform in a suit carrier, my highly polished boots in a holdall, I nervously sat in the train carriage, constantly considering getting off at the next stop and heading back to Windsor.

I was worried I'd be the only person there. I was worried that I'd turn up and be pressured into something I didn't particularly want to do. But at the same time I wondered who I might meet. Would I make some new friends? I felt nervous right until I arrived at the hotel where we were meeting. I'd made the right choice to stick it out. In front of me at the hotel reception stood about fifty other uniformed men and women from across all three services.

There was a larger contingent of the Royal Navy men and women, with their smart dark blue sailors' uniforms and white caps. The RAF had slightly more personnel in the hotel foyer than the army did, too. To be surrounded by so many other different uniformed soldiers, sailors and airmen all proudly gay and ready to march at Gay Pride was the most surreal of experiences. Where had all these people been until now?

We were ushered out of the foyer and into a conference room where a gentleman, not in uniform, introduced himself as a colonel. He welcomed us along and told us why he felt it was important we were there.

'This is the military's opportunity to show the world we're gay-friendly and proud.' His words were met with applause. They struck a real chord, too. For five years I'd served and never been reassured officially by the army that I was fully accepted and, more so, wanted.

The starting point of the procession was miles across London and two coaches were needed to get us there. I'd been taken in by a group of Royal Navy sailors, by which I was delighted. They'd all been in London since the previous evening and were a little hungover to say the least. It was bizarre to be in the company of like-minded people who'd had similar experiences to me, to be unified with these people because we were gay. The conversations the sailors were having at the back of the coach were the kind I couldn't begin to repeat. The navy boys have always enjoyed limitless banter. I loved it.

As the coach door closed and we prepared to drive away, I noticed a uniformed soldier running along the pavement urgently trying to stop the coach from driving off. It was a late arrival, whom I slightly recognised. The coach stopped and the lad climbed on board. I was amazed to see the figure of a soldier in the same uniform as me and wearing the same Household

Cavalry badges. His eyes met mine and we both looked at each other with surprise. The soldier stood before me was also based in Windsor, but working in a different squadron. Marc, who was not 'out of the closet', had found the information about the pride march in the same manner I had and hadn't spoken to anybody about it. This was his coming-out day and I was gobsmacked to see him there. He told me nobody knew and I respected that. He was still finding himself, as I had done throughout my teenage years, but I knew that on that day of celebration and unity, he'd be reassured with confidence that he was not alone.

I'd never really done the whole Gay Pride thing before that day. It wasn't just my first Pride wearing uniform, but actually my first Pride full stop. As the coach meandered its way through the busy London streets, I was amazed to see so much colour and so many different people, all out to celebrate gay pride. The excitement began to build. I wondered just how loud a reception we'd get as we marched by. How would the day unfold and where would we all go after the march? Where would we party?

The coach pulled up at the starting point of the march through London and, immediately, we were hit by wave after wave of photographers and journalists. The very first time all three services were allowing personnel to take part in Gay Pride celebrations was of huge interest to the media. I was completely taken by surprise. Yes, I had a vague idea of what the whole thing was about. I understood the difficulties and discrimination the gay community had endured to be able to get to that moment of acceptance and celebration, but what hadn't occurred to me was that it was essentially a protest. A protest that signified to the world that there was still much more to be done. At the front of that protest was us, the British military. It was a hugely symbolic image.

Waiting for the nod to step off, I was repeatedly moved by people, particularly older people, who were out to celebrate,

waving rainbow flags. People would come up to us with tears
in their eyes, thanking us. Men and women who'd been on the
Section 28 marches in the 1980s against Thatcher and her homophobic policies; men and women who knew fully what it was to
be overtly discriminated against and chastised in public. People
who had been through the most horrific of experiences, who'd
fought for their rights and mine. On that day in 2008 they were
moved to tears to see us there in our uniforms, proudly wearing our medals as we proclaimed: 'We're gay!' Meeting these
people and realising that there was a whole deeper meaning
to why exactly Gay Pride existed struck a chord in me; it was
the moment I realised that the torch had been passed to a new
generation; it was the moment I realised I was an activist. And I
was proud to be one.

The two hours that followed passed by in a bubble. With the
cheers of support and well-wishing spurring us on, we marched
along, our heads held high, to the sound of a sergeant shouting
'left, right, left, right', stopping us occasionally and then setting us
back on our way. Every second of the march, people applauded
us and cheered. Thousands upon thousands of photographs were
taken of us all in our smart uniforms by members of the public,
some just ordinary people caught up in their Saturday afternoon
shopping along Oxford Street. It was quite a sight seeing the
three uniformed services all smartly marching together in step,
every single one of us smiling away to the crowd as we made our
way along the route. The feeling of exhilaration and pride will
never leave me. It was the day the British Army came out of the
closet and said, 'We're here!'

The march concluded at Trafalgar Square, where there was
a concert planned and speeches from political figures, but the
armed forces contingent marched on past the rally point. It had
been decided that we'd march down Whitehall and past the

Cenotaph, signifying a historic moment for gay servicemen and women to salute fallen comrades, comrades who'd never had the chance to do what we'd just done. In a personal note for me, we were also passing by Horse Guards on the way along Whitehall, the place I'd spent so many days on Queen's Life Guard. As we marched by, the two soldiers sitting on their horses carried their swords and saluted. I felt enormously proud. For 350 years the Household Cavalry has had a guard on Whitehall in one way or another and never before had they carried swords and saluted a body of gay men and women celebrating who they really were and the service those people were giving to the country.

As we approached the Cenotaph, the national focal point of mourning every November, the adrenalin in me began to rocket once more. I thought about all those soldiers who'd fought in both wars and in conflicts since who'd never been able to talk about their sexuality. I thought of all those soldiers who'd been criminalised for being gay and discharged from service in dishonour, just for being true to themselves. More than anything, I thought about my American friend Sammy, still serving in Iraq, his sexuality a secret to everyone around him. Tears filled my eyes as we saluted the Cenotaph. I was saluting Sammy.

After the march, instead of dispersing into the busy London scene for the evening, we found ourselves drinking together in uniform. I'd become friendly with three sailors from Portsmouth, Travis, Sam and Steffan, who were all great company. It was a pleasure to be sharing the entire experience with the three of them.

While having fun with the three sailors I noticed a very good-looking guy sitting alone, not in uniform and looking a little detached from what was going on around him. He wore a light blue jacket and had a woolly knitted hat on his head. I thought I saw him looking at me too, but wondered if I was just misreading the situation. By the time I got the opportunity to say hello, a guy in a navy outfit had sat down and was talking away with this mysterious chap. Soon, I realised that the two were a couple.

A senior officer in the navy circled the room and told people to get changed. We were getting a little too drunk to be dressed in uniform. It had taken years of difficult persuading to get us to Pride in uniform that day and nobody wanted to spoil things by being photographed in uniform misbehaving... We agreed to head into Soho a little later on and hit a few of the different bars, starting with G-A-Y, and then perhaps a club, such as Heaven. The thing about bringing a lot of out-of-towners into London was that they were clear about what they wanted to do and where they wanted to go. Personally, I'd moved on somewhat from my late nights and endless drinking in G-A-Y but understood how much of a focal point it was and a place of interest for so many. I was happy to go with the flow and, as the resident Londoner, I led the way to Soho.

Walking up to Leicester Square, I noticed the nice guy in the knitted hat had joined us with his fairly large boyfriend. There seemed to be a bit of tension between them so I thought it best not to talk to them. I was glad he was joining us, though.

An hour later we found ourselves in the main bar at G-A-Y, cramped together and fairly unable to move; it didn't dampen our fun though. Everyone was so delighted to be out together. I was having fun; I was pleased to be making new friends with like-minded people. The night continued and in the commotion of being crammed together and pushed around, I suddenly found myself stood closely next to the guy in the hat. We smiled awkwardly at each other and both struggled for some initial conversation.

'Hi... I'm Ryan.' Ryan held out his hand and smiled at me with a fixed grin. He sounded really sweet and looked amazing. His

skin was perfect, quite different from mine, and his long blond
hair just poked through the bottom of his knitted hat. I wanted
to tell him how hot I thought he looked but thought better of it.

'I'm James, I'm a soldier.'

'I know, I saw you on the march.'

'Who are you here with?'

Ryan gave a little laugh at my question. 'Yeah, he's my
boyfriend. His name is Sam.' I knew what Ryan was laughing
at. I was clearly snooping around trying to find out if he had a
boyfriend or not. I'm sure I looked more than a little disappointed.

Ryan was the first guy I'd really found myself drawn to since
Sammy. But I couldn't work out whether he was just overly
polite or actually quite interested in me and being flirtatious.
Throughout the night I saw him looking at me again and again. I
was doing exactly the same thing and I wondered if he'd noticed
me staring at him.

The night continued and the guys stuck true to their wishes
and headed down to Heaven. I took them there but the queue
was far too long and I decided not to stick around. I had thought
I might have gone home with someone as the night continued
but after meeting Ryan, I didn't really want to see anybody else.
I'd certainly grown up and changed since my younger days on
the scene, when going home alone wouldn't have been an option.
I said my goodbyes to the navy boys I'd shared the day with,
thanked them all profusely, and made my way back to my hotel.

Lying alone in my hotel bed thirty minutes later, I considered
the day's events. From feeling nervous, anxious and considering
turning around on the train in the morning, to arriving and discov-
ering so many fellow military personnel in the hotel lobby, the
huge amount of pride I had felt while marching through the capital's streets, lined with thousands upon thousands of well-wishers,
and the poignant moment of remembrance at the Cenotaph.

I'll never forget that Saturday in July 2008. It was a historic day for the military but, more than that, a historic day for me. I'd become empowered by what we'd achieved and desperately wanted the feeling to continue. But I was off to Canada.

18

CANADA: A ROYAL AFFAIR

When I look back over my decade-long journey in the army, I will always consider my four months in Canada in 2008 as the happiest. There wasn't a single second of the day that I wasn't walking around in high spirits, feeling proud of the job I was chosen to do. We worked with a variety of different regiments and, on occasion, soldiers from the Canadian military. There was plenty of chance to travel and also the opportunity to try something completely new and courageous. By the end of my time out there I was frantically trying to find a job within the army that would allow me to stay even longer. I totally fell in love with Canada and it's somewhere I really intend to spend much more time.

Two weeks after the adventure of London Pride, I was en route to Calgary, which I'd been told was a city in a place called Alberta. The plane journey seemed to take a lifetime and, it being an old RAF passenger carrier with no in-flight entertainment, I read a book cover to cover on the way over there.

We knew what job we were heading out to Alberta to do. A handful of the guys had been to Canada a few years before and carried out a similar role. From what I understood, Canada was generally a place to let your hair down. They spoke of tales involving very late nights and very drunken soldiers getting up to all sorts of mischief. I was alarmed, however, by some of their recollections of a couple of soldiers dying from excessive boozing and troublesome carryings on. Canada certainly promised to deliver on the age-old army saying 'work hard, play hard'.

The facility we were being based at was known as BATUS, standing for British Army Training Unit Suffield. Suffield was a tiny little place in the middle of the vast Canadian prairie, about three hours away from Calgary in the west. To the east, our nearest town was a place called Medicine Hut, which again was a long drive in an almost straight line. Med Hat, as it would be known, was the place we'd escape to in the evenings, without much regard for its distance. It was nowhere near as far away as Calgary, but it still took almost an hour of driving to get to. We were in the middle of nowhere.

The beautiful thing about BATUS was its sheer size. With the space to replicate the real thing, the army could conduct full warlike scenarios. It completely outweighed anything the Ministry of Defence had in the UK for troops to train at.

We were considered 'staff' while at BATUS, acting as the enemy for the troops who would be coming to Canada to train, and were put in an accommodation building that closely resembled a large block of flats, as opposed to the usual barrack-style set-up I was used to. I was to share my room with a lad called Joe Pank, who was one of the new boys in A SQN. Pank was from north London and his father was a guitarist in a famous band in the 1980s. He had plenty of tales to tell and was quite a normal bloke, until it turned out he had a nasty habit of urinating in the middle of our room when intoxicated, which was quite often.

The bar on camp was called the Longhorn and was solely for the use of permanent staff, allowing us a place to let our hair down away from the soldiers who we'd be up against out on the prairie.

It was astonishingly cheap and a place that was regularly smashed up when conflicting soldiers sought to resolve their issues.

Soon after arriving in BATUS, we headed out on exercise for a three-day opportunity to refresh our skills before going head to head against our 'enemy'. For the first four weeks of our Canadian adventure we'd be working with the Welsh Guards, a regiment we had close ties with, both being members of the Household Division, but it would play out quite differently. From the off we could see the tension between them and us. It was impossible not to notice the difference between the Welsh Guards and the Household Cavalry in terms of general behaviour and attitudes. I was very comfortable within my squadron as we had an environment of mutual respect. In the Welsh Guards, it was obvious that there was a divide between soldiers of rank and the rest. We didn't interact with them much.

Driving the squadron leader went well over the initial three days of preparation. He was happy with me and I was certainly very happy with him. As a leader he was calm under pressure, rarely getting overexcited about things, and he was somebody who took the time to talk to people. Over those three days of 'dry training', I felt a rapport had developed between us.

Immediately following our three days of training on the prairie, us 'enemy' soldiers were given a week off to undertake adventurous training. Adventurous training in the army had a bit of a poor reputation as something billed as amazing but in reality often a bit of a let-down and waste of time. In Canada, however, we had the natural resources to really kick the arse out of doing something fun, exciting and somewhat challenging.

I outright refused to participate in anything that involved jumping out of a plane, which thankfully was noted. On the other hand, some of the boys did decide that parachuting was their thing and headed off to Calgary for a week's worth of skydiving.

Some of the lads chose to do something called glacier walking in the Rocky Mountains, which I was tempted to join in with, but the extreme coldness turned me off. Pank and I and, much to my annoyance, a number of Welsh Guards opted to do something a little more pleasant: Western-style horse riding in the Rocky Mountains. It was essentially a four-day holiday on horseback, climbing the idyllic scenery of the Canadian Rockies. It was brilliant. I remember getting halfway up a mountain, surrounded by what looked like thousands of other mountains, and being completely swept away by the view. The view, the fresh air, the beautiful brown horse underneath me; it all moved me. By the end of the experience I felt like I'd seen one of the earth's most elegant sights and the whole thing had cost me nothing save a sore bottom.

We headed back to BATUS and prepared for our first go at the job we'd been sent out to do. We had two days of packing, vehicle preparation and a chance to let off some final steam in the Longhorn bar before causing the visiting troops havoc.

Our first bite at the cherry involved us heading out for fourteen continuous days of mock war fighting. It wasn't insurgency-style warfare: we'd returned to the old 'fighting the Russians' or 'conventional' warfare, which in the past had sometimes been a little boring. This, however, was not. There was a clear line of good guys – our enemy – and bad guys – us and the Welsh Guards. The organisers of the battles would give us a time and a location, radio through when to set off, and at some point we'd encounter the advancing British forces and give them a run for their money. It was bloody good training and turned out to be far more exciting than the relatively mundane tasks we'd faced twelve months earlier in a real war situation. I suppose we had the added bonus of knowing the ammunition we faced was never going to actually hurt anybody. We'd fire lasers at the enemy and, if we hit, the sensors on their vehicle would acknowledge the fact and disable their controls, making them redundant from the war game. We had the same equipment fitted to our tanks and if they scored a direct hit on us we'd be reduced to cyber rubble and face a lengthy spell immobilised on the spot. It was clever kit, but very complex and would often break down. If a cable was unplugged or a sensor knocked out of place, the alarm would sound and we'd face the same fate as if we'd suffered a direct hit. We'd work this to our advantage, too.

Our first fortnight on the prairie participating in war games had been a success, with lots of lessons learned about how we could outmanoeuvre large bodies of men and tanks, but also about how we could pull together and push forward, even under extreme fatigue. The staff running the exercises really demanded a lot from us. We'd fight a battle for ten hours, re-form to rest and conduct administration, and then move on to a new location, often dozens of miles away, with a fresh set of orders. At the end of every battle we knew not to switch off because we would have a forty-mile move to conduct. It didn't take long for most of us to realise that being 'killed' in a battle early on offered the best chance of prolonged rest. Once you'd been destroyed and taken out of a battle scenario, you were left alone until the battle was over. Some vehicle commanders were pulling off suicide-style missions with the specific intention of being destroyed by the enemy.

On the final day of the first exercise, word began to spread that we were getting ten days off to do whatever we pleased. Excitement shot through the ranks as hasty plans were drawn up. We'd been in Canada for over a month and, if our pay had been sorted accordingly, we'd all have a hell of a lot of extra cash in our wages conveniently heading our way on the first day of leave.

It seemed I'd done a good job driving the leader throughout

our first exercise and I was already looking forward to returning to the job after leave and driving for him again, but that
wasn't to be. Driving back into Suffield, the leader spoke with
me about my aspirations. He told me I ought to be thinking
about the future and that I really needed to be heading towards
a gunner's seat. I wanted to tell him that I was more than ready
and, more to the point, actually desperate to move out of the
driving seat and into the turret, but I didn't need to.

'So I've decided that I will find a new driver for the remaining
three months of BATUS. I'm moving you into a gunner's seat.' It
felt like all my Christmases had come at once. I was delighted!

'Am I to be your gunner, sir?'

'Ha! No chance. I need an experienced gunner. You're going to
gun for the new 2IC [second-in-command]. You two will work
nicely together.'

'Who's the new 2IC then, sir?'

It wasn't known at that point that we were getting a new
second-in-command. The squadron leader had been doing a fine
job on his own. Of all the names the leader was to tell me, I least
expected the one that he muttered down his microphone and
into my headset as we drove our tank home in the darkness.

'Somebody you know actually... Lieutenant Wales.'

It took me a few seconds to consider exactly who Lieutenant
Wales was. Surely it wasn't...? 'Fucking hell. Which one?'

'Harry. He's arriving next week. Don't tell the guys... most of
them have never met him.'

I finished my drive back into Suffield with the leader, thinking
about my future role as Prince Harry's gunner. I couldn't believe
events had taken such an incredible, and quite unbelievable, turn
for the better. I'd desperately wanted to be a gunner from the off
and now the job was heading my way – but I'd be the gunner to
the third in line to the throne. I couldn't believe it.

I hated that the leader had asked me not to tell the boys. I was one of the boys and keeping something as major as that quiet was a difficult task, but I knew I had to. The leader would know for sure it had come from me if the boys found out.

I parked my vehicle and closed it down accordingly. We were done. Ten days off would follow, with the whole squadron going on their various travels. The leader was off to visit a friend in New York. Three of the lads and I were off to Cancun. Canada was about to pay off!

Happily, when booking our holiday we'd seen a poster on a billboard advertising something that caught all our attentions. Oasis! One of my favourite bands of all time was throwing a concert in Calgary. In a stroke of good fortune, the concert was the night before our flight to Mexico from Calgary. We boarded a Greyhound bus, carrying our luggage and passports, and made our way to the big city in the hope of seeing the Gallagher brothers before jetting off to Mexico.

Four hours later, we rocked up at the ice hockey stadium where the concert was taking place. Purchasing tickets, we made our way into the venue and patiently awaited the arrival of the Gallaghers. When they walked onto the stage the place erupted and as soon as they finished their opening song they told the crowd that there were a lot of British soldiers among them, dedicating the gig to us all. It was amazing. The perfect start to our Mexican adventure, albeit still firmly in Canada.

After the concert, and more than a little drunk, we caught a cab to the airport and slept off our hangovers on a group of seats in the departure hall before waking up and checking in for our four-hour flight to Cancun. We were off!

We spent the week unwinding and letting off steam. Away from camp we could get up to all sorts, and we generally did. One of the boys lost his passport, however, which caused him a world of misery as he wasn't allowed to board the plane back to Canada; we had to leave him there. The squadron leader was less than impressed about this and blamed the whole debacle on the rest of us. The guy ended up flying back to the UK and remaining there.

I couldn't stop thinking about my role as Prince Harry's gunner throughout my week on holiday. I was paranoid throughout that the plans would, for whatever reason, change and I'd miss out on an opportunity of a lifetime. Somehow I'd managed not to let out the news to the other boys but it was rarely out of my mind. I did tell my mum on the phone, though; she considered it to be the biggest news the family had ever received. Everyone in the family was informed of my role in the space of about two hours. Nan, as the royal family's number one fan, was more than proud. I would tell her hundreds of stories about my time with Harry in the years that followed and they helped our relationship become closer than ever.

The squadron leader arranged for an A SQN night out in Med Hat at a bowling alley, during which Harry would be introduced to the boys. I was one of the few who'd worked with him in the past and knew a little of what he was like as a person, but for the likes of Pank, my roommate, and a number of other new faces within the squadron, it would be their first look at just who and what Harry was. There was no prior announcement, Harry just showed up with his protection officer mid-evening and said hello to the boys.

Pank's face dropped as he spotted him over my shoulder.

'Holy fuck! Fucking Prince Harry is here,' he quipped in his cockney accent.

I told him I'd known for over a week and that I hadn't been allowed to say.

'But what's he doing here? What's he going to be doing?'

'He's our new 2IC. And I'm his gunner.'

'FUCK OFF!'

I'd got over the initial excitement about the job, it was fairly old news for me, but I could see the excitement on everybody's faces. By just turning up and saying hello to everyone, he'd made morale rocket through the roof.

We played a few rounds of ten-pin bowling, at the end of which the leader brought Lieutenant Wales over to me.

'And you remember Trooper Wharton?'

'Of course I do! How are you, Ronald?' Harry offered his hand to me and I shook it, telling him I was fine.

'I'm your gunner for the next four weeks.'

'Brilliant. Are you any good?'

'Well, you're my first commander. So we'll have to wait and see, sir.'

'Well, I hope you gun better than you bowl, Ron.'

The ice was broken. I'd wondered whether Harry was going to remember me. I worried that he wouldn't and I'd have to go through the whole 'who am I' situation, which would have involved coming out to him. But he'd remembered exactly who I was.

Almost two years earlier, during the build-up to Iraq, I had a couple of the boys in my room playing on my Xbox one afternoon. Harry had joined us for a bit of fun on Call of Duty. Before he left us, he had scouted over my photos which were blu-tacked on the wall and asked me a few questions about who people were and what we were getting up to. I'd pointed out Thom to him and he'd asked if he was my boyfriend. He told me we looked good together. Having a prince tell me that my boyfriend and I looked good together always stuck in my mind. It was a surreal conversation. Over the course of the coming weeks, we'd share an awkward chat about what had happened with Thom. He was both gutted and surprised by the news.

The icebreaker night had worked well, and I could tell the boys were both enthused and encouraged by the arrival of Lieutenant Wales. As we were leaving the bowling alley, I was stopped by two middle-aged Canadian ladies.

'Is that Prince Henry of Wales over there?' The ladies were pointing at Harry.

'Oh yeah, that's him alright.' I walked off and left the women shocked by my confirmation. That would happen a lot over the following weeks.

We had about a week to prepare for our second exercise against a new force of British regiments, during which we put a lot of effort into making sure our vehicles were ready and up for the job. We still enjoyed plenty of downtime as the week went by, finishing early in the afternoon, relaxing a little and then heading out, either to the Longhorn bar or down to Medicine Hat.

Working with us for the next stage of our time in Canada was another infantry regiment. Having had a generally bad experience with the Welsh Guards, a lot of us wondered if we'd see much of the same with the new guys, but fairly soon after being introduced we found they were quite different and, similarly to us, extremely close and loyal to each other.

By the time we'd spent three full days on the tank park, tinkering away at our vehicles and preparing to deploy, everybody who worked within BATUS had become aware of Prince Harry's presence and, due to my close link to him, I found that everybody began to know me. I became aware of people pointing at me in the NAAFI during the mid-morning break or in the Longhorn bar in the evenings. I could see people mouthing the words 'Prince Harry' and 'gay gunner'. Clearly word had got around that not only was I the lucky person who was sharing a turret with the prince but also that I was gay. It didn't seem to cause me much trouble – until one evening in the bar.

The clock had been slowly ticking down to the start of our

two-week deployment, so we'd automatically kicked things up a notch and were really enjoying ourselves. My good friend Danny had been in Canada with us from the start, as had Scoffy. I'd also become very close to a guy called Alex who loved a good time, and my roommate Pank was part of our clique too. After a fairly straightforward day on the tank park, we all decided to head to the Longhorn bar and have a boozy night.

The night progressed and we found ourselves chatting away with some of the infantry guys at the bar. After a little while the conversation had drifted on to Prince Harry.

'Ask James, he's his gunner.'

I found myself talking about my commander at length, which was fine as all they really wanted to know was if he was a good guy. It was quite a good chance to break the ice a little with the people we'd be spending the next fortnight on the prairie with.

Mid-chat, one of the infantry soldiers leaned over to me and asked if he could buy me a drink. I was delighted and naturally accepted the offer. He was a younger chap, about nineteen, and looked fairly new to the whole soldier game. I took his beer and carried on the conversation but, for some reason, I felt something in the air between us.

Without wanting to make a fool of myself, I checked with Danny what his thoughts were.

'Danny, this lad talking to me at the bar. I'm sure he's trying to chat me up.'

'Really? Are you not just wishful thinking?' It was a good point. I might have been completely reading the wrong messages. I had been drinking for about two hours.

'Maybe, but he's just bought me a beer and he keeps trying to strike up a conversation.'

'I'll keep my eye on him and let you know. Fucking James! You're always a drama!'

The truth was, if the guy was trying to hit on me I wanted him to continue. I was certainly attracted to him. I went back to the bar and finished the pint the guy had bought me. After, I thought it only polite to offer him the same. He accepted my offer and, more than that, he placed his hand on my arm as I asked him. I could see Danny's eyes light up from across the bar and soon after felt my phone vibrate in my pocket. It was a text from Danny: 'Well in!'

The night continued, as did my conversation with the guy from the infantry. I've never been a betting man but I was totally convinced that this character who'd been talking to me all evening was gay and looking for a friend for the evening. He even asked me which room I was staying in and if anybody else stayed in there. I told him I had my own room as the guy I shared with was away. I texted Pank, who was stood with Danny at the bar, telling him to stay out of the room for the next hour or so. I could see them both shaking their heads at me from across the room. I smirked back at them.

'I'm heading up to my room now, actually. It was really nice to meet you.'

'Have you got any DVDs?'

'I have a few, yeah... Why? Do you want to borrow one?'

'Yeah, can I? I've seen all mine a million times!'

I couldn't believe what was happening. The guy had invited himself back to my room. He was making his intentions obvious. He knew my room was empty, he knew it was the floor below where he lived and he knew I was gay. It was a full-drawn conclusion to me. I'd pulled.

He told me he'd meet me at my room in about fifteen minutes. I thought he was a little worried about being seen leaving the bar with me. I was used to how curious straight guys operated. My life had been made a million times easier by just being open and honest about my sexual feelings.

I reminded Pank that I needed privacy for at least an hour and hastily tidied the room for my impending visitor. I also got a collection of DVDs out on the side ready for him to look through on the off-chance that he was actually coming to borrow an action movie.

Right on cue, a knock came at the door. I opened and he hastily made his way inside. He was a lot more nervous than he'd seemed earlier.

'The DVDs are there, dude.' I pointed over to them but as soon as I finished the sentence, the guy grabbed me and began to kiss me. I didn't need encouraging. We ripped each other's clothes off and spent the next hour having sex.

Afterwards, he got his stuff together and, in the darkness, left my room and went back upstairs, saying very few words before closing the door behind him. I laughed to myself about the whole thing.

The following morning was when I made my fatal mistake.

Some of the boys had been in competition as to who had got 'laid' the most while in Canada. It's something I've seen often... The boys go out and the following day they exchange their sordid tales and have a general laugh over each other's escapades. Pank was finding it particularly painful as the majority of the boys had at least got off the starting line and slept with someone while in Canada. I stupidly allowed myself to enter these discussions the following day, stating very proudly that I'd scored the night before.

Immediately, everyone knew who I was talking about. They'd all seen me spending hours chatting away to the lad and found it convenient that we'd both left in fairly close proximity to each other. The worst thing was the lad in question actually worked in the same tank hangar as us. I knew from my own experiences that it wouldn't take five minutes for the story to swoop the tank park, putting him in a very uncomfortable position.

Prince Harry entered our conversation and found the whole thing quite amusing. He jokingly referred to me as a dirty dog before walking off to do something on our vehicle.

As feared, soon enough the news had circulated and I became aware that the story had sent the infantry boys into overdrive. I could see from the turret of my tank that some of the boys had circled the poor lad and were taunting him and giving him hassle. I felt crushed that I'd caused the whole thing by opening my big mouth. I'd practically outed the poor guy.

Panicking, I dropped down into the turret and began carrying out some maintenance on the gun, hoping that the whole thing would blow over.

'James? James? Are you in there?' It was Danny. Standing up, I saw him looking at me with panic on his face.

'Mate, you need to come down here, it's all kicking off.'

What on earth was happening? I climbed down and walked over to Danny, who was surrounded by about six of the infantry guys.

The poor lad from the previous night had had a very tough morning. Everybody had heard that he'd spent the night with me in my room and everybody was taunting him. The guy was nowhere to be seen, but standing in front of me were six sergeants and Danny, and they looked extremely angry with me.

'Have you been spreading rumours about our Martin?' I didn't even know that was his name.

'What?'

'Why have you been lying, saying you've slept with one of our guys? He's no faggot!'

It appeared that in the heat of everything, Martin had denied the whole thing, understandably I suppose. This was turning into a bit of a situation. Danny was right on my side. He told them everything he'd seen and to back off. Standing in front of the angry soldiers, I felt under huge pressure. They were looking at me with such disgust.

Danny sent the angry sergeants away and I walked back to my vehicle to find Prince Harry working away at something in the turret. He asked me to help him but I just couldn't stop the feeling of complete dread in my stomach. I could tell I was about to be beaten up.

'Sir, I need to talk to you.'

'Why? What's up? Are you OK?' Harry instantly looked concerned.

'I think I'm about to be murdered by the infantry guys.'

I climbed into the turret and Harry and I talked through exactly what had happened. He had a complete look of bewilderment on his face. I didn't hold back. I told him about Martin buying me drinks, chatting me up, about my discussion with Danny. I went through the whole thing, including everything that had gone on in my room and then in the tank park that morning.

'He's saying I'm lying about the whole thing!' I really didn't want to, but I just couldn't stop the tears from welling up in my eyes.

'Right. I'm going to sort this shit out once and for all.'

Harry climbed out of the tank and left me and my tears in the turret. Across the tank park I could see Harry having a go at people while trying to collect a group of the infantrymen together. I worried he was about to make the whole thing worse, but I could see he wasn't holding back. Prince Harry was sorting out my drama. He was actually sticking up for me and my interests, and completely putting a stop to the trouble I was facing that morning. Until Harry went over and dealt with everything, I was on track for a battering. I felt rescued.

He came back ten minutes later and told me the problem had been 'sorted'. I wanted to know what had been said. Was the guy still insisting that I'd made the whole thing up?

'I knew one of his officers and we both pulled him to one side and cleared everything up. I also told those other lads to back the fuck off, too.'

The feeling of relief was beyond words. A potential nightmare had been averted thanks to Lieutenant Wales. Prince Harry had saved the day.

The day ticked on and, as it did, I could still feel the tension in the air between the infantry guys and me, despite Prince Harry's efforts. I talked with Scoffy and he told me, in a typical Scoffy way, to 'man up'.

'You've got your mates around you. What are they really going to do?'

I felt reassured by Scoffy's words, but I knew walking into the Longhorn later that evening was going to be a nightmare. I decided I wouldn't head there that night, but Danny and Scoffy insisted I went and 'faced the music'.

I walked in alone, twenty minutes behind Danny and Scoffy, expecting trouble to ignite immediately. Soldiers put their pints down and looked at me. It seemed to me that it was going to be an evening of unpleasantness. I made my way over to my friends regardless. I was over the difficult part, I thought, to hell with it. After all, I'd done nothing wrong.

An hour went by and the tension was noticeably getting worse by the minute. Danny told a few of the boys to stay behind in case it did kick off and we needed numbers. I was incredibly moved and felt well protected with Danny and Scoffy by my side. It was clear to me that my friends were ready to fight for me against a force that quite considerably outnumbered our own.

Another hour went by and, with a few pints in me, I'd found some courage. 'Fuck it,' I thought. I wanted to sort the problem out.

Among the infantry guys stood a chap a little older than me who seemed to be the centre of attention. He was tall with short blond hair and was quite an athletic-looking chap; a token rugby player and probably the 'popular' guy of the gang.

From somewhere I found the courage to approach him directly. I wanted to speak with the guys and just attempt to put my point across. Without a doubt, our two regiments were heading for a violent clash that night; by making the first move, in a somewhat diplomatic manner, I realised I had nothing to lose.

Dreading the worst, I tapped the guy on his shoulder.

I expected to be punched square in the face but, very much to my relief, my direct approach and confidence paid off. The guy agreed to talk with me.

We both grabbed an empty table and he eyed me with curiosity. I began explaining that I knew there was a clear problem between them and me, and that I thought it best to tackle the issue head on. He seemed to listen, leaning forward and scratching his chin. To my surprise, he stopped me thirty or so seconds into my speech and offered me a drink. I told him I'd appreciate a pint and he waved to a friend to get two beers for us both. The situation was bizarre. I looked over my shoulder at Danny and the boys and saw them all sat in silence, watching over us eagerly.

The guy, called Josh, listened to my story and surprised me by saying he understood. He had thought Martin had been making up stories about the previous night's events to keep face.

'But I'm angry with you for telling everyone the way you did... He's been getting picked on non-stop all day. He was crying his eyes out!'

I couldn't believe what I was hearing. Was this whole show of aggression over me outing one of their guys? All day I'd regretted gobbing off about my escapades the night before, but I'd spent the day thinking the guys were out for me for another reason, a more homophobic reason.

'I told the boys we should teach you a lesson.' Josh spoke with a strong Yorkshire accent and, despite the awkwardness of the conversation, I couldn't help finding him deeply attractive.

'I'm so sorry... and if there was some way you could tell him, I'd be so glad.'

'But it is true though, isn't it? He is gay?' Josh leaned closer to me as he asked.

'I don't know. He might not be...'

'But last night. It definitely did happen, right?'

'Yes. Of course.'

Josh sat back in his seat and pondered over our conversation for a few moments.

'And are you, like, proper gay?'

'Yes. I'm proper gay.'

'When did you know?'

Was this actually happening? Josh had now deserted our original, somewhat hostile, conversation, and gone down the road of sexuality in general. His entire body language had changed, too. He became a lot more likeable.

I appeased his curiosity for some time. Answering his questions, it dawned on me that perhaps Josh was asking them for a different reason. I wondered if Josh had ever questioned his own sexuality, but in the aftermath of the previous night's events, I was too weary to play detective.

Josh and I ended our conversation and I returned to Danny and the boys. I wanted to tell them about the bizarre turn of events and the randomness of our conversation, but I thought it best not to. I assured them that the trouble was over and that I no longer felt in danger.

Leaving the bar, I went off to check my emails. As I flicked through messages from family and friends, I noticed Josh walk past the window of the room, glancing at me and nodding as he did. I nodded back, half wondering if I wanted to continue our earlier conversation. Still twice shy from earlier events, I decided against it. It was quite a difficult choice; the more I looked at him the more attractive I found him, and the more I became curious.

After sending a summary of my activities back home, carefully missing out the details of the previous day's events, I logged off and made my way up the stairs to the middle floor, where Pank and I lived. A communal TV room joined four corridors filled with two-man rooms. I was pretty sure only the Household Cavalry occupied the floor, but on walking past the TV room I noticed through the glass windows the figure of Josh sat in the darkness. I naturally wanted to walk by, feeling that this was becoming a little awkward, but as soon as our eyes met he sprang to his feet and opened the door.

'I didn't realise you lived on this floor.' I actually knew full well he didn't.

'No, I don't. I live upstairs,' he replied. I giggled a little at the toughness of his accent.

'So what are you doing here then?' I had completely reverted to my old flirtatious self.

'I just thought we could chat.'

I sat myself down, trying to avoid looking too keen.

'No, not in here. Can I come to your room?' Was there a chance I was misreading the entire situation? Was I hoping for something that just wasn't going to happen? Did Josh simply need somebody to talk to and nothing else? I suddenly realised that Pank had left the bar before me and was now very likely fast asleep in our room. This was a problem.

'Wait here. Give me two minutes.' I rushed off to wake Pank and kick him out, panicking that Josh would get second thoughts and dash off in my absence. I unlocked my room to find Pank sat up in his bed watching a DVD.

Clearly very reluctant to leave his bed and very unwilling to vacate the room for yet another occasion, Pank responded to my plea with a simple 'Fuck right off!'

'Please Pank... I'll love you forever and I'll never forget it!'

'For fuck's sake! This is so unfair. You're outrageous!'

I left Pank to get dressed, having agreed he would vacate the room for an hour, and hurried back to Josh, who I was expecting to be gone. Much to my relief he was still sat in front of the large TV, his hood now pulled over his head.

From being the cocksure, centre-of-attention, popular guy I'd just met, Josh, who was suddenly in my room taking off his jeans, was a completely different person. He was visibly nervous about the entire situation he'd put himself in, looking to me and asking questions with a certain innocence. He was still confident but somehow more submissive, impressionable and boyish.

Hardly any words were spoken; simply, 'Tell anybody and I'll kill you.' The whole thing happened quickly. Josh was, in my opinion, far more repressed than Martin had been the night before. He had a very clear understanding of the things he was doing and the messages he was giving off. I really liked the guy, although the memories of my stint in Chelsea and Westminster hospital after a similar situation three years ago kept creeping into my mind. To begin with I could tell he was on the verge of grabbing his stuff and walking out at any moment, but once he was over his nervousness, Josh let himself go with the moment. I wondered if he'd ever done this before. Once things got underway, he seemed to be pretty fluent in the things we were doing. I almost felt like he was setting the pace. When we finished, he barely said a word, just quickly dressed himself and headed for the door. Before unlocking it, he turned to me and reiterated his message: 'Tell anybody and I'll kill you.' I didn't intend to tell a soul.

Pank returned to the room soon after, prompting me to ask how he'd known we'd finished.

'I saw him walk past the TV room, his shirt was on inside out and he was sweating. Doesn't take the brains of a mathematician to figure out he was your guest and you'd fucked him!'

Pank, who'd I'd considered quite straightforward and perhaps even a little dim-witted on occasions, was right on the money. I asked him to respect Josh's privacy and he agreed. All things considered, I was a much worse roommate to him than he could ever have been to me, even if he did piss on the carpet every time he was drunk. Maybe he did it as payback.

The following morning I intended to maintain my promise to Josh about the things we'd done the night before, even though I thought it unfair the other guys were able to head into Med Hat, sleep with a random stranger, sometimes a hooker, and be able to brag and boast to their hearts' content the following morning in work. I was unable to do that; anybody I slept with immediately became everyone's business and gossip always ensued.

When Lieutenant Wales turned up and began packing some personal effects away in the stowage bins at the side of our tank, he looked a little surprised to see me in one piece, unbeaten, and mentioned that I'd 'survived the night'.

I knew I could trust him and that he was a man of principle, so I leaned over to him and told him I'd done more than survive. 'Fuck off! Who?' He looked at me straight in the eyes. He couldn't believe that I'd done exactly the same thing again.

I left the information there but it was enough for Harry to chew over for the rest of the day. As the morning continued he'd keep muttering words like 'outrageous' and the like. He joked that I'd be put on a 'sex ban', which I laughed off.

It was the day before our two-week exercise was due to get underway. Our enemy for the fortnight had already been on the prairie for a week, undergoing training in preparation for our arrival. The squadron, with the morale boost that Prince Harry had brought out to Canada with him, was extremely eager to get out there and give the new enemy a run for their money.

Quite unexpectedly and while we were still pottering around the vehicle, Harry's mobile phone rang and, much to my fascination, he answered it with a 'Hey Dad! How's it going?' I found it incredible that stood next to me was the third in line to the throne, casually on the phone to the first in line to the throne. I chuckled to myself, thinking that all we needed next was Her Majesty to call.

A message got to me from one of the boys that the squadron leader needed to see me in his office at the other side of the tank hangar. Walking over, I thought it must be to do with the shenanigans of the past two days and perhaps he was just going to have a quiet word in my ear. Arriving at his office, I knocked on his door and peered in, looking quite sheepish.

'Ah, Trooper Wharton. Excellent. Come in and sit down.' Maybe I wasn't in trouble.

'I have a very important job I need you to carry out in secrecy.'

I wondered what on earth I could possibly be asked to do. The office door was shut behind me and the leader leaned forward to discuss the important details.

'Tomorrow is Lieutenant Wales's twenty-fourth birthday. I want us to mark the occasion when we get out onto the prairie with the whole squadron.'

'Erm, OK, sir.'

'I want you to get a birthday cake from somewhere. Can you get transport to the Walmart in Medicine Hat?' I'd been in the army long enough to know full well that the leader was basically saying 'Go to the Walmart and buy him a cake.' It didn't matter whether I had transport available or not.

'Righto, sir, mum's the word.'

The leader thanked me for my time and discretion then sent

me on my way. On reaching the vehicle Harry asked me if all was OK. Making something up on the spot, I told him I had to sort out a clerical issue. He bought it and let me go.

Brilliantly, the motor transport team at BATUS allowed me to loan a vehicle from them just as long as I had it back fairly quickly. I didn't want to waste my time explaining what I needed it for, although they did persist. I lied and told them one of the boys was very ill and needed treatment. Original, I thought, if not a little inappropriate.

The cake selection at the Walmart in Medicine Hat was slim to none. I had the choice between Sesame Street and 101 Dalmatians. The leader had not provided any money for the task, I was making the shortfall in that department, but I opted for the Sesame Street offering and paid $20. I wasn't at all bothered about forking out myself; this would be a great tale to tell the family.

An hour later and once the borrowed car had been returned, I headed back to my room, Sesame Street cake underarm, to store it for safekeeping. Pank laughed as I entered the room and made a joke about me holding the cake.

'Is that for your new friends in the infantry?'

'No, you dick. It's for Prince Harry. It's his birthday tomorrow. And don't say a fucking word!'

I spent the rest of the night preparing for our time away. I stocked up on Haribo and Liquorice Allsorts, bought copious amounts of Spam and packet after packet of Super Noodles, which I thought were considerably overpriced in Canada as compared to the UK. We sorted our kit out and en masse entered the Longhorn for a final few drinks before deployment.

The following morning would be the beginning of two weeks that would test my professional relationship with Prince Harry, and deal with the highs and lows of hard, conventional war training. It would be two weeks I'd never forget.

19

THREE MEN IN A TANK

The following morning, I fully took charge of the loading of kit onto our vehicle, having carefully placed the Sesame Street cake in the back bin and covered it with camouflage and a water-proof protective sheet. Our driver, a lad called Dan, was in on my secret as I didn't want him to throw a heavy bag in the back bin and squash Big Bird. The squadron leader gave me an awkward wink, looking for reassurance I'd followed his plans to the letter. I gave him a thumbs-up and pointed to the back bin.

Eventually we rolled out of the back gates and onto the vastness of the Canadian prairie. I enjoyed being a passenger rather than the driver, where I would constantly have my ability scrutinised. I'd vowed never to be as ridiculous as some previous gunners I'd had the displeasure of driving for. Some could be unfair and, to be blunt, turn into whinging backseat drivers.

Initially we had a large move to carry out. We were travelling to the extreme north of the area, a trip that would take three hours easily. In the fortnight since we'd last been out, I could feel the temperature had dropped; to me this was a good thing as I'd found the heat overpowering on occasion during the first exercise. As we bobbed along, occasionally banging our hips on the hatches to our turret, Harry and I shared Haribo and the three of us participated in light conversation and banter over the vehicle's intercom system, which was crucial to communication because of the noise of the diesel engine and constant sound of tracks cutting up the ground.

Harry mentioned that he and his brother had been informed some time ago that they were both gay icons. This caused me to laugh.

'What? What? We are!'

'I don't think you are, sir!'

'Why? We are! Our press people told us!'

'Honestly, I'm sure you're not...'

'Is it because I'm fucking ginger?'

I could hear Dan giggling. Harry laughed a little and we returned our concentration to the task at hand. After what seemed like an eternity, we finally reached our location.

Almost immediately, the leader spoke with me on the quiet and told me to prepare the cake, shoving a bunch of feeble candles into my hand. I carried the cake in secrecy to the back of a Land Rover. The last thing in the world I needed at that moment, as the entire squadron and our infantry friends grouped together to listen to the leader's address, was gusting wind but guess what? It seemed windier than it had ever been.

I lit the candles, nervously looking over to the men who were about to sing 'Happy Birthday' to the prince. The leader was buying me time by welcoming everyone to the exercise but I could tell he was getting impatient.

Realising I had little choice other than to hope for the best, I shielded the cake and candles from the wind as best I could and made my way into sight of the boys and Prince Harry. On cue, the guys burst into jubilant song.

Upon reaching the prince, who'd been ushered into the centre, I presented his cake, with its extinguished candles, and wished him a happy twenty-fourth birthday. 'You've fucked this up,' he joked, shaking my hand. It was exactly the right level of humour required at that very moment. The leader led the applause and everyone wished Harry three cheers. Our entertainment was over.

'Where the hell did you find that cake?' the leader asked afterwards. I resisted boring him with endless points about the lack of resources available to me considering the time frame I had to work in. In fact, he loved the cake, everybody did. The staff responsible for conducting the exercise told Harry and me that we were the prize target for the training troops, who'd caught wind that Harry was one of the enemies out to get them. They warned us that we would probably be the priority target in every battle throughout the two-week war and that we shouldn't become too disheartened by the fact.

The enemy had carried out their intel and discovered what call sign our vehicle was. 9.1 had become the main effort for the training troops, but Harry was ready to take on their fight and outsmarted them from the start.

Cleverly, Harry decided to change the numbers on our vehicle with another. The commander of the vehicle in question was quite put out about the whole thing, but Harry held more weight as an officer than the corporal in command of the now doomed vehicle. The decision was made. I'd find this was just one example of the sharp wit and clever tactics I'd remember Harry for.

The exercise got off to a flying start. Between the two of us we had a good tally of confirmed kills and Dan was an excellent getaway driver. We'd taken on some pretty large outfits of men and generally come off the better.

As our time on the prairie progressed, the activities we were asked to undertake gradually became more and more challenging. One night we were given a long move to carry out, under the cover of darkness and in full tactical conditions.

It was a painstakingly long drive, which minute by minute became more stressful for me as a passenger in the turret of our vehicle. I realised that I was a much calmer soldier being responsible for the safe delivery of a crew, in the driver's seat as opposed to standing by and relying on someone else.

The calm prairie landscape was interrupted occasionally by a sombre lone white cross, signifying the precise spot where a soldier had lost his life in a training incident. I'd have felt more at ease if there was only the odd one of these but, much to my distress, there were many. I considered the sadness a loved one must feel on hearing the news that their soldier had died in a peacetime accident while training in Canada. After the previous year spent abroad in hostility, I know that news would crush my own mother.

Throughout the move, Harry, much to my relief, had decided on occasion that the landscape was too severe and gave the order for Dan to switch on our headlights. As soon as the immediate danger had past, Harry had the lights turned off again, in keeping with our orders.

Dan also had his night-vision sight, used from inside his driver's cab; Harry was using a night-vision device he'd acquired from somewhere, too. I spent most of the journey hoping for the best with my bare eye.

Suddenly, chaos ensued. We'd been driving along at an incredibly steady speed, a little over ten miles per hour, when out of the complete blue, smash! We'd landed in trouble.

The whole thing happened in an instant. While crawling along, none of us had noticed a sudden drop in our path, completely undetectable in the sheer darkness of the vast Canadian plain. The moment we rolled off the edge of the drop, I thought we were driving off a high cliff, heading for the ground far below and our death. The drop seemed to last forever and as soon as we hit the bottom of the hole we'd driven into, the three of us were knocked and tossed around our small armoured vehicle. I was thrown forward and my head hit the sighting equipment to the main weapon system. I could hear through my headset that Dan was conscious and making a noise. I looked over to Harry, sat just a foot away from me in the centre of the turret, dreading what I'd see.

Like me, he'd been thrown face first into his sights and was rubbing his face after the knock he had just taken. The commander and gunner relationship was quickly forgotten as I grabbed him to make sure he was OK. He was. Although I'd not totally switched off from the fact that he was a high-ranking member of the royal family, he had become familiar enough to me and enough a part of my everyday life to be considered one of the lads.

The three of us climbed out and drew what artificial light we could onto our damned vehicle to survey the damage. The drop, although it had felt severe and long, was actually about two metres. Initially I'd considered the vehicle to be in a desperately poor state, but apart from the crushed stowage bins at the front and a couple of smashed headlights, it looked in good working order.

Throughout the move Danny and his crew had been driving behind us. As soon as we were no longer detectable in front, he'd switched his headlights on. With his wealth of experience, he took charge of the situation and oversaw the recovery of our vehicle.

The accident did nothing for my confidence with regard to being a passenger rather than a driver, and I couldn't help feeling that the incident had really knocked my courage levels in being a gunner. The ditch we'd driven into could easily have been a cliff or even simply a larger hole, resulting in a much worse outcome.

I also felt that Harry had to an extent enjoyed the experience; I think it underlined the dangers associated with armoured vehicle tactics and the realism of training for war, maybe reigniting feelings he'd experienced earlier in the year while fighting in Afghanistan. In the hours that followed, after endless worrying, Harry told me to 'man the fuck up and stop acting like a fanny'.

Mid-exercise, Harry was called to a briefing along with the other commanders, reviewing the progress of the exercise. When he returned, he looked more than a little excited.

'Great news, we're the call sign with the most confirmed kills!'

He was right, this was great news. To be in the running for 'top gunner' on my first exercise was pretty incredible.

'I want to win this title!' Harry exclaimed.

We had our carrot, and we intended to see the job through. The infantry soldiers, who like us were steeped in tradition and history, were offering a medal to the call sign crowned Top Gun at the end of the exercise. Within their regiment, one of these medals was seen as a very notable achievement. Although fairly insignificant to us Household Cavalrymen, in reality the competitive streak in both Harry and me really whetted our appetite. We wanted that medal.

Our hunting began in earnest the following day. At one point, it was going so well I couldn't help considering why we were achieving so many 'confirmed kills'. Was our enemy simply not as good as us or were they just not putting enough effort into their training?

Throughout our trials, there was one recurring point that marred our impressive tally: my fairly inexperienced drills in turret. Yes, I was getting the kills, but carrying out the correct drills in order for me to get a shot off onto the enemy was continually going wrong. The news that another call sign in our enemy collective was catching up fast with us only fuelled tensions in our turret.

Harry had tapped into a member of the exercise staff who was feeding him information on how many kills we were on and how many our closest contender was on too. He'd hear daily if we were in a comfortable lead or if things weren't looking great.

Three days before the end, the gap between us and the other call sign, manned by soldiers from the Royal Tank Regiment, was down to just two. All our hard work had been closely matched and we worried the chance of winning Top Gun was slipping away from us.

Patrolling along in an area where we knew the enemy was hiding, suddenly we encountered a fully exposed main battle tank sat broadside on the top of a hill. It was a dream of a target for me, as all I really needed to do was aim into the centre and fire. I was in position quickly and when Harry gave the order to fire, much to his and my annoyance, nothing happened. Immediately I knew I'd made the same mistake again, only this time things really mattered as we desperately needed to improve our kill tally. By the time I'd sorted the problem and pressed the button I was continuously forgetting to press, the tank had driven off and into cover. A missed opportunity.

Annoyed, Harry turned to me. I knew I was in for an ear bashing.

'If you forget to do that again, I'm seriously going to knock you the fuck out!' He wasn't joking.

I could hear Dan cough uncomfortably in his driver's seat. Harry was understandably frustrated. It was my responsibility to carry out the drills properly in order to successfully destroy the enemy without hindrance. I'd failed and he was furious.

For about an hour hardly a word was spoken and, as if our day couldn't get any worse, somebody managed to get a shot off on us which took us out of the battle. We'd hopelessly managed to add nothing to our kill count, and we fretted thinking about how many kills the other team was getting in our absence.

We remained at the location we'd been destroyed at for about six hours, mock battles still raging around us. We displayed our shamed green flag, signifying our redundancy from the game.

Dan was becoming chattier as the exercise continued. At first, I think he was quiet due to the situation he found himself in. Among the squadron, apart from Scoffy, I was probably the loudest character. The added weight of having Lieutenant Wales meant that he just didn't seem to make much noise. It was good to get to know him.

Harry took the opportunity of being alone in the middle of nowhere with the two of us to have a bit of a chat. Thankfully, he seemed to have forgotten about the whole gunnery incident and the three of us passed the time by discussing each other's backgrounds.

Harry asked what our plans were for Christmas and in turn we both told him. The hours passed by nicely and I realised how very surreal and rare an opportunity it was to hold a personal discussion with one of the most famous men in the world.

'When did you realise you were gay?'

'I always knew to be honest. Just never really wanted to say.' Harry nodded in understanding. Dan piped up with another question.

'Have you ever had a girlfriend, like?'

'Yeah... I had one when I was growing up, nothing too serious though.' I thought that might have been the end of the conversation.

'Did you ever sleep with her?' asked Harry.

'I did, actually. I don't think I was ever any good at it though. I certainly didn't enjoy it.' The three of us laughed at the thought.

'How old were you?' asked Harry.

'About fifteen. It was more about keeping face.'

Dan then explained the circumstances surrounding the loss of his virginity, captivating both Harry and me.

'Well, you've heard ours,' I said, turning to Harry. 'What about you? When did you pop your cherry?'

Harry told us both an extraordinary tale about what exactly happened in the lead-up to the first time he'd had sex. It was fascinating. Afterwards, I considered what diverse backgrounds the three of us had, but how we'd all completely accepted the differences in our lives and shared our stories. Dan's was interesting because of the environment he was raised in; mine was different as it involved both boys and girls, and Harry's was unique simply because he was born into the royal family. Class went out of the window, as did upbringing and sexuality. While we shared our personal stories, the three of us leaned on an unspoken pillar of respect that bonded us as a team. It was incredible.

The exercise team resurrected our vehicle overnight and at six the following morning we were ready to embark on our penultimate day of hunting. We had no idea if we still held the lead on the kill front, but we desperately wanted to take the crown upon the call of 'end-ex' the following day. The usual excitement surrounding 'end-ex' was fairly insignificant to me on this occasion; I knew it would mark the end of mine and Harry's time working together.

The day started off well. I'd consciously made an effort to rid myself of my repeated mistake behind the gun. Our enemy were as professional as they'd been throughout – so, not very – and we tallied our way through the morning.

After one such battle, Harry decided we could have a break and I dropped into the turret to make the three of us coffee, using the boiling vessel stored inconveniently in the corner. Harry's thermal mug was bright orange and I joked that it matched his hair.

Over the radio, while enjoying the lull in activity, the three of us heard a call for help. Harry answered, stating our position. The call was for medical assistance after a crash of some sort.

'They need a medic!'

'I'm a team medic if that's any help?' I returned.

A team medic was a soldier who wasn't a professional medic but trained as much as possible to step up into the medic role if the situation ever called for it. They were introduced for the Iraq and Afghanistan conflicts as a way to deal with the endless streams of casualties and the fairly small number of 'proper' medics on hand at the time.

'I've got a team medic here, we're 2 km away from you,' Harry told the worried person over the radio.

Suddenly we had our green flag flying and were on our way to help somebody. The pair of us mentioned that it was far from what we'd have wanted, but ultimately the right thing to do. We got to the stricken vehicle and spent about thirty minutes with them, giving what immediate care I could. Soon enough a safety vehicle came and took the injured guy, and his crew, away.

The day was over not so long after. The battle had purposely ended early to give everyone the chance to rest ahead of the final push. Harry had been briefed and found that we were completely level pegging with the Tank Regiment call sign and the competition for Top Gun was going to run right to the end.

The vehicle in question, our nemesis in the running for the Top Gun award, parked right up next to us that night. It was a nice opportunity to talk with the guys from the Royal Tank Regiment. They teased that we might as well forget about winning the prize and we returned with, as expected, like-for-like comment. I had somewhat forgotten about the status of our crew with our very special commander, but seeing the jubilant faces on the visiting Royal Tank Regiment crew's faces, at once I was aware of our situation again. I wondered if Harry knew how important and proud a moment it was for people to see him and serve with him? Harry's – and William's – story was one the whole nation had been caught up in. Every single person in the country had a vested interest in their livelihood. We'd all seen them grow up on our screens, in our papers, and to suddenly be thrown into the middle of that whirlwind of a life was simply remarkable.

Our final day started early. We were to lie in ambush awaiting the passing of the enemy troops. They appeared right on time and we opened up on them, claiming an easy three kills in the process. We dampened our own celebrations, knowing that our rival call sign would have probably had the same success from their vantage point. A little after our ambush we carried on the hunting game and took out another two vehicles. I imagined the pride of marching out and collecting our medal. It was my first time in the turret and I might be awarded from the start.

Out of absolutely nowhere, our sirens started to sound and our lights began to flash. We'd been hit. I dropped down into the turret to read the display screen. We'd been destroyed. Our fight was over. I stood back up and saw Harry swearing at someone. A sneaky enemy Challenger Two tank had crept up on us from behind a hill. It took one shot. Our running for Top Gun was over. We were in the hands of the gods as far as victory was concerned.

In an incredible turn of events, our rival vehicle drove straight into our area and entered a battle with a group of infantry soldiers who were heavily armed with anti-tank weapons. The three of us sat on our doomed vehicle and watched as they drove right into the path of the waiting troops. In a flash, they'd been destroyed.

From the distance we could see their commander throw his

headset off. He was having a right go at his gunner, who just stood there looking sheepish. Harry and I laughed. They reversed and pulled up next to us.

'How many kills did you get?' the young commander shouted over. I was about to reply with the truth, but Harry beat me to it.

'About twelve!' The face on the commander dropped. They drove off and settled in the spot they'd been destroyed in. Defeated, the commander displayed his green flag.

'I'm not letting on to those cunts!' Harry said afterwards, a grin on his face.

Shortly after, the 'good guys' had defeated all of us 'baddies'. The war was over. End-ex!

We had a long journey back to Suffield, which took about two hours. Nobody spoke about the result; we were left brewing for the entire journey. Upon finally reaching our hangar, Harry dashed away to sniff out a potential result, leaving Dan and me to unpack our kit and put the vehicle to bed. He returned some time later, expressionless.

'Well... Did you learn anything?'

'WE GOT IT!'

The three of us jumped up and down with joy. It was like winning the FA Cup. I couldn't believe it. Trooper Wharton: Top Gun at the first attempt. I put it down to the winning combination of a prince and a commoner from North Wales.

Danny and Scoffy were both chuffed for us. Danny bought lots of drinks at the bar that night and referred to me as 'Top Gun' constantly. I was over the moon.

The following day, the entire group of enemy troops was pulled together. The colonel from the infantry regiment wanted to say a few words about the exercise and, of course, present me with my Top Gun award. I was extra smart that day and walked with a spring in my step.

All 200 of us formed up. Harry, Dan and I stood together, so the three of us could lap up praise when the right moment came. The colonel began with the usual spiel about effort and congratulated us all for performing well throughout. Then it was on to the prize.

'The crew with the most kills has performed far better than anyone ever expected. They showed grit and determination throughout.' I was struggling to keep the smug grin off my face. 'So I'd like the commander of 9.1 to come out and collect this award, Lieutenant Wales!'

Harry sprang to attention and marched out. I couldn't believe he was being rewarded for my skill behind the gun. Where was the justice? He accepted the award and the entire enemy force applauded. No award for me!

Afterwards, the squadron leader came to congratulate me and patted me on the back. I thanked him but moaned that I'd not received a medal, to which he laughed. 'That's how it works, Trooper Wharton. The commander always takes the glory.'

And he was right. It was, of course, Harry's strong leadership – far stronger than most of the officers I'd ever worked with before – that had got us to the level we were at. From his relatively short experience, I'd learned a hell of a lot about commanding. He'd shown me how to navigate best with a GPS, how to 'sneak' around hillsides and land features without exposing the vehicle and, more than anything, he'd shown me how to command with real leadership. Without his motivation and attributes as a boss, undoubtedly we'd not have achieved the Top Gun status we had.

I knew that Lieutenant Wales wasn't staying with us for our final exercise in Canada, but had to head back to the UK to be a prince again for a while. Throughout our time together in the turret of 9.1, there wasn't a single moment that I didn't cherish. I'll probably never meet him again but I enjoyed every bit of the exercise with him. I appreciated his openness, the way he spoke with personality on almost anything, the way he almost stripped his royal title off himself every time he entered the turret next to me. Most of all, I admired his kindness. I'll never forget the four weeks we worked together and the incredible conversations we shared. Today, whenever I see him on TV, I want to tell the person next to me that I 'knew him once', but every time I do, I stop myself. The four weeks I spent with him were, of course, professional and part of my duty as a soldier. On leaving the service and moving into the civilian world, the experience lives on in my memories as the single most stand-out period of my decade in the military. I will never forget the time I spent with Prince Harry.

20

THE POSTER BOY OF
MODERN EQUALITY

I returned from Canada on 11 November 2008 to some very pleasant news. Ryan, the mysterious guy from Gay Pride four months earlier, the chap who was in a relationship with a sailor from the Royal Navy, had tracked me down on Facebook and sent me a very nice message. The message was quite short and to the point: He and his boyfriend were no longer an item and he'd very much like to go out for dinner with me. I was thrilled.

Ryan was studying journalism at the University of Winchester, a whole hour away by car from Windsor. Initially I didn't mind the prospect of driving the distance to meet up with him, but in the weeks that followed, when it became more obvious that we both really liked each other, the driving became quite heavy, day in day out. But, it was certainly worth it. Ryan was the first person I'd been seriously keen on since my short-lived experience with Sammy in southern Iraq over twelve months ago.

We didn't rush anything, indeed it took two whole months before we made it 'official', but with Ryan I found a character with lots of charm and with a lot of love to give.

In March, after Ryan and I had been together for nearly three months, I was pulled into a meeting with some high-ranking officials within the army, a meeting that would change my future in the military and, to an extent, my life in general.

The army, apparently, just didn't look gay-friendly enough. Someone, somewhere high up in the chambers of power within the Ministry of Defence, had been put under pressure to make the British Army more appealing to the gay community and, in turn, make it more gay-friendly overall. They wanted my help.

The officers had a plan that involved me talking about my positive experiences as a soldier with the press. To be fair, on the whole, I'd had a reasonably pleasant time, but just in case I was thinking of talking about the time I was beaten up for being gay or my first day in the army when I was told 'faggots' wouldn't be tolerated, I was completely banned from talking about any negative experiences I might have had.

The whole thing was billed as being an exercise that would score the army more points in the equality league tables, but the results of the PR work would turn out to be far more significant.

I went along to the offices of *Soldier*, the British Army's internal magazine, read by every soldier every month, to do an interview and have my picture taken a few times. Like the officers who'd arranged the interview, the journalists there were playing the whole thing quite calmly, suggesting that it might be half a page or, at best, a full page in the middle of the magazine where I'd discuss and explore my experiences.

The afternoon went fine and the questions were pretty general on the face of things. When did you realise you were gay? When did you come out? Has it ever affected your ability to be a soldier? Do you have a boyfriend? Is he a soldier? I answered the gentleman's questions, posed for a few shots and went on my way. I met Ryan after the interview and we both headed off to London to see Britney Spears in concert.

Three weeks went by without a word. Day after day, I

wondered what the article would look like and if anybody would even notice it. Maybe they wouldn't even run it. The guys at the magazine said it wouldn't be possible to send me a copy before publication due to time constraints, so I had to just sit patiently until it arrived in camp. Then, all of a sudden, it did.

I walked into the NAAFI to see about thirty soldiers sat around all holding copies of the magazine, which had, to my huge surprise, me on its front cover. I couldn't believe it. There I was in my ceremonial uniform holding my cap in one arm with the word 'Pride' below me.

I grabbed a copy and began flicking through. Three whole pages about me and my life! All the guys were reading it with interest, which was a little too much for me at that point, so I dashed out of there and headed to my room, clutching a copy close to my chest.

The interview was great. It wasn't unfairly written, which I have to admit was a worry of mine leading up to publication, and the pictures were very professionally done. I very much liked the whole thing, it was just the thought that everyone in the regiment was, at that time, reading it and probably making comments that worried me.

The magazine hadn't just turned up in Windsor that day, it had been delivered everywhere and the constant text messages and Facebook comments I received reminded me of the fact. It seemed the magazine had been received rather well. More so, at the end of the interview it had a contact number for information, including a plug for London Pride, which was fast approaching. As far as I was concerned, I'd done my bit and, potentially, a few more gay people might find the confidence to be themselves as a result and perhaps even turn up and march at Pride. But it wasn't to be the end of my role in improving the image of the army.

The day after publication I received a phone call from one of the officers who'd been responsible for the press work. He said that a lot of newspapers had seen the magazine and that they wanted to interview me. My number was passed on and I spent an entire morning giving interviews to a number of British newspapers. *The Independent* even sent a journalist to the barracks in Windsor to question me.

I was the first openly gay person ever to appear on the cover and within the pages of *Soldier*, a historic publication serving members of the army since the Second World War, and that very fact was what the newspapers were mostly interested in. By the end of the week, my story had been in almost every major newspaper in the country and, all of a sudden, I was of interest to important people and large organisations. The *Daily Mail*, renowned for taking a somewhat right-wing approach to liberal matters, even dubbed me 'The Poster Boy of Modern Equality'. It was all very flattering.

The attention was surreal and I kept thinking that somewhere, someone who was not in a great place personally, or who was struggling to come to terms with their own sexuality or situation, would read about me, my good-news story, and somehow feel a little better about who they were.

I soon became aware that the publicity had caused a bit of a rift in some areas of the forces community. The Army Rumour Service website, aptly nicknamed ARRSE, became the centre of all things homophobic and hateful. *Soldier* was inundated with negative feedback and, quite frankly, hurtful letters about me and gay people in general. Much to my annoyance, *Soldier* concentrated on publishing these letters in the issues that followed, rarely mentioning any support that had been given. I could also tell that within my own regiment, the Household Cavalry, the senior echelons were taking a slightly dim view of the barrage of publicity the regiment was receiving as a result of my story. The boys, and the people I was surrounded by day in, day out, thought it was brilliant, but I was aware of some of the comments that were being made by colonels behind closed doors. The most traditional regiment in the entire world was suddenly in the media for also being the most gay-friendly.

Across the pond in America, much unknown to me at the time, my story had been picked up and repeatedly republished online and in newspapers all over the States. The positive story about me and my service, my frank account of how life had been, although missing some facts that it hadn't all been easy, was being used to apply pressure on the US government. Bloggers and gay rights campaigners lobbied the Senate to act on 'Don't Ask, Don't Tell', using me as their tool. As I became aware of this, I kept thinking about Sammy. I wondered if he'd seen the coverage. A little bit of me fantasised that I'd log onto Facebook and be greeted with an out-of-the-blue message of support from him, but it never came to be. I hoped he was OK and doing well.

All this sudden attention blurred slightly the responsibilities I had as a soldier. Whereas I should have been concentrating on my career, getting up early and being fully involved in my duties within the Household Cavalry, for a little while my life became about representing the army at the right events and talking positively about life as a gay soldier to important people. These events were mostly city-based, with large banks hosting receptions for cross-industry experts on equality. This was clearly very new ground for the army, but right among the middle of all those suits, well-paid bankers and politicians was me, often feeling like a fish out of water.

Things with Ryan gradually became strained as the weeks went by. It's a huge shame, because if both our situations had been just a little different, I'm almost certain we'd have maintained a long and happy relationship. He was extremely busy in his last year of university and, not at all to his discredit, often needed to spend evenings and weekends glued to his laptop typing up dissertations and essays. My new-found fame became quite a distraction too.

It's a very shaming fact that I now realise I was more interested in wining and dining with people in the City than sitting around a house in the middle of Winchester with the person I was supposed to be in love with.

A month later, in early July, the capital was playing host to Gay Pride once again. I was hugely excited for a repeat of the previous year's events, of the fun and all the friends I'd made. Incredibly, besides Ryan, I'd not seen any of the people I'd met the previous year since then, so I was keen to pick up where we'd left off and continue our camaraderie and support of each other. I intended to march once again, as did a number of other soldiers who'd made the journey to London. There was a notable increase in the number of soldiers who'd come to take part in the celebrations and I realised then how great the impact of the media work I'd been doing for the army had actually been.

The day before the march, on the Friday, senior officials in the Ministry of Defence had arranged a conference about lesbian and gay employees within the services. It was only really attended by civil servants who worked within the MOD, but I had been invited along as a guest.

I was delighted to be there and very much enjoyed hearing the stories of other gay and lesbian people who'd spent a long time in the closet. Their stories resonated with my own and, suddenly, the penny dropped. I realised that gay people, particularly in the military, performed better as a result of being accepted for who they really were. I realised that my service could have been enormously different if I'd remained in the closet or if I'd come out and not had the support I'd had from the likes of Dean and Faulkner.

At the end of the conference, before the wine began to pour, the gentleman who was hosting the event, a person who is still a very good friend today, informed the audience that the 'cover star of *Soldier* magazine', which he held up high in the air, was sat among them. He encouraged me to stand up, which I nervously did, and I was met with rapturous applause. I was incredibly moved. Everyone at the conference, most of whom I'd never even met, clapped and cheered. I felt honoured. It underlined again just how much of a difference my article had made.

Pride weekend 2009 was significant. The year before had been a moment for the world to take note and see that there were gay people in the military and that those people mattered; 2009 was all about moving forward, cementing support for each other and realising that change does happen, however gradually.

We marched proudly and partied the night away. It was a hugely successful turn-out and I loved meeting so many new people from across the three services. The peak of the day was watching Lady Gaga, who threw a gig for the gay revellers in Heaven at midnight. It was magical.

On the Sunday, a large group of us met at the lobby of the hotel we were staying in. We had breakfast together and, one by one, people said their goodbyes, heading off to catch trains and coaches back home. There was a fairly sombre feeling in the air as each person left; the idea that it would be another twelve months until we'd all see each other again was quite a depressing thought. Soon there were just a handful of us left and it was almost time for me to say my goodbyes. It occurred to me that, actually, there was nothing stopping us from meeting up again before the next Pride. As the person who lived closest to London, and probably knew London best, I realised that I could simply arrange a gathering of people, to just mix and socialise, with relative ease. All I really needed to do was invite people to the city and go with the flow. It was the moment the Gay Members of the Public Services social group was created.

The following month, as easy as that, a group of gay servicemen and women met up at a central London venue and carried on almost exactly as we'd left off. Sensing the general success of the evening,

I repeated the event the following month, booking a proper space in a well-known gay bar, Ku, in Soho and inviting gay people from other uniformed services. The night went brilliantly and it became clear that such social events had been missing from the gay scene. My group was backed by senior support from the three services, with regular attendees including wing commanders and lieutenant colonels. The event still runs today. Though I have passed the management of the social group on, I am extremely proud that I created a regular event that has supported hundreds of gay people across the public services, and has also raised thousands of pounds for a number of charities. It's almost impossible to feel isolated in the armed services as a gay person today, unlike I did when I first came out, and I'm certain that's due to the huge level of support on offer to servicemen and women that was created by the establishment of the Gay Members of the Public Services monthly social in London. An infantry soldier, higher in rank than me, pulled me aside one evening and thanked me personally for creating a culture where he felt able to be himself. The words struck a very deep chord. I was a trooper, the very bottom of the ladder, and I'd implemented this.

Summer leave arrived in August 2009 and with it came the news that I was to be promoted. At last, after six years of working hard as a trooper, I was rewarded with a promotion, but with it came a career move. I was to head back to central London and ceremonial duties in the capital. My time at the armoured regiment was over.

I embarked on my three weeks' leave with an elevated level of satisfaction due to my new appointment. Ryan and I made plans that involved time apart and time together. He'd completed his last year of studying and was looking for somewhere to live. I was heading to North Wales to see my folks alone for a few days, before Ryan caught a train up to meet me.

By the time he arrived in Wrexham, he'd arranged to move in

temporarily with his brother and sister-in-law in Oxfordshire. I knew he was unhappy with how life was going for him at the time and that he wanted to feel settled in his own home.

When he got to Wrexham, we both tried to put the issue out of our minds and attempted to enjoy a week in the countryside, but almost immediately cracks started to show in our relationship.

I took him to the coast, north-west of Wrexham, to the towns of Rhyl and Colwyn Bay for a day out. I wanted to show him where I'd grown up and show him the places my mum used to take me as a child, but Ryan wasn't at all interested in any of it and really upset me when he commented on how 'chavvy' he thought the place was. It wasn't very pleasant, but I knew he was having a tough time. The economy was in a bad state in the autumn of 2009 and with Ryan fresh out of university and looking for a job he was facing several unwanted changes in his life.

By the end of the week, however, I'd had enough of Ryan and our constant bickering. I was really upset that within eight months of meeting him we were in a very unhappy state. It wasn't at all his fault and I wish I'd had the ability to wave a magic wand and make all the problems disappear, but I simply didn't. I waved him goodbye from the train station in Wrexham knowing the end of our relationship was imminent.

There was another reason for my change in feelings towards Ryan. My ex-boyfriend Thom was turning twenty-one in the next few days and there was a party organised for him that many people were talking about going along to. To my surprise, the party was happening in Wrexham. It was the last place I'd have thought Thom would have wanted to celebrate his twenty-first birthday. I hadn't seen him since the awful events of his nineteenth birthday, two years before in Windsor. I didn't at all think about turning up and expressing my birthday wishes, but it certainly played on my mind that we were both in the same small town in Wales.

On the Saturday, the day of Thom's birthday, I headed into the town centre in the evening with an old schoolmate from Gwersyllt. We had a great night out and partied hard to the very early hours. At the end of the night, instead of heading home, I said my goodbyes and headed off into the darkness.

An hour before and after a few drinks, I had texted Thom to wish him a happy birthday, thinking he'd either ignore it or maybe even reply with something quite nasty. Happily, I received a pleasant message which asked where in the world I was.

'I'm actually in Wrexham!' I replied, pretending I didn't know he was only a handful of miles away from me. After a few text messages, I agreed to go and meet the guy who had broken my heart and left me during one of the most stressful periods of my life.

I met Thom at his auntie's house an hour later and we sat outside in the darkness talking over the minutiae of our relationship, the good times and the bad. He admitted the mistakes he'd made and, somehow, during the hours we chatted away until the sun began to rise, I forgave him. I accepted his reasons, although not overly agreeing with them, and understood why exactly he'd deserted me.

All we did was talk, but as soon as I left him, as soon as I was away from him again, deep down I wanted to see him. I wanted to carry on talking about our past. I wanted to be with him. He'd grown up considerably, was doing pretty well for himself and, ultimately, had changed. He told me he'd been single for some time and really longed for something back in his life. Something he'd thrown away two years ago.

I knew my time with Ryan was over.

He was beautiful. He was exceptionally kind. I loved how intelligent he was and the way we'd talk away for hours. But, unfortunately, Ryan just wasn't Thom.

21

THE AMERICANS

My return to work after summer leave and the start of my new posting back in central London coincided with two major events. Firstly, the ending of my relationship with Ryan, which I knew I had to do, particularly after Thom and I had begun to put right the wrongs of our past; and secondly, a visit from American officials, representing the Pentagon, who were in the process of designing the bill that would eventually bring an end to 'Don't Ask, Don't Tell', the highly homophobic law banning gay people from the military.

Thom and I had been texting each other daily since our all-night meeting after his twenty-first birthday celebrations. Every time my phone buzzed with another message, my heart skipped a beat and I felt excited. I knew it was wrong and that the two of us were slowly rekindling our love while I was still officially involved with Ryan, but I couldn't resist how I felt. The daily texts led to phone calls within the space of a week, during which we'd talk like we used to when we first got together three years before. Soon, and I'd known it would happen, Thom asked me out for a drink and a chance to chat further over some food.

While all of this was going on, I all but shut Ryan out from my life. I can't imagine the frustration he must have felt as I spinelessly ignored his calls and avoided all conversation with him.

Then one evening, while I was getting ready to meet Thom for a drink on the river, I read a text from him telling me he knew I was getting back with Thom. That caught my attention, so I called him.

On the other end of the phone was a very hurt person. Ryan and I had started off strongly and with so much potential. I'm not sure I ever loved him completely, and I think if he's honest he might say the same, but we were extremely close. When our relationship ended, we were on the brink of true and meaningful love and would, I'm sure, be still together today had the events of those few weeks not occurred.

The bounding factor with Thom and me was that we knew each other so well. I knew all his secrets, he knew all of mine. We were each other's first loves and we'd had a blast before things went sour. Incredibly, even when discussing Thom with Ryan, as new partners do in the early stages of a relationship, I caused friction by exclaiming that Thom was my one true love. I even remember saying to Ryan one night after some drinks that I still thought Thom was the most beautiful person in the world. It's amazing Ryan gave me the time of day.

I told Ryan on the phone – and again, I'm not proud – that he was wrong to assume Thom and I had rekindled our love. I blamed my apparent sudden change of heart on the changes I was experiencing, or was about to experience, in work. Ryan didn't buy it and we ended our conversation with him crying down the phone. It's awful to think that I was able to switch off from the stresses I was causing my then boyfriend but the reason I was able to do that was that I knew I might have Thom back again.

Thom had done the same to me two years ago. When we spoke later that night about Ryan, Thom gave me great comfort, explaining he knew exactly how I felt. Thom had left me when

I was vulnerable and at a time in life when things were rough. I was doing that to Ryan; he had just finished his studies and was waiting for his university grades, and was basically homeless and living with his relatives because he had nowhere else to go. My mum would not be proud and it wouldn't be long before she'd give me her honest opinion on how I'd treated Ryan.

†

Momentum in America had been steadily increasing around what was widely considered (not least by me) the discriminative policy of 'Don't Ask, Don't Tell' (DADT).

I'd been pulled into the debate across the Atlantic due to the publicity showered on me throughout the *Soldier* episode. Bloggers and even TV talk show hosts were using my example to lobby the US government into ending the rule, bringing gay equality into the US military.

While on summer leave I received a phone call from the same officer who'd spoken to me about doing the magazine earlier in the year. He quickly got to the point and informed me that President Obama was hurrying his government into ending DADT and that a group of officials were flying over to learn from the British Army how to lift the rules on gay servicemen and women. These people had the incredible responsibility of drafting the bill that would eventually be passed through Congress and finally signed off by the President himself, and they wanted to talk with me.

I was given a date and told not to worry about getting time off work. The meeting was of the highest priority and, actually, I didn't have much of a choice. The meeting was taking place at Uphaven, the then headquarters of the British Army's Land Force.

Driving to the meeting, a lot went through my mind. Who

were these people? Would they really care about what I had to say? Should I mention my brief relationship with Sammy in Iraq? I felt that the Americans would get as close to passing the bill as possible, then stop it going through in the last moments, leaving the whole process pointless.

Turning into the camp, it dawned on me that thousands of gay servicemen and women in America, who were hiding their true selves away, were counting on me to make the right statements. For a few hours that grey autumn morning, the responsibility of gaining gay equality in the US military lay fully on my shoulders; me, a 22-year-old lance corporal from a small town in North Wales.

The annoying thing about the affair was, as usual, the military were adamant I remained discreet about the entire business. I wasn't allowed to tell people who I was meeting or what the meeting was about.

What struck me about the officials who'd flown over to Britain to conduct their initial research was just how extremely polite they were. In the ice-breaking coffee session between me and them, I was surprised by just how very pleasant they came across as. I realised later that they needed to be because they were about to sit me down and ask some pretty blunt, and hugely private, questions about my life as a gay soldier.

The chap who led the questioning was called Gary and he sat in front of me, as if I were at a job interview, with a number of sheets with his many questions clearly set out. It started off lightly, asking easy things like the age I was when I started to tell people in the military I was gay. Naturally the topic moved on to the initial reaction from colleagues and, remembering the significance of the meeting and the potentially life-changing outcome for the gay American service population, I decided to skip the tales of being hit on in the army bar and beaten severely. My natural instinct told me that those stories would have a negative effect on the outcome of their visit. Soon the questions turned to the more sensitive issue of service abroad and mostly what being in a war zone while openly gay was like.

'How was it?' Gary sat back as I began to answer, sensing that I might have a lot to say.

'Well, to put it simply, I performed better because I was able to be myself.'

The three Americans looked at each other with wide eyes. Gary stirred in his seat, turning to make eye contact with the lady sat behind his right shoulder.

'Do you mean being gay made you a better soldier?'

'No, that's not what I mean at all. I mean, being able to be gay and being able to say without any fear that I was gay, helped me serve better. It made me more operationally effective. If I'd had the constant worry that I could be outed at any point or that some suspicious police officer could read through my letters to find I was secretly hiding away a boyfriend, other people's lives would have been in danger. I'd have spent more time worrying about my fate and being found out than worrying about being shot at or blown up. That could have cost lives.'

I thought my opinion was a generally accepted fact, but the American officials looked at each other in revelation. The woman beamed. Had my remarks really not occurred to them before? Of course they hadn't. I was speaking to three hetero-sexual Americans who'd never known personally what it meant to be different from the crowd or what it meant to hide away something that was of such ultimate importance. The words I'd just muttered to them were of massive significance and the only person in the world I could think about was Sammy. Where was Sammy now?

The meeting continued, but nothing else I said that day was as significant as my remarks about being a better soldier and saving lives. I was asked a slightly awkward question about showering with other soldiers and sleeping under the same roof, which I was able to answer honestly, telling them that a bunch of straight, highly strung soldiers would misbehave regardless of a gay person being present in a shower room. Boys would always be boys. It was a bit of light relief after the charged-up conversation beforehand.

At the end of our meeting, which had lasted several hours and even included lunch, at which I still faced the American inquisition, I was given a small medallion by way of thanks from Gary and the rest of his team. They were deeply grateful that I'd answered their questions as honestly as I had, and told me that the words I'd spoken that day would be repeated at the White House in the weeks and months that would follow. I'm still waiting for my call from the President today, though.

Out of all my campaigning moments to date, nearly all of which have been in the UK, I'm not sure anything I've done, not ever, will be as crucial and defining as that day at Uphaven. The Americans left the meeting, boarded a plane and flew back to the US to begin writing their recommendations. It's a highly emotive issue for me. When the President finally delivered on 'Don't Ask, Don't Tell' in late 2011, I opened a bottle of champagne and toasted the bill. I also poured a second glass for my dear friend Sammy, imagining he'd be doing the same somewhere, wherever he was serving. I just hope to God he made it to the end and that he didn't become one of the thousands of military personnel to have his life unfairly ruined at the hands of legislative homophobia.

✝

Back in London, life was rather more complicated. Everything would have been much easier, and quicker in fact, if I'd just met with Ryan, face to face, and told him I was leaving him. Due to my cowardice and inability to confront the situation, I was stringing Ryan along in the hope he'd make it easier and finish with me first. As a result of my diabolical behaviour, Ryan thinks that the only reason I left him was because of Thom. It's a huge factor in the running of events, but it wasn't the only one. But it's also fair to say that if Thom hadn't turned up when he did, all the other problems between Ryan and me could possibly have been worked through. We'll never know.

I met with Thom once again for drinks at a nice pub on the river Thames. I had absolutely no intention of misbehaving and felt I owed it to Ryan to at least not go down the avenue of sleeping with somebody else while still in a relationship, but that night I took the decision to accompany Thom back to his house in Chiswick. When I woke up the following morning, I knew I had to end it with Ryan. How could I continue to mess the poor lad around?

The conversation was dreadful. Ryan didn't cry and I realised that he'd lost all hope for our relationship over the course of the previous two weeks when I'd practically ignored him. He'd also seen a few comments by Thom on social media, with Thom inappropriately saying that he was going on a date with me and that we might be getting back together. The whole thing was a nightmare and completely unfair on Ryan. Ryan might not have cried, but when I came off the phone, I did. I cried a lot.

How could I have put someone through the same heart-stopping pain that I'd been put through by Thom? How could I turn my back on the guy who'd been so nice to me and been genuinely interested in me as a person? I felt low, but I was lucky to have one very significant source of support. I had Thom.

Thom had truly changed. He'd needed to do what I and a lot of other young gay people do when they first move to the big city.

He needed to get everything out of his system and see what was around. Like me, he'd found that, actually, there wasn't anything overly amazing about hitting the scene hard and making lots of new friends. As a result of our two-year break, Thom and I are stronger today than ever. I'm certain we'll be together for the rest of our lives.

A few weeks went by and I was seeing Thom on an almost daily basis. Eventually he asked me if we were going to get on with it and get back together. It was a very easy answer for me. I wanted to be the main person in his life, forever. From the moment I first laid eyes on his profile on the internet when he was seventeen, I wanted to be the only person in his life. For whatever reasons, life had taken us both on a different course, but right then we were back in each other's worlds. We were back together, and it was the start of a very happy and enduring romance. I hope Ryan will understand one day that had I have left him on a whim for anybody off the street, his anger and frustration would be understandable and right. I left Ryan for the only man in the world I preferred to be with: my first love and, honestly, my only love. I know Ryan will find the right person in life, but unfortunately I wasn't that person.

22

'WEDDING' BELLS

In the three months leading up to Christmas 2009, I settled in to my new role as a troop corporal, dealing with the day-in, day-out tasks of middle-managing a troop of twenty eighteen-year-olds and thirty, mostly grumpy, horses.

I'd been promoted and sent to a new working environment, which made my transition from trooper to lance corporal fairly straightforward. I didn't know any of the boys who were junior to me, so they listened to what I said and gave me little grief in return. Often, soldiers are promoted and sent to work over the lads they've spent three or four years with as fellow troopers, causing obvious difficulties.

Working in 2 Troop, where I'd served as a trooper during my first time at the ceremonial regiment, my corporal of horse was a chap called Geoff. Geoff embodied the remnants of the Victorian era of values and discipline that were gradually being ironed out of the regimental make-up as it slowly embraced modernism. I really liked the guy, despite his robustness with the boys. I personally preferred his style of management, because you knew exactly where you stood with him. Rule-breakers were punished severely and seeing a young trooper in tears was a common sight. Geoff had turned 2 Troop into the pride of the regiment and flaggers were dealt with accordingly, often being removed and re-trooped somewhere else if they continuously failed to adhere to Geoff's strict rules.

During my three-year break from all things equine, save the four days I'd hitched a ride on the back of a horse up the Rocky Mountains in Canada, I'd not really had much to do with the creatures at all. People kept telling me that horses were like bikes, one never forgets how to ride one, but from the very start I realised I'd lost a sense of fearlessness in handling the animals.

When Dean and I were in riding school, and even when we'd joined the ranks of the regiment escorting the Queen along the Mall, we were both completely fearless when it came to riding. We'd both go into Hyde Park and kick the hell out of horses, each trying to go faster than the other. No horse was too fast for us and we'd often fall off or just bounce out of the saddle before simply jumping back on and carrying on as before. Now, alone back in London, I'd gained a sense of fear and wariness around the creatures born from being away at the armoured regiment. Even standing behind a horse or lifting a foot up to pick clean took a lot of bravery. Geoff had his work cut out with me for some weeks trying to re-instil that sense of confidence and professionalism. In good news, however, after some years apart I finally had the opportunity to work closely again with my old friend Faulkner, who was also a troop corporal in Knightsbridge. It was just like it used to be, although we'd both grown up considerably since our days as troopers. He'd recovered from his blast injuries, now over two years old, and was enjoying love with a lady called Charlotte.

Outside of work, Thom and I saw each other when time allowed. Sometimes he'd be away flying with work or I'd be on Queen's Life Guard as the guard NCO, essentially the second-in-command of the Queen's Life Guard, but otherwise we'd both be together, either in my seventh-floor room overlooking Hyde

Park or at his Chiswick townhouse which he shared with two of his girlfriends. My room in the barracks wasn't ideal at all, with the 200 or so eighteen-year-olds who lived both below and above me constantly blasting music. Thom's house in leafy Chiswick was very much the opposite.

The weeks disappeared as Christmas drew closer and my two roles carried on without much excitement. In the day, I'd ride to and from Horse Guards Parade, passing Buckingham Palace as I went; in the evenings, I'd sometimes find myself at a posh dinner or drinks party in the city talking about my experiences as a gay person in the army. Some nights Thom and I would just sit in and watch a movie. I was much happier in life now things were continuing with the guy I loved.

Soon everybody's favourite time of the year was upon us. I was happy to have Thom with me for almost every aspect of regimental Christmas life. As the nights continued to draw in, the days ticked down until leave: two weeks of festive fun culminating in a trip to New York which Thom had organised for the Christmas holiday.

We'd made the plans earlier in October. It was a place I'd always wanted to visit, though Thom had been there many times. We flew out on the twenty-third, spending the three days of Christmas in the city before flying home late on Boxing Day.

We walked up and down the streets of Manhattan for hours and hours. My eyes rarely looked down from the magnificent skyscrapers that make up the skyline of the Big Apple. We ate in fabulous places and even found ourselves in an Irish bar late on Christmas Eve singing 'Fairy Tale of New York'. I couldn't have asked for a grander way of spending Christmas with the one person in the world I truly loved.

New York was significant for one other reason, too. On Christmas Eve, stopping off in Grand Central Station for cocktails while enjoying our whistle-stop tour of the city, Thom and

I had a deep conversation about ourselves as a couple. Neither could deny that since the moment we'd rekindled our friendship and then romance earlier in the year, we'd both fallen head over heels for each other again. We'd been far closer and stronger as a partnership since our reprise than we'd ever been before. I was glad things had worked out as they had done. It felt like nothing could tear us apart now. We'd been through a lot together.

'Why don't we go all out and get married?' I said it with an air of humour, but he knew I was being semi-serious, too.

'Ha! Don't be ridiculous!'

'Why not? We love each other.'

We both sat in silence on a raised balcony overlooking the vastness of the open hall inside Grand Central Station, watching the thousands of people go by.

'When?'

'Well... There's no rush, is there?'

Thom sipped his cocktail and I continued looking down at the huge hall below us. It was like a scene from the movies. I didn't panic about the conversation we found ourselves having, I just worried a little that Thom hadn't taken me seriously enough. I really wasn't joking.

'OK then. Let's do it!'

And, as simple as that, Thom and I were engaged. No ring, no tears, no over-emotion. Simply put, we were very serious and extremely happy about the impending future that was awaiting us around the corner. We were to plan a civil partnership and we'd begin almost immediately.

We both automatically made plans for a 'wedding'. I remembered just how very long my sister Liza had planned her wedding for; we'd had a lengthy three-year countdown to her big day. Thom and I visited hotels and locations we liked and soon we both came to the same, eye-opening conclusion: weddings were mightily expensive and regardless of how long you wanted to prepare for the big day, the cost was still significant and rather instantaneous.

We realised that to get married in eighteen months' time we'd still have to pay the same amount of money straight away. I decided that I didn't want to wait around for a year and a half for something to go wrong having spent a fortune on a ceremony that might never come to pass, and we changed our plans, paid the balance required and suddenly found ourselves on a countdown to marriage that was only three months long.

Three months. Thom had three months to plan the day of his dreams. I knew from the start that I would have little involvement. I knew I'd just need to arrange my uniform. Thom assumed all command of the occasion, and though I knew he really loved doing it, the stresses of the short time frame would often get to him.

A Household Cavalry tradition that has survived a century too long in my opinion is that a soldier has to ask permission to marry before he can commit to the occasion and, indeed, to his partner. Geoff sat me down in his office and congratulated me on the news, but added that I needed to write a formal letter to the squadron leader asking for his blessing.

It was something I knew I'd have to do, even if I didn't like the fact. For the first time in the history of the Household Cavalry, a letter was drawn up between a soldier and his superior officer formally asking permission for him to 'marry' his partner of the same sex. The letter was submitted and I continued with my duties while I awaited the response. I was really peeved that in an instant our wishes could be ignored and we'd be unable to go on with our plans.

Major Twumasi-Ankrah, the squadron leader of the Blues and Royals, a man I'd long respected from his early days as a junior officer in the regiment, called me into his office to hear more about my relationship with Thom and our plans for a civil partnership.

I told him that Thom and I had met some years before (true) and that we'd been very happy together as a couple (almost true). I didn't want to offer him any chance of rejecting our wishes so I ironed out any details of our past that might have given him an opportunity to deny us our potential married life.

It's important to note that a large part of this process of asking permission to marry is because a soldier will leave the barracks upon marriage. Before formalising a relationship, a soldier is still expected to live in the barracks with the remainder of the regiment. Upon marriage – or, in my case, civil partnership – a soldier is free to leave the barracks and set up home with his new wife – or, in my case, husband.

Major Twumasi-Ankrah sat forward in his chair and leaned across his desk.

'Corporal Wharton, nothing would make me more happy than seeing you marry Thom. You have my 100 per cent blessing. Congratulations!'

I could have kissed the major on the head, I was so delighted. He'd gone a stage further than just approve my wishes, he'd added his personal feelings to the blessing at the same time. It was an incredible moment for me, and the major became my favourite squadron leader. Nothing was going to stop us now.

I really wanted to enjoy my big day within the walls in which I'd spent so many happy times. Yes, I'd also had my fair share of unhappiness within Hyde Park barracks but, on the whole, the place was the centre of the universe as far as I was concerned. I wanted my reception to be there, in the mess I'd recently become a member of after my promotion. This required further permission, but this time from the regimental corporal major, the most senior non-commissioned officer on camp.

He gave his preliminary blessing but warned that if a fellow mess member raised a complaint at the monthly mess meeting, he'd have to listen to that complaint and put a stop to the event. Again, I was grateful for his initial blessing, but annoyed that someone had the right to complain about it and then halt the proceedings. I asked him how many heterosexual weddings had been stopped due to a complaint in the past, to which he returned, quite sheepishly, that none had. I pushed him slightly more and asked how many weddings had even been brought before a mess meeting for discussion, and again he said none.

I wanted to get on my box and scream discrimination, but I thought better of it. These were still progressive times and, actually, I honestly couldn't think of a single person in the mess who'd be bothered at all about the event. I thought it more likely most mess members would quite enjoy gatecrashing the reception and having a good time – something that any mess member was entitled to do. I bit my lip and kept quiet about my annoyance and, as I'd expected, nobody in the mess cared one bit, in fact, almost everyone was delighted.

In the weeks that followed, as the clock slowly counted down, Geoff became more of a friend than a boss. He'd been married twice and knew just about everything there was to know about getting married from a groom's point of view. He was invaluable, and one afternoon over a beer, he told me something that really underlined to me how far the army had come in a relatively short amount of time regarding gay equality.

'All my life I've been homophobic, James.' This was a little uncomfortable.

'Well, why?'

'You have to understand, when I joined the army, it wasn't allowed.' This was a similar conversation to the one I'd had with Warren two years ago. 'If someone was gay, they got beaten up and the army, instead of helping them and stopping the bullying, turned their backs on them and kicked them out. It was basically encouraged.'

Geoff was making a point I'd heard before, but what struck me was that he showed real emotion while talking about it. He'd come to the conclusion that for most of his life he'd thought wrongly about gay people and the reason for that was that the army had told him to. The homophobic image the army had me working so hard to change was caused by the army itself to suit a time when being gay wasn't acceptable.

'Before I met you, James, I honestly couldn't even bear the thought of homosexuals. I've completely changed my opinion on the matter.'

Was it any surprise the media had made a big deal out of my *Soldier* magazine feature? The army had created its own image of homophobia through decades of overt discrimination and now, after being forced to change their rules, desperately needed to change their image. But why had it taken so long?

As my impending civil partnership became more widely known among the senior ranks of the military and, in particular, the PR department that had put me on the cover of *Soldier* a year earlier, so it spread among the media. Two weeks before the ceremony, it was arranged for a national newspaper to have their own photographer and reporter come to the event. That newspaper then had the exclusive on our wedding, which was preferred by the army and, to an extent, Thom and me.

Both our families were descending upon London for the big day, as were friends from both sets of families, some of whom Thom and I hadn't seen for a long time. The plan was to put everyone in the same hotel and keep our home for just the two of us. In keeping with the army rules, we were given a property in south-west London, a reasonable distance from the barracks, to live in as a married couple.

In the mail, quite unexpectedly, a fancy letter arrived in what I remember was a posh-looking envelope. I opened it up and saw immediately at the top of the small-sized note the words '10 Downing Street'. Inside was a card invitation which read:

The Prime Minister
requests the company of
LCpl James Wharton
at a reception celebrating the LGBT community
at 10 Downing Street

I read the note and was alarmed to see that the date of the event was the following day, allowing hardly any time to prepare for such an occasion. What on earth would I wear? What would I say to the Prime Minister? I hurried to the squadron leader's office and showed him the invite.

Major T-A did a double-take at the note I handed him. 'Wow, well I've never been invited to the Prime Minister's house!'

Major T-A told me to wear uniform, which I was relieved about. The plus side to being in one of the fanciest regiments in the world was the array of different posh uniforms ready to be worn which would all turn heads in a room full of important people. It was decided I should go wearing 2 Dress Mounted, a uniform consisting of knee-high riding boots and spurs, with khaki-coloured riding breeches and my usual dark-brown coloured jacket, finished off with my Iraq medal and service cap. It was possibly my favourite outfit hanging up in the wardrobe, alongside my Blues and other uniforms that were generally reserved for the Queen.

Awkwardly, the regiment had some work on that week, too. There was a state visit planned for the following Thursday, just a day before my wedding, and we had our usual set of

early-morning rehearsals in preparation for the occasion. One
of those early rehearsals was scheduled for the Thursday morning, only hours after my evening with Gordon Brown was set to
finish. According to the invitation, the reception would be over
by 9 p.m., which would give me six hours before having to wake
my horse and ride through the escort. It was annoying, but something I was used to with the Household Cavalry.

The following evening, after spending the day answering
questions from people in work, and even a brief chat in the
commanding officer's office, listening to him tell me how pleased
he was about the affair, a car from the barracks drove me the
small distance down the Mall and onto Whitehall, before pulling
up outside the gates of Downing Street, where a small line of
people were queuing to pass through security.

The feelings I experienced handing over my invitation, passing through the metal scanner and casually chit-chatting with
the officers charged with the security of the Prime Minister were
bizarre. I'd always been hugely interested in British politics and
always wondered what it would be like to be in the company of the
most important man in the country, and I was about to find out.

The door was opened for me and I walked in. My phone was
taken off me and my chance of a sneaky picture of the loo disappeared in an instant. I decided to keep hold of my hat and of
course my whip, which was a custom with the uniform I was
wearing, as something to hide behind and grip as the event took
its course. I was incredibly nervous.

Ushered upstairs, I entered a large room with many paintings
on the wall which overlooked my usual place of work, Horse
Guards, the very place I'd be bouncing around on a horse in the
hours that would follow. The room was filling fast. Stood near
the front shaking the hands of the many assembled guests
was the wife of the Prime Minister, Sarah Brown.

I was handed a glass of white wine and moved towards the centre of the room, where people began talking to me, mostly asking about my uniform. My whip was quite the centre of interest for the majority of folk I spoke to, which delighted me as it meant I didn't find myself in complex conversations about equality in the army.

It didn't take long for me to realise that the majority of people in the room were famous personalities from one area of the media or another. There were TV stars, pop stars, famous journalists and the occasional well-known politician. It was an incredible experience to be talking to such an impressive collective from the gay community, but what I found even more amazing was that these people wanted to talk to me. By the end of the evening, Paul O'Grady had taken my whip off me and was carrying out an amusing gesture with the end of it, to the gasps and delight of the massed audience.

The Prime Minister eventually made an appearance, shaking the hands of many as he made his way to the front of the room and onto an assembled stage where he made an address. He made reference to the number of famous people in the room and also highlighted the few of us who weren't off the TV but who were, in his opinion, equally relevant on a 'night like this' to be recognised for our commitment to the gay community.

After he spoke, Gordon Brown made his way to the exit, where I'm sure he returned to the busy duty of running the country, but before leaving he stopped to say a few words to me.

'It's brilliant you are here tonight,' he said while holding his hand out to shake mine. The memory of my briefest of conversations with his predecessor, Tony Blair, on the steps of Windsor Castle six years before entered my mind. I was about to repeat the only words I had said then to another Prime Minister.

'Good evening, Prime Minister...' I couldn't leave it there. 'And thank you for inviting me, I'm honoured!'

The Prime Minister nodded as he pulled his hand away and walked towards the door. At that point, I assumed the wine would be taken away and everyone would be ushered out of the door, but that didn't happen at all. Instead, we were all left to enjoy another hour of mixing and wine sipping, before most headed on to another venue. I, of course, needed to head back to Hyde Park barracks and get what little sleep I could before the following morning's early rehearsal. Such is life.

That evening at Downing Street is a wonderful memory. In the years that followed, going to Downing Street would become a regular occurrence but that night, heading back to camp in a taxi, I couldn't believe that the Prime Minister of Great Britain had 'requested the pleasure of my company', and when it actually came to chatting with me, knew full well who I was and, more so, what I'd done.

In work, some hours later, Major T-A, while showing the commanding officer around the Blues and Royals stables, stopped me grooming my horse to ask questions about the experience at Downing Street. Once I'd told them both about the run of events, Major T-A joked that I should have stayed in bed and taken the morning off.

'You'd have got away with saying the party with the PM over-ran. What on earth could we possibly say to that?'

As much as I'd probably have enjoyed staying in bed while the rest of the regiment were out practising for the forthcoming escort, I had no need to. I'd enjoyed the evening enormously but at the end of it I was happy to return to my duties with the Blues and Royals squadron. I had a day job to do, after all.

23

MR & MR

The morning of our civil partnership finally arrived. I woke up in Putney alone, save for the new addition to our family, Pickle, our half-pug, half-Jack Russell puppy that I'd bought Thom as a gift leading up to the big day. It was quite a lonely feeling waking up that Friday morning, my face being licked to death by Pickle. Across town, and in a somewhat different environment, Thom was waking up surrounded by friends, before being pampered as the morning continued and sipping the occasional glass of champagne as he went.

Our ceremony was taking place at Old Marylebone Town Hall, which was also the venue of Paul McCartney's wedding to Linda some decades before. It was a lovely, historic building, with grand steps leading up to the large entrance. Every aspect of the day had been chosen by us, down to the reading my sister was to give and the colour of the Range Rover that was to take us on to the reception.

My best man was the only person it could ever have been, the person who'd been there for me on that day back in 2005, knocking at my door holding a coffee for me to sip over while he counselled me through my difficulties: Faulkner. Of all the people who had passed through my life in the military, soldiers coming and going as our careers took different paths, Faulkner was the one person who'd been pretty constant.

Faulkner and I both wore the ceremonial uniform of the

Blues and Royals, and the two of us looked, as usual, very smart. Another friend and confidant, Pikey, acted as my usher and wore a different uniform to Faulkner and me, though he looked equally as sharp. As the three of us walked along the Marylebone Road towards the venue, dozens of cars beeped their horns and shouted messages of good wishes as they passed.

Thom had kept his outfit hidden from me and when I arrived at the steps of the building with Faulkner and Pikey, I was moved to tears by how beautiful he looked. He had chosen a grey three-piece, formal morning suit that fitted him perfectly. He looked smarter than me even though I was in regalia. In the commotion of everything that was going on, our parents and friends standing on the steps applauding our arrival, Thom began to cry. I guess it was just all a little too much.

Pikey sprang into action on my nod and started to usher everyone up the steps and into the room on the first floor that was housing our special occasion. Thom and I stayed back while everyone filed in. I grabbed his hand and asked if he was OK. Our hearts were beating fast and we were both visibly nervous about the magnitude of what we were about to do together. Everything we'd been through as a couple, the highs and the lows, was about to take its place in the past as we cemented our lives together. What was done was done, we were now sealing our love and the future was ours.

We entered the ceremony to the music of Sir Elton John; 'Rocket Man' is Thom's favourite song. Flashes from the photographer lit up the room intermittently; we could hear the click each time he aimed his machine at us. Behind me I could hear the sniffles of one of our mothers. Our wedding was actually happening. The music came to a stop and the registrar began with our chosen words.

Half an hour later, the business was done and we were officially civil partners. We'd planned a few moments of light-hearted humour to break up the formality of the occasion, with music from our favourite show, *Priscilla, Queen of the Desert*, playing while we signed the relevant paperwork that accompanied the ceremony.

Outside, on the steps of the Old Town Hall, passing vehicles again beeped and honked their horns to the sight of us both walking, hand in hand, down the steps, confetti passing over us and the photographer aiming to capture as much of the moment as possible. In the days that followed, the many different shots captured by the photographer would appear, firstly in the newspaper that had the exclusive on our special day, but then in almost every newspaper in the land. The image that adorned the many articles was the same striking picture of a soldier, decorated in state regalia, grasping his new, beautifully dressed husband with a loving embrace and kissing him on the lips as they sealed their ceremony with a moment of intimacy.

Pikey took us to the waiting Range Rover and we were whizzed to Hyde Park barracks, where our reception was to be held. The short time it took for us to travel the distance to the barracks was the only period of solace and privacy the two of us would enjoy for the rest of the day. I deeply appreciated how far some friends had travelled to be with us and I loved catching up with members of both of our families who we'd not seen for some time, but those few minutes alone in the back of the car, my new husband and me, were perfect and I wished the journey had taken longer.

The cake we'd chosen, a beautiful, fresh cream-filled, profiterole-stuffed, white chocolate-laced magnitude of baking, had been successfully delivered to the mess and was now pride of place in the centre of the room, where we were to all enjoy a curry lunch. It was utterly breathtaking to look at and it certainly tasted delicious; Thom and I had enjoyed a tasting session with the bakery, Patisserie Valerie, three weeks before. My state sword had been placed on the table next to it, still sheathed in its scabbard, and Thom and I would later use it to cut the cake. It was the very same sword I'd carried in my right hand so often when escorting the Queen.

The guests began to file into the mess, initially into the bar, before taking their seats. The food was served and everyone enjoyed tucking into the curry, even Thom's father, who, as a master chef in the military himself, I was sure would find fault in the offerings.

I'd written a speech and was anxious to get the words out of the way, feeling I wasn't able to fully let my hair down and enjoy the day until it was done. Thom's dad wanted to say some words, as did Phil. Faulkner didn't write a speech, but calmly pulled off a few words in a cool manner, thanking everyone for coming along and looking so fabulous.

We had about forty close friends and family for the formalities of the day and had invited close to 200 for the night, including top brass from within the Household Cavalry, like Major T-A and the corporal majors of both the Blues and Royals and the Life Guards, as well as the policy-making high-ranking officials who'd put me on the cover of *Soldier* and were behind a lot of the media that were reporting on the occasion.

Some might think I would be a little hostile to those who placed this high degree of responsibility on my shoulders with all this heavy press exposure, but in all honesty, at the time of my wedding, I didn't mind it at all. I could see the benefit to having gay relationships covered in the national media. I knew people would see the images and read the words and begin to change their opinions on gay people and gay equality. I also knew that there was a chance that gay people might feel inspired to be themselves and even come out of the closet as a result of the images in the newspapers and online. I didn't just wear the uniform to look good, I wore it because I was incredibly proud of the status that came with being part of the Sovereign's Escort and, to an extent, I knew it would be challenging to some old conservative right-wingers, who'd see my picture in the *Daily Mail* in the days that followed and be forced to comment on it. I enjoyed the thought of challenging people's perspectives on what exactly a gay man was in the twenty-first century. Two years later, when media interest in me continued, I began to feel differently towards some of those people who'd tarted me around to the army's benefit, but in March 2010, I certainly didn't feel put out by the work they were having me do. It made the army a much more gay-friendly place and of that I'm incredibly proud.

In true mess tradition, the party ended the following morning at 6 a.m., the last person to leave being Bruce, the Life Guard corporal major, who in the early hours after Thom and I departed took over as host for the remaining guests who wanted to continue with the show. Thom and I got a car home, and in my drunken state I carried what was left of our wedding cake, deciding that none of it should go to waste.

We'd received hundreds of cards from well-wishers and, thankfully, the mess allowed us to leave some gifts securely behind, to save me carrying yet more heavy items home. It had been the greatest of occasions. A friend, some weeks before, warned me that the entire episode would flash by in an instant, and it certainly had. At about midnight, just before guests started to leave, I took a moment on my own, sat in the corner of the mess, to look at all our friends and family, enjoying themselves and being happy. I realised that everyone had come to share our special day with us and that tomorrow it would all be over. It was a very comforting thought that all our friends and family had come along to support us on our big day with so much love and acceptance. I remember talking to my mum on the day, and on a number of occasions since, and she spoke of her pride in seeing the second of her children marry the person they loved. Liza had married in 2006 and it was a wonderful occasion. Her wedding occurred just a handful of weeks after I'd told my family I was gay, and I took Thom along as my guest. Back then, I considered some of the feelings Mum might have been having, watching her only daughter marry. I know she worried that I, as a gay person, would never have the white wedding she'd always dreamed of for me. On the day of my civil partnership with Thom, I know she felt relieved that her grand plans for me, which I suppose every mother makes for their children, had come to pass in one way or another. She was incredibly proud, and for that I love her.

Nothing else could have made the day any more perfect than it was. Since, and quite recently, I've been asked if Thom and I would marry properly if the law changed and, if we did, what our plans would be. The answer from me is simple: nothing could ever live up to the magic of that special day in March 2010 and there is nothing in the world that would make me want to undermine the magnitude of the occasion by 'upgrading' to marriage just because the government of the day had finally got its act together and was affording equality in marriage to all. It should have been on offer to us then and, if it had, we'd have enjoyed a formal wedding. That chance has now gone, and we will never change the past, nor replace the memories we have of our civil partnership ceremony. It was the happiest day of my life.

Just ten years after the lifting of the ban on gay people serving in the British Army, the celebrations of my civil partnership were held within the walls of the most traditional environment in the country. I felt hugely privileged and immensely proud of my regiment for taking such a lead with the occasion. To quote my commanding officer at the time, 'The Household Cavalry has a fine tradition of leading from the front; it's only natural for us to be the leader in this exciting new world, too.'

24

JIMMY AND JESSICA

In the weeks that followed our civil partnership, Thom and I were busy giving short interviews or comments to various people about our ceremony. Across the pond in the States our civil partnership had caused news and again I found myself being used as a key tool for the campaign against 'Don't Ask, Don't Tell'. Every time the phone rang and it would turn out to be *The Sun* or the *Daily Mirror*, I considered how annoying all this press attention must have been for my ex, Ryan, who would have undoubtedly seen at least one of the many articles about our civil partnership. I still felt incredibly guilty over the way our relationship had ended.

Thom and I delayed our honeymoon by a few weeks, waiting for more time off work to allow it. We jetted off to Boston for three days before flying back and heading north to Edinburgh for an additional five days of honeymooning, having a perfect time throughout. I didn't feel any different in my day-to-day relationship with Thom; the only change was the addition of a ring on both our left hands.

The Trooping of the Colour, that quaint and typically British occasion, was approaching fast. After seven years of service, I was still a virgin with regard to participating in the Queen's Birthday Parade; 2010 would finally bring an end to that wait.

I always remember Mum telling me that the Trooping of the Colour was an event I had to take part in and that if I never did manage a seat on a horse for that grandest of occasions, I'd have to just stay put in the regiment until the day eventually came. I know her and my nan especially were a little underwhelmed when during my first tenure at the mounted regiment at the age of eighteen, I didn't manage to take part. Much to their relief more than mine, in the summer of that year I would finally take my place in the parade.

Adding to the family pride of the occasion, the horse I was charged with riding was named Jimmy, like my grandfather, who was still always in my memory eight years after his death at the age of eighty.

Jimmy was the source of family inspiration and after his death in 2002 he left a gaping hole as the father figure of the family. He was a hero. He'd endured a long life, often with hardship, the peak of which came as a Japanese prisoner of war during the Second World War.

He served on a battlecruiser called the *Repulse* and was sunk three days after Pearl Harbor in the South Pacific. After rescue he was taken to Singapore to recover, but during the respite Singapore fell to the Japanese and Jimmy was captured as a POW, interned into the Changi jail. There followed four long years of incredible suffering, laying the Burma railway, and eventually he was transferred to Japan on the hell ships, being sunk yet again, this time by the Americans. Finally, the Japanese had him labouring in a salt mine in Nagasaki, where he witnessed the atomic bomb explode. After release he was sent to Australia for recovery, finally returning home to my nan. The telegram he received from the King wishing him a long and happy life after his release from captivity in 1945 is at the centre of our family pride.

He seldom talked of his suffering, but every now and then he'd pass a comment about the Japanese; he never had any respect for either the nation or its people for the rest of his life.

Mum picked him up from his house in Liverpool one morning in her shiny new Nissan Micra and Jimmy outright refused to get in, spitting at the car in protest. Only five years old, I stood by, confused. Mum sold the car within two months. Another early memory of mine is playing toy soldiers with little plastic army men Mum had bought me. Granddad was sat in his usual position, in front of the TV with the remote control carefully guarded, bouncing from one news bulletin to another. I set up camp for one set of toy soldiers in front of the TV, placing the flag that had come with the soldiers in the centre of the little plastic men.

'A German flag? Have you not got another one to put in front of your granddad?' He didn't want to be staring at a German flag, understandably.

I looked into the plastic bag, rummaged around and pulled out another. Swapping the two, I called for Granddad to approve.

'Sweet suffering Jesus Christ!' Granddad shouted at the top of his elderly voice, kicking the flag and all my little plastic soldiers over before walking off into the kitchen to make himself a cup of tea. The flag I'd replaced the German one with was, unfortunately, a Japanese one. In the end, he allowed the German one but there was no chance the red sun of Japan was going anywhere near him.

Jimmy the horse was quite a character, too. As ever, there would be lots of rehearsals and therefore lots of time for us to bond. Jimmy wasn't a horse from my own troop, which made our companionship that little bit more peculiar. The thirty horses on offer to me in 2 Troop had somehow been handed out to everyone before taking me into account. The Blues and Royals squadron corporal major, a great Welshman called Kerry, had to loan a horse to me from 1 Troop, so I knew very little about Jimmy and his behaviour. Most of the info on Jimmy I learned either first-hand, bouncing around on him in Hyde Park, or through my old friend Donna, who looked after him daily and knew him well.

Huge and towering far over me, Jimmy was quite a boy. He was incredibly playful and very cute with his mannerisms. He loved being entertained and I'd often find myself just nattering away to him in the run-up to the Trooping of the Colour.

By the time the second rehearsal arrived, Jimmy and I had a relationship that rivalled some of the longest riding partnerships in the world. He knew me and I knew him, and there was no doubt at all that anything would go wrong between us.

In the parade I was the centre number two, meaning I was responsible for the dressing of the entire line as the Blues and Royals trooped past Her Majesty; this was the moment her meticulous eye for detail would look upon us all and judge our professionalism. I'd mastered this important role fully in the many rehearsals leading up to the day, barking orders left and right along the line for men to either kick on or rein back in order to hold the perfect line.

The mounted troops on parade at the Trooping of the Colour ride past the Queen twice, once at the walk, and then again at the trot. It's one of the smartest sights in British tradition, witnessing 100 horses of the Queen's own regiment fleeting past her in perfect dress, saluting the Sovereign as they do so. Having watched the moment on TV for most of my life, witnessing it from behind the scenes earlier in my cavalry career was stomach-churning enough; sat on a beautifully turned-out Jimmy, carrying my plume smartly and keeping the dressing of the Blues and Royals around me was a moment of sheer pride that can't easily be described. It was the one occasion I'd waited for since signing up to the Household Cavalry years earlier and back home my mum watched the events live, as did my nan, surrounded by family. James Wharton, a boy from North Wales, responsible for the smartness of the entire line of Blues and Royals on the occasion of Her Majesty's official birthday, riding a horse called Jimmy in a final nod of remembrance to a fallen veteran of the Second World War. It was an incredible moment for our family.

†

In the week following the Trooping, yet again I found myself with an invite to 10 Downing Street, this time from the newly elected coalition government. I wore my mounted uniform accompanied by a smart thin whip again. On this occasion, the event was taking place in the garden.

What struck me about meeting David Cameron was the way he held conversation. I really enjoyed meeting his predecessor, Gordon Brown, but was on reflection slightly underwhelmed by the lack of conversation. With David Cameron, I had a five-minute chat about how brilliantly the Trooping of the Colour had gone just days before. He asked where I was on the parade and if I knew of any mistakes that had happened. Joining me at Downing Street was Thom, for the first time, who then went on to have a conversation with the Prime Minister about his job in the airline industry. The man completely won me over, even before his famous speech pledging full government support on the progression of gay equality. The picture I have of me chatting to the Prime Minister takes pride of place on the centre of my mantelpiece.

Summer leave was fast approaching and with it the usual three-week break from all things army. Thom and I had a quick trip to Orlando to start the holiday off before travelling up to North Wales to visit family for a week. As usual, we had a great time together and it was really nice to catch up with family and friends back home in Wrexham.

On the Sunday morning of our week-long visit home, while Thom and I were having an extended lie-in until the mid-morning, I was awoken by the sound of my mobile phone springing into song every few minutes with text message after text message. At first I thought I'd leave it on charge at the other side of the room, reading the messages when I eventually got out of bed, but due to the continual incoming flow of texts, I was encouraged to get up and read the many messages, worrying something was wrong somewhere.

'Congrats on your Pink Listing! Very proud!'

What the hell did that mean? I read it out aloud to Thom, who looked as bewildered as me.

'Brilliant to see you ranked on the Pink List, James. Much Love! xx'

I quickly opened my Facebook account to find more messages and a link to the *Independent on Sunday*'s Pink List 2010.

Much to my astonishment, I'd been ranked on the list as someone who was influential in the gay community. More so, I hadn't just been added to the end of the list, I'd made it into the top twenty, ranking nineteenth. The news was incredible. I'd heard of the Pink List and read it with interest in the years prior, once even joking with Kempy that I'd make it on there one day; all of a sudden, I was on it. I rang my mum and told her I'd been ranked as one of the most influential gay men in the country and told her to go and buy the newspaper to read it herself. Thom and I laughed about the news, finding it all unbelievable. What made me so special? All I'd done was enter a civil partnership with the person I loved most.

Stonewall, a charity committed to lesbian and gay equality, had become aware of me thanks to my appearance on the cover of *Soldier* and then more so from the media surrounding my civil partnership with Thom. Shortly after the ceremony, the chief executive of the charity sent Thom and me a congratulations card, with a wonderful handwritten message of support. I, like many gay people, had been familiar with them for many years, always finding their research on homophobia and the like extremely interesting. Mostly I remembered how successfully they'd lobbied for civil partnerships in the run-up to them being introduced in 2004. Out of the blue, in September 2010, I received an email from them inviting me into their offices for a meeting.

Sir Ian McKellen, who'd been key in the founding of Stonewall in the late 1980s, had been working with the charity again, touring secondary schools and talking to youngsters about homophobia and gay equality. I'd read a piece about his visits in a newspaper, which explored the impact Sir Ian was having on the audiences he'd visited. It was fascinating stuff. Stonewall was inviting me to become involved in the same scheme, talking to school kids about my own experiences and offering them an alternative role model. I had to go away and think about it, and of course gain permission from the army, but in my own mind, I'd already decided it was crucial to accept the offer.

Alongside the school visit request from Stonewall, they also asked how I'd feel talking at their workplace conference, making a speech about my time as a soldier and the challenges I'd overcome during my service. Again, I was honoured to have been asked and desperately wanted to say yes immediately, but I needed the go-ahead from the army.

The officials in the PR department of the army, those chaps who'd started off this media campaign with me at its centre, were the ones who had to give their nod of approval. The conference was of immediate priority as it was fast approaching, and was the major event in the workplace equality calendar. From the start, I could tell that the powers that be were not overjoyed at the prospect of me having a microphone and the opportunity to speak freely of my own experiences.

I met with them at the newly moved Army HQ in Andover to discuss my plans for the speech and listen to their thoughts. It would have been impossible for the army to prevent me from speaking, as they were a paying member of the Stonewall Diversity Champions scheme, and blocking me from talking would have been really bad press for them. They gave their blessing, but analysed my speech word by word.

I wasn't allowed to mention that I'd been beaten up soon after coming out; I wasn't allowed to mention the early experience of being told 'faggots are not welcome' on my first day in the army. I also wanted to say that Turkey was the only country left in NATO that actively banned gay people from service, apart from the US, which was completely ruled out from the speech. As frustrating as this was, I understood that it would be inappropriate to criticise our nation's allies in public in that way. I did, however, know one or two people who'd be in the crowd and I planted questions with those people, which would allow me to answer them and make the points I wanted to make. For instance, I had someone ask if there was anywhere in Europe that banned gay people from service, and I was able to say that Turkey was homophobic in that regard. I had a minder from the Ministry of Defence with me throughout the occasion to ensure I didn't say anything that would cause trouble for the army. All this aside, I made a keynote speech which was very well received and which got a standing ovation from the 300 or so delegates. To have shared such a stage, a stage that the Home Secretary herself had stood on just before me, welcoming the delegates to the conference, was hugely exciting.

The school tour business was handed back to my regiment to

decide whether or not it was appropriate for me to undertake. The army powers were, I know, not overly keen on the idea and I'm sure they hoped my commanding officer would decline the request, citing workload as a key reason, but much to my relief, the colonel allowed me to go ahead with the visits, just as long as I used my own leave to do them. I was a little frustrated I had to book days off to carry the visits out, but was delighted to have the chance to go out and make a difference to schoolchildren around the country.

The night before my first visit, to a school in rural Wiltshire, I found myself more nervous than the night before my civil partnership, even more nervous than I'd felt in the hours leading up to my keynote speech at the Stonewall conference some weeks earlier. What if the kids hated me? What if they laughed at me and called me names for being gay? I was anxious about the episode, but I boarded the train the following morning, smartly turned out in my Blues, and headed off to the school to give my talk to the waiting assembly of teenagers.

Stonewall sent a very nice lady along with me, to hold my hand, as it were, and prep me before facing the audience. After chats with teachers and a handful of youngsters over coffee, it was time to go on stage. I adjusted my uniform, took a sip of water and walked out to the expectant crowd of schoolchildren.

As I walked out on to the stage, I could feel the eyes of every person in the school hall fix on me, looking at my smart uniform, stirring in their seats, ready to hear my message.

Cleverly, the school kids hadn't been prepped before my arrival. At the moment I walked onstage, the majority of school pupils probably would have thought I was there to give a presentation on being a soldier, but the moment I began to speak, the reaction from the kids was astonishing.

'I'm a gay man. I'm also a professional soldier.'

The teenagers began to natter at my sudden admission. A gay soldier?

'I've come to talk with you today about breaking down stereotypes and tackling homophobia.'

For the following forty-five minutes, you could hear a pin drop. The room was that silent. Every member of the audience, including the teaching staff, was captivated by my tale of service, both in Britain and abroad, and how I'd faced every day of my service authentically, as an openly gay person. When I reached the end of my story, and after I'd pleaded with everybody to think twice before using homophobic language and to consider the potentially dreadful effects of bullying within the community, I was met by rapturous applause. The entire school hall was clapping and smiling at me. I found it incredible. Here was a mixture of thirteen- to sixteen-year-old boys and girls, an age group that's known for being difficult sometimes, embracing a real story and listening with interest. I'd won them over and, it has to be said, they'd won me over, too. If my reception had been hostile in the least, I might have reconsidered participating in the school visits for Stonewall completely. The opposite was true and the visit spurred me on to continue with the work.

At the end of the school day I was being taken for coffee with an official from the education board in Wiltshire to discuss equality, before dropping by to an LGBT youth group, where gay and lesbian teens hung out safely and accessed advice and support.

I'd noticed the youth-group visit on the timetable of events for the day, and considered briefly while scouting over it how brilliant it would have been to have such a resource when I was growing up. It led me to realise that if I had had access to an established youth group, I'd have 'come out' at a much younger age. By growing up in a community that, in my opinion, was very enclosed and not very diverse, I'd felt a little entrapped by my own diversity, leading to me refusing to accept how different I was. If I'd known there was a safe place to access help and make friends confidentially, I know I'd have sought the support I craved.

I arrived at the youth group, which was based out of a community resource centre and run by the local authority. The nice lady from the council had briefed me fully on the establishment of the youth club, which was quite an astonishing story in itself.

A fourteen-year-old girl called Jessica had been on a journey of self-discovery for some years as she accepted and understood the fact that she was quite different from her school friends, finally concluding that she was a lesbian. Instead of keeping her thoughts and feelings bottled up for years, she decided to fully embrace who she was and went in search of support.

She found it incredible that there was no overt, easily available resource for her to access as a young LGBT person within her county and, feeling quite alone, she decided to do something about it.

Jessica had lobbied her local authority to provide her, and people like her, with support and a place to access information and make friends. She demanded a youth group for LGBT teens and campaigned hard for her wishes.

After numerous knock-backs, two years later the council gave in and provided her and other youngsters the resource of an official LGBT youth group, which would meet twice weekly, just like any other youth club. Jessica had won, and in doing so she became a hugely influential young person and a bit of an unsung hero along the way.

What struck me about meeting Jessica and the other LGBT teens was how open and honest they were with each other about the daily struggles each had faced or were facing. After being introduced to them and accepting a cup of tea, we all sat down and discussed homophobia. I asked the group how many of them had been bullied for being different, and was heartbroken to see every single hand go up in the group. I looked at the adult staff member who ran the group alongside another, and she nodded and said to me that it was a very awkward, uncomfortable and hard-hitting truth. Gay kids get bullied, full stop.

Jessica, who as a young gay rights activist had developed an incredible presence when speaking publicly, sat in the centre of the group of teens and said that the only way each person gets through the daily struggle is by coming to the youth group twice a week and being in an environment where everyone has something in common. Jessica told me that they'd survived the daily bullying because the youth group existed, and they each were able to support each other in the manner they'd become accustomed to.

I knew instantly that I needed to help these youngsters and the thousands like them all over the UK. Jessica became my new hero. Through her tireless campaigning as a teenager, she'd pushed the local council into providing her and the youngsters like her with a valuable service that arguably saved lives. She was a true role model if ever there was one and I certainly gained something from meeting her.

My first day volunteering with Stonewall was over. I'd planned to use the day as a trial, to gauge how difficult a challenge it was that was being asked of me, and I had concluded that the decision had been made almost entirely for me by someone else. The moment I sat and listened to the gay teens open their hearts to me and speak honestly about the daily bullying they'd received for being who they were, I realised that the choice had disappeared. This was something I now had to do and it was something I certainly was going to do, regardless of whether the army would support me or not.

25

THE ROYAL WEDDING

The royal wedding of 2011 will remain with me for two significant reasons. It was the professional peak for me as a serving member of the Household Cavalry Mounted Regiment and also my swansong as a member of that elite outfit. Throwing down the reins and getting out of the saddle after the parade that day was symbolic for me, as I knew it would be my last time riding alongside Her Majesty the Queen.

I was never supposed to be riding on the occasion. Weeks before I'd accepted a job with the commanding officer, working as his orderly and being singularly responsible for his movements, his bearing and his turn-out. When the world was informed of Prince William and Kate's wedding plans, I walked into the commanding officer's Knightsbridge office and expressed my hopes to ride on the occasion. Being the leader he was, he sanctioned my wishes immediately; it did mean, however, I'd have to turn both myself and him out for the big day. Turning one person out for a parade was usually difficult enough.

The weeks ticked by quickly and before anyone knew it, the royal wedding was on us.

In the ten days that led up to the occasion, London, and in particular, royal London, the area surrounding the palace and the abbey, became a global media hub as the world's press moved in and set up camp. An incredible construction of TV studios had been assembled opposite the balcony of Buckingham Palace, awaiting the famous kiss.

Trepidation for us soldiers, the showmen of this global centre of attention, had grown steadily, while the construction of the media city and the visible clean-up of the streets of the West End was undertaken by the many thousands of workmen and women who, like us, would always be able to talk about their little part in that big day.

But what was my part in this big day?

I was to be the Rear Guard of the Sovereign's Escort for Her Majesty's return trip to Buckingham Palace after the ceremony at Westminster Abbey. Once back at the palace, we, the Sovereign's Escort, would form up on the spot and give a final royal salute to our Queen, before getting the hell out of there ahead of the fly-past of the Royal Air Force. On exiting Buckingham Palace I would become the Advance Guard and singlehandedly lead the regiment back to our Hyde Park home.

The magnitude of the role I'd been handed played on my mind constantly in the run-up to the day itself. I was to lead the regiment home after the biggest ceremonial occasion since the coronation of the Queen almost sixty years earlier. Every single person on parade, including the commanding officer, was going to be following my lead. And then, back at barracks, the ceremonial dismount of the entire regiment would be on my nod. To say I was proud is an understatement; to say I was nervous was an even bigger understatement.

The day before, at an early hour, a full rehearsal was held for everyone on parade. It was going to be quite an affair, more so because of the length of time we'd be atop our horses. We were to leave Hyde Park barracks, head right along the park to Wellington Arch, then down Constitution Hill eventually passing in between the palace and the temporary construction of Media City, before heading into Victoria – quite unusual for us – and coming to a halt about 200 metres short of Westminster Abbey. Here we'd wait forty or so minutes for the happy couple to emerge, newly married, when a small escort of Household Cavalrymen would zoom off with the new Duke and Duchess of Cambridge. The rest of us were there for the Queen, who was due to appear at the west door precisely five minutes after the newlyweds had departed. At this point we'd kick into a full ceremonial escort for the Queen as she waved her way home to Buckingham Palace, along Whitehall, through Horse Guards and up the Mall.

The rehearsal almost felt like the real occasion. The large numbers of people who'd already taken up home on the streets of the route, not wanting to miss out on the best spot, made our practice far more real than it should have been. When we rocked up the day before the wedding to carry out drills, it made global headlines on news networks around the world, defying the point of early-morning rehearsal. Alas, it was what it was and everybody had a taste of what to expect the following morning.

While waiting outside the abbey, going through the motions of picking up the Queen in the early-morning light, I found myself saying a cheery hello to some American supporters who'd travelled from afar to witness the celebrations first-hand. They'd camped out for days in a little tent, which they'd eventually lose before the big event, in order to secure the prime location. I was struck by how friendly everyone outside the abbey and at other key locations along the route was being to each other. There was a huge sense of historic occasion in everyone's behaviour. Everybody was in this together.

Our rehearsal went well, and before I knew it I was undertaking a last-chance practice of the regimental dismount, which was solely my responsibility. I was too long in the tooth, and far more prepared than needed, to get this crucial moment wrong. Often, people think that the parade is over as soon as the Queen has been safely delivered back to the palace. In actual fact, we ceremonial troops have our work cut out for some time after. The regimental dismount, a historic tradition dating back to 1660, is the culmination of any cavalry movement, and has to be carried out to the highest standard every time. In almost a decade of service, the responsibility had never lain on my shoulders. I'd dodged the bullet, as it were, but at the royal wedding of 2011, the job was completely in my hands.

As expected, Mum and Phil descended upon London the day before the royal wedding – to be part of the occasion, but also to support me, their son, in what was, unknown to them, the last occasion I'd wear the uniform and accompany the monarch.

It started early. My drive across the capital into Knightsbridge was joyously straightforward. Of course, that Friday had been deemed a bank holiday, so my usual impatient drive through Chelsea wasn't marred with the endless traffic associated with west London in the morning. Within ten minutes of arriv- ing at the barracks I was dressed in my stable fatigues, waking Doncaster and mucking out his stall in preparation for the morning's activities.

Hyde Park barracks was alive with activity. Dozens of news crews circulated the base, hoping to capture every moment of this important event. The BBC, NBS, Forces Radio, ITV and Sky were just a few of the many recognisable logos floating around on the side of giant cameras. The occasional celebrity TV presenter stopped a soldier and offered questions trying to gain an insight into the routine of a state escort.

In a trick I'd learned years before from Faulkner, Doncaster had been on a reduced diet of just chaff for the day preceding the event; I didn't want him too energetic and giddy for my big moment.

After my initial dressing of Doncaster and his stall, I gave him some food and left him to his own devices while I grabbed my own breakfast. I'd spent hours and hours all week sorting my kit out as well as the commanding officer's kit, which he'd be wearing as he inspected the entire regiment. As he would be looking over the boys, the boys would be doing the exact same thing to him, and if he didn't look as smart as possible, comments would be made and everyone would know I was the person who'd turned him out poorly for the royal wedding. I dashed from one side of the barracks to the other many times that morning, titivating both our uniforms.

The colonel was turned out immaculately, as was I, and – it has to be said, quite unusually – so was everyone on parade; there was usually at least someone who let the side down. Not at the royal wedding.

The time came for us to get on top, and after spending three hours slowly dressing Doncaster and making him look as beautiful as possible, I was glad to have the chance to sit down, even if it was on top of a horse. By the time the regiment started to form up on the square for the colonel's inspection, our families and loved ones had filled the area at the back of the regimental square, standing on a balcony looking over the sight of the entire regiment formed up and ready to make history.

I took up my position as the very last man, ahead of my duty as the Rear Guard for the most part of the parade. I rode over to Thom and my parents and they wished me luck and took many photographs. Soon the regimental corporal major, who by chance was Warren, my old boss and friend from my days in Iraq and Canada, called for us to form up and settle down before getting started.

We were brought to attention and the commanding officer smartly but gracefully swaggered into the centre of the square, chatting briefly to Warren before starting his inspection.

Following the old Faulkner formula of 'time available and number of men on parade', I figured the colonel had about eight seconds to inspect each person. All that stood between a soldier leaving the gates and riding his part in history was eight seconds of inspection. It was make-or-break time.

I could see him getting nearer and nearer through the corner of my eye, and when he got into my vision directly, I gave the colonel and the kit I'd spent so long cleaning a good look over. Thankfully, he looked perfect. The colonel got to me, stood in front of me and looked me square in the face.

'Excellent turn-out, Corporal Wharton.'

What else could he have said? I expected nothing less; I was ready to go.

Out of absolutely nowhere, an eruption of noise filled the air across London and every horse on the square replied by tossing and jerking, some more than others. Doncaster gave out an extremely long and loud sigh. I had never heard anything like it and my heart skipped a beat as I considered all the awful things the noise could have been. Soon I realised it was the sound of cheers, the sound of an entire world cheering, and after the parade I learned it was the moment the Duchess was sighted for the first time in her beautiful dress as she appeared at the front of her hotel in Belgravia.

Our horses knew this was something none of them had ever done before. I tried to consider quickly when I'd last been on a parade like this, and of course the answer was never. The sixtieth anniversary of VE/VJ Day back in 2005 had been pretty spectacular, especially as it was just three days after the London bombings, but it didn't compare to hearing an entire city shout with joy at the sight of a lady in her wedding dress, our future Queen.

The colonel gave the regiment his nod of approval, and took

the fairly unusual step of addressing us all before giving the command to move off. His words were a moment of privacy between him, the command element of the most traditional establishment in the world, and us, the men charged with the honour of carrying out his commands.

We left the base and rode into history.

26

DISMOUNT

Sitting in the forecourt of Buckingham Palace, once the centre-piece of the glorious British Empire, keeping still as possible and Doncaster's reins in my hands, I carried my sword proudly as we performed a royal salute while the Queen's carriage pulled into the tunnel leading to the privacy of the palace. Now we had to get out of there fast.

I kicked Doncaster into action and we flew into position exactly on command. Behind me, almost 200 men and horses followed, each painstakingly trying to keep their beasts calm against the constant cheers of happiness for which the royal wedding will always be remembered. Never before had I witnessed so much jubilation and joy. Even with a recession on and the lives of many millions of people around the country marred with difficulty, on that day, 29 April 2011, the world put its worries aside. Happiness was the theme, celebration and joy was the way to express it. Like too many of these great occasions that come along once in a generation, the event passed by incredibly quickly. We were now, led by me, on the home stretch to camp. The job was done, as was my life's duty as escort to the Sovereign.

Breaking with tradition, at Wellington Arch on Hyde Park Corner, I turned myself around and looked back at the spectacle, sensing that I may never have the opportunity to do so again.

Behind me, beautifully smart and riding along with glee, every single member of the regiment rode on, following in Doncaster's footsteps. It was something I had to do, something I needed to witness with my own eyes, instead of having to imagine what it must have looked like from the very front for the rest of my life. Albeit a little naughty, I'm glad I did it. The sight was breathtaking.

As we approached the ceremonial gates of our regimental home, the trumpeter, a few paces behind me and riding alongside the commanding officer, sounded the royal salute, signifying our return to barracks. As my eyes caught sight of the hundreds of friends and families of soldiers of the regiment who'd piled into the barracks to witness their sons ride out of camp and back in again on this huge occasion, I began to feel overcome with emotion. I led the way for the hundreds of troops behind me and slowed Doncaster down for the command to form up and halt from the colonel, who'd taken up position in the centre of the square.

'Without advancing, escort to the left!'

The colonel's command thundered across the barracks and on his final word, I turned Doncaster to the left and the regiment formed up in two huge lines, me at the extreme right-hand side of everybody.

The ceremonial goings-on that follow an escort occurred and all the officers, bar the colonel himself, fell out and left us to it. It was almost time for the moment I'd been waiting for: the regimental dismount.

The colonel demanded we return our swords, and we duly obeyed. The moment was here.

'From the right, in twos... NUMBER!'

Without hesitation, I screamed 'ONE!' at the top of my voice, and the person next to me replied with 'TWO!' This continued

– 'ONE! TWO! ONE! TWO! ONE! TWO!' – all the way along the line until the very last person screamed out 'TWO!'

The colonel waited a few seconds and my heartbeat increased in the silence.

'Prepare to dismount!' Again, his words were thunderous.

I kicked Doncaster to life and rode forward four horse lengths. I held the reins in my left hand and raised my right arm out straight in front of me, my white leather gauntlet visible for the hundreds of men looking to me for the next command. I halted Doncaster and remained dead still, listening for the silence of hooves behind me before giving the nod to continue. I waited for the token six seconds, the eyes of everybody piercing me, and then I had the guts to wait a little longer. This was my moment.

Sharply, I tucked my chin into my chest and threw my head back, my scarlet plume flickering through the air as I did. On cue, the entire regiment slapped the side of the neck of the horse they were each sat on, signifying the end of the day. The regiment's eyes were back on me as they waited for my next nod. I swiftly struck my head to the left and gave each man a split second of a glance, ensuring everyone was ready to get off. I threw my head forward and gave the expected nod. On that nod, the regiment threw away the tension in the reins and removed their right legs from the stirrup irons that held them in place. The colonel now needed to give the actual word to get off.

'Dismount!'

And on command, everyone pulled themselves out of the saddle and held themselves in mid-air, to the side of their saddles, again looking at me. I had one arm raised high in the air, which I suddenly and with force slapped on the side of Doncaster's saddle flap, creating a loud bang, giving the cue for everyone to land on the floor. I'd dismounted for the last time and as I gave that final smack to Doncaster, notifying the regiment to step down, I knew

I was never getting back on again. I had tears in my eyes as the inevitable dawned on me. Never again would I have the honour of escorting the Sovereign, my Queen, at a state occasion.

I'm not sure what it was that struck me so deeply. I hadn't particularly considered leaving the army before then, all I knew for sure was that my time on ceremonial duties was again coming to an end. I was heading back to the operational regiment soon, and as my life had started to build around Thom and the home we had started together, I felt that the commitment I'd shown the army since the age of sixteen couldn't be maintained. I felt it was becoming time to move on.

It's certainly fair to say that I was a much happier person when in London, as opposed to Windsor, where nobody was likely to pull you into an office and send you off to war. I'd also agree that, all things considered, I'd been exceptionally fortunate with my war experience. I hadn't lost any limbs and I wasn't injured in any way. I have friends who've not been so lucky. But in 2011, settled down in a meaningful relationship with my husband, I really didn't overly enjoy the prospect of having to deploy abroad again. It was very often in my mind how much the tour to Iraq in 2007 had cost me personally and I honestly didn't feel able to put myself in that position again.

Separately from all of this there was my new-found hunger to make right something that was utterly wrong: my ongoing attempt to offer youngsters an insight into my achievements as an openly gay man. The army just wasn't supportive enough of my continuing efforts in that area. I could sense the uneasiness towards my work each time I submitted a leave request to carry out a school visit. Press coverage of my visits was greeted with annoyance by some factions of the military. Some officers just couldn't stop themselves dissenting in public places such as Facebook. It got to the point where I decided to stop telling the army I was working with Stonewall for fear that they'd put an all-out ban on the activity. I hated that they didn't see the importance of the work; I hated that it wasn't as high on their agenda as it was on mine, but I guess it was still progressive times.

In 2011 I'd been ranked again in the Pink List, rising two places to seventeen. I was very honoured of course, but the powers that be in some corners of the military saw it as too much. 'How can a junior rank be getting so much attention?' commented a senior officer from the Royal Air Force in a letter to my commanding officer. To top everything off, I received an invitation to a reception at Downing Street for the third time in eighteen months, and on that occasion I'd be the only representative there from the military. Once word was out, it led to a lot of complaining from jealous but influential people high up the command chain. As a junior-ranking lance corporal, elevated by the army to a position of significance in the public eye, I felt completely let down by my employer, as nobody seemed to defend me and tell them to back off. I couldn't do that myself; how could a junior NCO tell a senior officer to fuck off? The tipping point came when I attended an army LGBT forum meeting, a group I'd been instrumental in establishing, at the Army HQ in Andover. The same officer who'd asked me to go on the cover of *Soldier* magazine three years earlier told me, with resentment in his eyes, that they were 'done' with my story and that I'd received far more than my fair share of attention and special treatment. There were also comments made about my ongoing youth work with Stonewall and how I ought to leave talking to youngsters to professionals in the army. These remarks echoed some of the others I'd experienced from factions in the military that just didn't want to support the grass-roots anti-homophobia work I was doing with Stonewall. What was the point in being out yet invisible? Where was the commitment to activism, to combating discrimination? I left the LGBT forum that day and never went back to it.

I did consider that perhaps enough was enough but, sitting at my desk at home, I read through the letters I'd received from delighted head teachers, thanking me for giving my time and visiting their schoolchildren to talk so openly about my positive experiences as a soldier. I realised that the school visits were vital and if the price for such a job was having to put up with a little bit of crap from jealous old men who'd failed to act as role models themselves, mostly remaining in the closet until it was safe to creep out, then it was a price worth paying.

I was posted back to the armoured regiment in Windsor, understanding that deployment to Afghanistan would follow in due course. This, however, would never come to pass. The reduction in troop levels meant A Squadron would be stood down.

Instead I was posted to the south coast of England, to the Crew Training School as an instructor of Jackal, a modern vehicle available to troops deploying overseas. I settled into the job well and was able to continue with my youth work on Fridays thanks to the lenience of a very good boss.

The equal marriage debate ignited in the UK, grabbing my attention and driving emotive feelings to the surface as the opposition made their case against equality. I was utterly gobsmacked by how overtly homophobic some public officials were being in response to the prospect of equality filtering down to all sections of society. One Member of Parliament commented, 'Gay marriage is an equality too far.' The oppression didn't sit comfortably with me in the slightest and due to the publicity created surrounding my civil partnership two years prior, my name kept popping up in the media.

I realised the homophobic actions of public figures on TV and in the press, and the plight of the many thousands, potentially millions, of school kids up and down the country who were being taunted daily for being different, went hand in hand. I considered Jessica and the other teens I'd met around the country who'd informed me that they'd been bullied daily for being gay or lesbian. How could a cardinal or a senior Member of Parliament get away with making such direct attacks on the gay community? How could they validate the behaviour of bullies and brush off the suffering endured by thousands of kids like Jessica and her friends? I just couldn't sit by and do nothing.

The editor of *Attitude* magazine, the most successful and popular gay monthly magazine, had become somebody I spoke and met with quite frequently since I'd become involved in the gay movement.

Matt Todd had taken *Attitude* to great success since becoming editor and had plans to enter into the very heart of the debate with a striking feature magazine on marriage. He agreed with my thoughts on the matter and had been moved to tears over the course of his tenure as a gay journalist to report on death after death of gay teens, bullied to suicide as a result of being different. Every time a cardinal or a politician appeared on the news, linking equal marriage to slavery or, in one case, bestiality, he was filled with anger and felt the need to act. When he asked me to do a front cover with Thom, in uniform, to signify that I was man enough to go to war but not man enough to be entitled to full marriage equality, I knew the feature would be controversial. I also knew, without doubt, the army would not give their blessing for it to go ahead and would probably outright refuse to give me permission. It was a very serious matter and a decision I didn't take lightly.

In my ninth year as a soldier, Thom and I were discussing our plans for the future, exploring when would be best to think about having kids of our own and the like. Since dismounting from Doncaster at the royal wedding nine months earlier, I knew my time in the army was fast coming to an end. What was left for me to achieve? What was important for me in the future? Being honest, I knew my commitment to the army was far less significant than it had been earlier in life. It was time to go. Stubbornly, I was adamant that I would reach my tenth year in the job, so I bided my time to achieve this final goal. On 1 April 2012 I tendered my twelve months' notice and began to prepare for life after the army; a life I'd never known.

I went ahead with the magazine cover without permission, cementing the end of my career as a soldier in the British Army. Politics was off limits to soldiers and I'd entered into the centre of a subject that was utterly political. But I was enormously proud of the cover and the feature and, even if it was the end of my career as a soldier, I knew it would give hope to youngsters up and down Britain.

When the magazine hit the shelves, Thom and I were purposely holidaying in San Francisco. I noticed the response while away and was overwhelmed by the support we received from the people who'd bought a copy and appreciated my decision to do it. But the military was not impressed. It seemed to me it was OK for me to talk on matters of equality that benefited the army, but certainly not on matters that were as divisive as marriage equality.

I arrived back in the UK and faced the wrath of the army. They had to make a response and that immediate reaction was that if I wasn't back at camp by 0800 hrs the following morning, I'd be arrested. I protested that I was on annual leave and to call someone in, unless crucially unavoidable, was quite wrong. The person on the phone, my corporal major back in Windsor, wasn't budging an inch. I was in serious trouble.

I was in camp by 8 a.m. the following morning, expecting to have the worst day ever imaginable, but was bewildered to find that the position of the army had seemingly changed overnight. I was no longer in trouble. For reasons unknown to me, someone, somewhere, had made a decision to just let everything go. I was told not to do anything again without express permission and sent on my way to finish my leave.

I'd escaped the assassin's bullet to an extent, but I could see the resentment in the senior officers' eyes as they 'dealt' with me that morning. Right then, I was relieved to be leaving the service. I'd become different. I couldn't believe that I was being judged for speaking out for gay equality as a gay person. The officers who were dealing with me, and especially the chap who'd been on the phone threatening me with arrest, were all straight and, to the point, married men. Marriage equality was in place for them, a luxury that was far from in place for me. I think the hypocrisy of that very point is what killed off any disciplinary action I might have faced that morning. I think once that fact would have been in the public domain, it might have created attention that the army didn't want to be associated with. There might have been a backlash from a lot of people in the gay community.

I embarked on my final few days of leave before having to return to the south coast to carry on with the teaching of Jackal to deploying troops. I would see the end of my army service out at that remote base on the southern coast.

27

ONE VERY SPECIAL ACHIEVEMENT

When I was thirteen, I got a job working in a local chippy as a potato peeler. I peeled for hours every day after school, constantly cutting my fingers on the sharp knives, but I loved the responsibility of having a job and earning my own money. Since then, I've always had money in my back pocket. At the end of my first week, I was handed a pay packet which I took across the road to the local supermarket and spent on an album I'd wanted for some time: Elton John, *One Night Only*, his greatest hits live from Madison Square Garden. I bought it because at that early age, I admired who he was and for reasons that weren't entirely known to me then, I identified him as a real role model. He was someone who'd had his fair share of knocks, but had come through the other end still standing, singing his songs to the world and being true to himself as he did so.

Late in 2011, I received a phone call from someone called Thomas, claiming to be the personal assistant to Sir Elton John. He had some news that was, in his words, 'exciting'. He wasn't wrong.

About six months earlier, a famous Australian artist called Ross Watson had got in touch with me through Stonewall with what, initially, I thought of as a bizarre request.

'I want to make a painting of you!'

Somewhat reluctantly, I went along with the request and Ross flew over to London to capture me some weeks later. I posed in my full military regalia, the same outfit I'd worn at my civil partnership, and Ross spent hours taking photos of me in different settings. He flew home and after some months eventually got back in touch to tell me he'd finished his painting.

The end result was utterly fascinating. In the days that followed seeing the painting for the first time, I couldn't quite put into words just exactly what I thought; I only knew it was breathtakingly impressive. Such skill, such delicacy, he was a true master of his field. Coupled with the painting, Ross had produced three photographic portraits of me, and in one of the works Thom posed next to me. Again they were captivating.

When I came off the phone to Sir Elton's assistant, I was at work, surrounded by other soldiers. One of them commented immediately.

'You've gone pale? Is everything OK?'

'Erm... I don't quite know how to say this, but Elton John has just bought a portrait of me!'

Sir Elton was a collector of Ross Watson's works and, as usual, had first offer on all his new pieces. He liked what he saw in my portrait and upon learning my story felt inspired to want to buy it. I couldn't believe it. Eleven years after I'd bought something of his, after feeling inspired by his work and his achievements, he'd done exactly the same for me.

My journey into manhood is similar in a way. I'd gone from peeling potatoes in a chip shop to escorting Her Majesty the Queen on a horse by day and drinking wine with the Prime Minister at Downing Street by night, an incredible turnaround in the space of ten or so years.

When I arrived at the crazy environment of 6 Platoon in 2003, where the homophobic platoon sergeant's early rule was 'no faggots', I didn't quite know what I was letting myself in for. I knew gay people were protected, at least legally, from discrimination but that information hadn't filtered through to those people who needed it most, the soldiers who were responsible for looking after the fresh recruits at their most vulnerable stage.

From day one, the soldiers I've counted as peers, those mostly in the same age group as me, joining around the same time as me, have on the whole been progressive and accepting of diversity. Being different, whether by race, religion or sexuality, is something they have been used to all their lives. The PlayStation generation has grown up with the internet and Sky TV, and have had regular access to diversity on a nightly basis.

The problem throughout has been the fallout of the army's old culture of homophobia. It was too much asking some soldiers to change their employer-driven, discriminatory opinions on gay people. And who can blame them really? The army had spent a lot of time, resources and money in actively hunting out homosexuals within the organisation, right up to the turn of the century. Then suddenly, literally overnight, they were made to change their policy, and instead of hunting us out and throwing us in the streets in shame, they embraced us and told everybody to be accepting of us. When I turned up three years later, over half of the army had served before the rules had changed and that generation of soldiers has struggled to embrace the new army. I can't hate my platoon sergeant too much for his words on that first night in the army; he was an example of the culture he'd signed up to in the 1980s. The times had changed so fast, in such a short amount of time, that many people were left behind, and right up to the last day of my service in 2013, it was still soldiers from that generation that I'd mostly hear using casually racist language or making silly comments about women or, indeed, sexuality.

These people are retiring gradually but until the remnants of that generation have fully left the service, the army won't be as gay-friendly an employer as its private sector counterparts. Significant to this too is the fact there are no openly gay senior officers within the ranks of the British Army. Nobody in a position of senior authority has stepped forward and said the words 'I'm gay', and the reason for that is simple: unless you are a married white man, preferably with a couple of kids to boot, it's very unlikely you'll become a general. The senior talent of the British Army is in no way reflective of the thousands of troops below; there isn't even a woman general up there. It's utterly disappointing and it leaves people like me, at the bottom end of the chain, without hope. Obviously I was never going to become a general, but my service in the army would have felt a billion times better if there was someone up there who wasn't just white, heterosexual and married with kids. There was no senior figure I could identify with at all; throughout ten whole years of service, there was no role model and, I would say, there probably won't be for another ten years yet. I hope I'm wrong.

Since I started on my journey of service, beginning at thirteen when I walked through the door of the army cadet hut in the middle of Gwersyllt, I have given my all to the army. After enlisting at sixteen, every hour of every day I've committed all my energy to the job I swore my allegiance to, and I have to say, on the whole it's been a pretty awesome experience. I've made friends I will never forget and will keep them close by for the rest of my life. Those three lads that I sat with the night I announced I was gay will be for ever in my gratitude: Dean Perryman, Josh Tate and Jamie McAllen, I couldn't have asked for a better reception to the words I'd fought so long with myself to say.

I came out when I did for no other reason than wanting to release something in me that I'd battled to accept for as long as I can remember. I didn't want to change the world, I just wanted to be happy, but I'm hugely proud that somewhere, someone might have felt empowered to be themselves and take that massive step out of the closet and into the unknown because of the actions I've taken over my fairly short career in the army.

But my greatest achievement is something outside of the military.

When my nan decided not to accept the news that I, her youngest grandson, was gay, my heart was broken. I cried on and off for years, mostly after talking to her on the phone. She was never nasty, but I always knew that behind her pleasantness she was harbouring feelings of resentment towards me and my life, and I hated myself for being the one person in the family who was different. She loved me completely, but there was one aspect of my life she just didn't.

In 2012, Nan accepted an invitation to come and stay and enjoy the Diamond Jubilee celebrations in London with me and Thom. For months I fretted over how the visit would go, worrying that she would be uncomfortable and, in turn, unhappy throughout her stay. The two of us, but in reality more Thom than me, went out of our way to make her holiday with us unforget- table, culminating in a grand day out watching the river pageant from the banks of the Thames before a night of patriotic singing in the Royal Albert Hall. She loved every minute of it, but more so, over the course of the six days, she witnessed how much love Thom and I have for one another, and how ordinary an environ- ment our home is, just like any other. She adored her time with us and left us feeling energised by her stay, taking home with her to Liverpool many tales and happy memories of her week- long adventure celebrating the Diamond Jubilee. She was great company and I didn't want her to leave.

In the weeks that followed, Nan sent a card addressed to her

'Grandson and Grandson-in-Law', and I knew we'd changed her entire opinion of us, and of gay people as a whole. The significance of her card changed my life. I was prouder at that moment than I have ever been and I thought, if an 85-year-old lady can change her mind on sexuality, there's no excuse for the rest of the world.

AUTHOR'S NOTE

In the weeks following the completion of this book, I wrote to the platoon sergeant who made those homophobic comments on my first day in the army back in 2003. I asked him if he remembered making such remarks and, if yes, why he had done – and, indeed, if he still felt that way. His response was incredibly revealing.

In my nearly forty years of living I have done things and said things that I now reflect on and think would I have done or said things differently? I am roughly fifteen years older than you and joined the army when you would have been a baby ... things were a lot different then. The army and world in general was a lot more conservative in regards to a lot of things, not just homosexuality, but generally anything that wasn't the norm. I have found out in the last eight years since leaving the army that there is life outside of the regiment and everything that you're told is not always the truth. The statement I made, upon reflection, was a statement I would definitely change.

He said it himself: the army was a different place when he joined. Homophobia and discrimination was acceptable then, actively encouraged in fact, and in some parts of the army today the hangover from that terrible time still exists. He continued:

I apologise for any comments I made in the past and now, with a few more years under my belt, I realise that everyone should be allowed to live their lives without judgement.

As I hope I have made evident in this book, the army has changed – and is still changing. It is trying, beyond belief, to better itself and to become a more equal and diverse body. To have my platoon sergeant acknowledge his comments, with such brutal honesty, and to apologise for them is deeply affecting. I'm extremely grateful for his response and hope that the army continues to recognise its recent past and look towards a more inclusive future.